THE GOOD GIRL SYNDROME

How Women Are Programmed to Fail in a Man's World— and How to Stop It

WILLIAM FEZLER, Ph.D.

ELEANOR S. FIELD, Ph.D.

D0009653

B

BERKLEY BOOKS, NEW YORK

This Berkley book contains the complete
text of the original hardcover edition.
It has been completely reset in a typeface
designed for easy reading, and was printed
from new film.

THE GOOD GIRL SYNDROME

A Berkley Book / published by arrangement with
Macmillan Publishing Company

PRINTING HISTORY
Macmillan edition published 1985
Berkley edition / August 1987

ISBN: 0-425-10108-8

A BERKLEY BOOK ® TM 757,375
Berkley Books are published by The Berkley Publishing Group,
200 Madison Avenue, New York, New York 10016.
The name ''BERKLEY'' and the ''B'' logo
are trademarks belonging to Berkley Publishing Corporation.

PRINTED IN THE UNITED STATES OF AMERICA

10 9 8 7 6 5 4 3 2 1

To Katharyn Powers, a Clear
who brings out the best in me by being herself—
WILLIAM FEZLER

CONTENTS

ACKNOWLEDGMENTS

I would like to express my deepest thanks to our editor, Melinda Corey, for putting her heart into our book. It was her project from the start and she was always there to give assistance and support throughout the long, many months of writing, polishing, and finding new sources of inspiration. Heartfelt thanks also to my literary agent, Evan Marshall, for his brilliance in putting the pieces together, knowledge of the business, and energetic, enthusiastic belief in me.

W.F.

In the process of writing this book, my gratitude expanded toward my patients and the participants in our Good Girl Syndrome seminars increased. They shared of their experiences and change to fulfill the promise of this book.

I wish to thank Fred Villani, actor-writer and friend, for his initial review of my manuscripts.

I received encouragement, support, and penetrating insights that enhanced the content of the book from many of my colleagues and from my editor, Melinda Corey, who reached into a deep store of patience to deal with two authors.

I wish to acknowledge my lover and husband Boris, for his encouragement and assistance; my parents, Goldie and Lou, for their unconditional love and for their worldly wisdom which they bestowed unto me; and my daughter, Noreen Barbara, who excels in self-reliance and independence.

Above all I wish to dedicate this book and express my gratitude to my late grandfather, Nathan Shusterman, who showed me I was unique and taught me to be a rebel and to love myself. He fostered within me the spirit of self-actualization that led me to achieve my highest potential. After all, for all of you, that is the purpose and goal of this book.

E.S.F.

HELP WANTED: MARTYR.

JOB DESCRIPTION: Cater to the needs of everyone but yourself. Sacrifice career, achievement, independence, identity.

REWARDS: Be called "virtuous," "an angel," "my sainted mother."

SALARY: Meager.

FRINGE BENEFITS: Anger. Unhappiness. Powerlessness.

Good Girls can be any age from sixteen to sixty-five, as long as they program themselves for failure in a man's world. Now you can live by your own rules by overcoming the myths that keep you down . . .

- "There is something wrong with me"
- "Men are better"
- "It is the right of the superior to govern"
- "The rules are sacred"
- "Self-sacrifice is a virtue"
- "Good girls don't *really* enjoy sex"
- "I am as men see me"
- "A woman's place is in the home"
- "Give me that old-time religion"
- "Those who deviate deserve to suffer"
- "Anger is unfeminine"
- "Independence is dangerous"

Stop believing in fairy tales. Start believing in yourself!

PREFACE
Learning To Succeed

Do you find that much of your life is spent doing what other people expect you to do? That while *they* think you're great for meeting their expectations, you feel achingly unsatisfied, unappreciated, and in a continual state of anger that seems to make no sense to you?

You are not alone. This condition is so prevalent among the women we see in our private practices in psychotherapy that it could well be called an emotional epidemic. All women from 16 to 65, single or married, career-oriented or family-oriented (or both), occasionally fall victim to devastating feelings of frustration and unworthiness *simply because they are women!*

Do you ever feel you don't deserve things you really want because your husband, not you, earns the money necessary to buy them? And if you work, do you find that men expect you to play by a different set of rules than they do? If you fight for what you need at work do you find that men look at you as if you're a barracuda? Have you noticed that men have specific expectations for your behavior down to the tiniest, simplest things in life? You are supposed to let the man order for you in a restaurant. . . . You are to defer to his opinion in business matters. . . . You are not to talk too much around his male friends. . . . You are to take your vacation when it is convenient for him. . . . You should always be there when he gets home from work. . . .

The list of expectations men may have of you is endless. Some items may apply to you and some may not. But there is a common thread that runs through all of them: You are "good" to the degree that you give men what they want and follow the rules that they have laid down for you. You sacrifice your own personal satisfaction in return for being told how nice and sweet you are by the men whose approval you are seeking. Unfortunately, this approval, which comes from meeting their needs, is no substitute for meeting your own needs. The inevitable consequence is a continual low-level anger that flares up periodically in "unexplainable" bursts that seem to mystify the men in your life.

While many girls brought up in the open atmosphere of today may not have the same prejudices as their mothers, these were the prevailing expectations for women as recently as ten or fifteen years ago. These ingrained expectations are what we're going to show you how to fight! For most women there is an enormous gap between their childhood conditioning and the process necessary to achieve growth and personal fulfillment today. The result is often tremendous conflict between the conscious needs of the '80s and the subconscious messages received in early childhood telling you what your needs *should* be.

The self-defeating messages that serve to satisfy the expectations of others rather than your own are grouped together into twelve basic areas, or programs, you may be having problems with (Chapters 1 through 12). Taken together, these programs make up what in psychology is called a syndrome, a collection of problems or symptoms that when combined make one major problem. We call this major problem the Good Girl Syndrome (GGS) because your reward for being a victim of it is being labeled "good" by the men who benefit from it.

You will come to see that although these programs were originally devised by men for their own benefit, the women who fall prey to the syndrome obey a staggering number of authorities, not just men. They obey almost everybody, because inherent in the Good Girl Syndrome is the belief that most people are better than you. This creates a vicious circle of frustration in which you feel unworthy because so many others are better, and you believe others are better because you feel unworthy. The only answer is to stop these programs that comprise the syndrome.

It's time for a change! . . . That's what patients are seeking when they come through our office doors. Some come to us because they are aware of their anger and resentment in their relationships with spouses, friends, bosses, men in general. Others come because they don't feel good about themselves or are depressed. Still others come with a myriad of complaints ranging from being overweight or smoking too much, to the fear of flying, driving, walking within crowds, traveling in elevators. Whether the pain is physical or emotional it really doesn't matter. It's the syndrome that has to be attacked.

Before we show you how to do this, we'd like to give you a little background on how we discovered GGS.

Many years ago, the two of us sat across from each other at a seminar dinner and began talking shop. We happened onto a subject of mutual concern—our female patients. We were amazed to discover that our experiences treating women over the years led us to the same conclusion. Traditional psychology seemed to work better for men than for women! It was as though the field had been designed by men for men. We don't know why we should have been so amazed at our discovery. It seems only logical now. Since men and women are different, their problems are also different.

First of all, we both had found that many women kept their anger much more bottled up than did men. On the outside they were Pollyannas, but inside they were boiling. Many patients have told us, "On the outside I'm a meek goody-goody, but on the inside I'm raging with anger." And we learned that the reason for containing all this wrath while outwardly showing a picture of sweetness and light was more often than not to please others, oftentimes men. We also discovered that most of the women who couldn't express their anger also had severe problems with their sense of identity and self-worth. They felt inferior. They got their sense of who they were from the men—or any authority figure—in their life.

Since that evening, we both continued to find still more self-defeating beliefs and behaviors common to women, all radiating from their image of, and lack of trust in, themselves. Many of the women realized that something was wrong and wanted to do something about it. As a result, we formed special support groups, which we called "Good Girl Seminars," to help women clear themselves of these problems. We've come to realize that there are many common ideas and problems that keep women from getting what they want in life. The twelve that we'll outline here are the ones that keep recurring. We've found that if women have one of these destructive beliefs, they usually have several others as well. GGS is a female phenomenon (though men may identify with parts of it), and its primary theme is the myth of "goodness." Whatever the variations, a "good girl" always sacrifices for others to the exclusion of herself and always has a sense of being let down. She is constantly angry inwardly and frustrated because doing the "right" thing never pays off completely.

We are glad we opened our minds to think about a new psychology of women, because nowhere else in the psychological, psychiatric or popular self-help literature is this collection of self-defeating beliefs common to women even hinted at. But now, thanks to the success and helpfulness of our patients and support groups, we are happy to bring you some good news. We believe we have found ways for other women to work out the problem of GGS.

Why have we spent so many years working on "The Good Girl Syndrome"?

We are therapists and healers. It's important for us to help people to feel better. Sometimes we can identify with the same problems our female clients are struggling with. While these problems take different forms, they all boil down to one common denominator: feeling inadequate because you don't meet someone else's expectations. Over the years, we've learned to set our own conditions for self-worth, and we're eager to aid you in doing the same for yourself!

We want to help you find that you *can* eliminate the GGS, to become a woman who feels she is at her natural best. "Clearing" allows you to *be* you, to make the most of what you are and what you want to be—all the time reveling in your womanhood. You are not a man in a woman's image, and you don't need to be. You are a totally new individual, a nurturing being of power who makes her own rules as a standard of self-worth.

We are offering you our best: a blueprint for change and a

call to action. The major theme for you to keep in mind is that you can change if you wish. Our methods are *behavioral* and therefore fast-acting. The books that have preceded ours have been much more analytical than ours will be. Although we are interested in analyzing *how* you became locked into a particular program, we are more interested in the behavior you will need in order to *change*. A behavioral approach means that you change your behavior *before* you expect an attitude change. For example, you assert yourself. *Then* you feel confident. You make your own rules. *Then* you feel independent. You go for what you want. *Then* you feel good about yourself.

Usually people unsuccessfully try to solve their problems in reverse. They want to feel better *before* they do the right things to make themselves feel better. Over and over we hear well-meaning women say, "I would get out of the house more if I felt more confident about myself," or "I know I'd speak up more at work if I thought more of my opinions," or "If I just didn't feel so dependent on my husband, I'd take a vacation by myself." They're asking to be made confident, self-assured and independent *before* they have any reason to feel this way! Get out of the house, speak up at work, take a vacation on your own. *Then* you will feel the confidence, self-assuredness and independence you hunger for. That is the behavioral approach. Change your behavior *first*. The good feelings will come as a natural result. Our thrust is on doing *first*. A healthy self-image will come *after*, not before, you take action. Our message is, don't sit around waiting till you feel like taking the necessary steps to freedom. Take them *now*. We'll show you how.

Many of you may be skeptical. You may have read about your problems, or thought about them, but felt, "Yes, these sound like me, but what do I *do* about them?" THE GOOD GIRL SYNDROME presents a new way of looking at things. Each of our chapters offers *definite* strategies for taking charge of the now, eliminating self-destructive behavior and helping you to become a woman free to succeed in the world as yourself. You'll learn what to expect and how to deal with men when you start to change. Even more important, you'll learn how to *maintain* your positive change once it's made. There are secrets to adapting to success as well as achieving it. Finally, you'll see the positive result of freeing yourself completely from the Good Girl Syndrome.

It takes time for a bright, sensitive child to become a frustrated, angry, adult "good girl." That is why it's so important for parents to read this book. They have a chance to help their children during their formative, most impressionable years. Even husbands and lovers can support the women they love. Relatives and friends also can help end your anger and frustration. This is a book for *anybody* who truly cares about your welfare. Ultimately, though, the responsibility for change lies with you. That's why this book will benefit most of the "good girls" who follow its blueprint to freedom. We have prepared your way with painstaking attention to detail . . . and much love. Get ready to embark on a wonderful adventure as you celebrate the birth of a new life—your own.

WILLIAM FEZLER
ELEANOR S. FIELD

INTRODUCTION
Do You Know This Woman?

> All my life I've always looked to men to tell me
> what to do.
>
> MARGIE N.
> *Patient*

Margie is 27, married to John, an ambitious computer systems
analyst. She is trying to grow, to become her own person
within the relationship. But whenever she attempts to take
charge and do things for herself, the people close to her try to
make her feel guilty.

Margie decided she wanted to become a court reporter. She
believed she had found a way to use her potential as well as
make more money for the two of them. John immediately
started to argue, "How can you have time for classes when
you don't have time for me?" John expected Margie to be on
call twenty-four hours a day to help him advance his career,
whether it be as secretary to him at night or as hostess for his
contacts over the weekend.

When her mother joined forces with John and told her it
wouldn't be nice to neglect her husband, Margie gave up her
plans. Although this decision made her mother and husband
very happy, Margie found herself pulling away from them in
anger and resentment. She rarely speaks to her mother anymore and dreads what was once exciting sex with her husband.

1

Sally, 44, is recently divorced and working in the business world for the first time, as a buyer for a chain of retail stores. Everybody loves "Sweet Sal," especially the wholesalers who up their prices whenever she goes to market. She doesn't wish to offend them, so she continually overpays for their products. Unfortunately, Sally will not last long in the world of finance if being loved is more important to her than making a profit.

Sandy, 36, is being run ragged by her husband, Jim, and her three children. She needs to take a vacation, just a few days away from them all, but doesn't know how to work it without losing her position as the house martyr. Jim is a big flatterer, and the kids have modeled his style to perfection. Whenever they want something they'll always begin it with, "Be an angel and . . ." or "Be a dear and . . ." or "Be a doll and . . ." In the eyes of her family Sandy is a saint, but in her own eyes she's searching for an identity not quite so entirely self-sacrificing.

One evening, as they were finishing the dinner Sandy had taken all day to prepare, she informed the family that she intended to spend five days at a girlfriend's retreat in Canada that coming summer. Nobody objected, but then nobody offered wholehearted approval either. "A lot of times you know what people are thinking without their saying it," Sandy explained. "I couldn't take their silence." Summer has come and gone and Sandy has yet to go to Canada.

These three women are very different from each other. But they hold at least one thing in common—they all have let other people control their lives in exchange for approval and being liked.

How many times have you been called a "good girl" or called someone else a "good girl"? And how many times have you wondered what was so good about being good? Have you ever questioned why being "good" often leaves you feeling inadequate, even inferior to someone more assertive? Do you ever ask yourself why most all the rules governing your life were made by someone else? Doesn't it sometimes seem strange that the more you give the less there is left for you? Did you ever stop yourself in the middle of a busy day and plain puzzle over why so much of what you do is motivated out of guilt or fear? How many times have you stopped yourself from getting what you wanted because it "wouldn't be nice"?

Where do all these blocks to happiness come from? Who is telling you that you must be "good"? And why are you listening? Do you need a source of authority in your life to tell you what to do or to affirm what you do? How to live? What is right, wrong and meaningful?

"Good girls" obey a breadth of authority that is amazing. Veronica never argues with the professors in college because it's "not nice" to disagree. Marilyn does exactly what her husband asks at home because it's part of her "wifely duties." Hazel steps and fetches for her boss in the office because "he expects it." Connie feels guilty when she's standing in the supermarket express line with eleven items instead of the allotted ten. It seems there are people telling you what to do and disapproving of you at every turn.

And when you follow these guides do you find yourself coming up short? Does it seem that often *they* benefit more from your following their rules than you do? There are many types of "good girls," but they all suffer from this common plight.

The funny thing is—it's very easy to be used and manipulated without realizing it. It's also easy to fall into the trap of believing you actually deserve to be mistreated. Some "good girls" go so far as to consider their ability to withstand the mistreatment as a sign of greater "goodness."

However, following the rules of others can lead only to the benefit of others. This is a book about fundamental rules of power. Principles described here are used by anyone who wishes to get something from another person, something that person would not normally be willing to give without a little manipulating from the "authority" figure. We put the word "authority" in quotes because the term is arbitrary. Most authorities on what is good for you are self-proclaimed, having only as much authority as you are willing to give them.

To win freedom and mastery over your own destiny, you need to clear yourself from your belief that other people are superior to you. You don't need to hate the person. You just don't need him or her to tell you who you are.

Discovery of the Good Girl Syndrome

As we mentioned, we discovered the Good Girl Syndrome quite by accident. We were spurred by our observations of the differences between men and women, especially in the way they handled anger. We were surprised at the similarities in the self-defeating belief systems held by women who were having problems in this area. For years we tried to analyze our findings, to make sense out of a latticework of beliefs. After sessions with dozens of women, we came to notice that inability to express anger was only one part of this complicated way of thinking. Eleven other problem areas prevented women from getting what they wanted in life as well.

For example, Sandy is not only having trouble expressing anger at her family's attempts to control her, she is a victim of a program we call "I am as men see me." She cannot bear to see any signs of disapproval coming from the significant men in her life, even signals as minor as a few moments of silence or a raised eyebrow. She gets her identity from the way her family reacts to her, and if they disapprove of her behavior, so does she. Rather than risk being seen as a "bad" girl in their eyes, she sacrifices the long overdue vacation she so richly deserves.

Probably the problem area we find most often in a woman is her belief that there is something inherently wrong with her. Rachel, who at 29 has been through nearly as many jobs and relationships, truly believes she is "doomed from the start" no matter what she attempts to accomplish. She always seems to be in the process of ending something because it is "too good to last." In other words, she believes herself too imperfect to *make* it last. Her last job as a counselor in a halfway house for drug abusers couldn't last because sooner or later the staff would discover she really wasn't "up" to the job. To save herself the trauma of an anticipated firing, she quit. Mark, her last love interest, was sure to realize eventually that she was not the girl of his dreams, so she left him first. "They're all bound to catch on to me sooner or later," she explained to us. "It's better I get out before they do."

Until Rachel can believe there is nothing wrong with her,

that she is complete as she is, she will live her life on the run—a fugitive from herself. There is nothing wrong with Rachel except her belief that there is.

Women who, like Rachel, believe they are defective or inferior usually fall prey to another common problem area: belief that men are superior or better than they are. "It would be a sorry world," laughs one of the victims of this program, "if I was the best there was."

Marcia, a 35-year-old attorney, is twice divorced and childless. She has a firm belief that men are better and wishes with all her heart that she had been born a man. Most of her life has been spent trying to be like a man. During her teens and twenties she devoted all her time to achieving in school, competing with men for academic excellence. She rarely dated, and then only to keep friends from thinking she was "weird." Marcia views both marriages as "experiments in living that just didn't work out."

Although she has yet to admit it, the possibility of motherhood scares her to death. Childbirth is too feminine a task for a woman whose sole goal in life is to attain masculine superiority. Not until Marcia gets in touch with her entrapment in this problem area of the Good Girl Syndrome will she be free to be what she is—a woman.

From the point in our practice that we discovered the Good Girl Syndrome, we chose to focus on adult women who were victims of any or all of these self-defeating belief systems. We knew we had to find out how they got that way and what could be done. By the time you reach the end of this chapter, you may even recognize yourself or a friend as a victim of The Good Girl Syndrome. This identification may give you a jolt—both because it is always unsettling to view yourself in a new way *and* because you may come to see how many very different kinds of women still suffer as unhappy "good girls."

The Prison of Living in an Externally-Controlled World

Victims of the Good Girl Syndrome live in an externally-controlled world, where rules for doing come from outside themselves. This outside world is dominated by men, and the rules that govern it are made by men for the benefit of men. *All* the myths comprising the Good Girl Syndrome were started by men for their own benefit. There can be no doubt that ours is a male-oriented society. Of course, to get women to play along, men also needed to devise some rewards or payoffs for getting you to let them have their own way. We'll discuss in depth what these prizes for your obedience are in the chapters that follow. Even if you consider yourself among the most sophisticated of women, we think you're in for some real surprises!

Traditionally women have been raised to be "good girls." They have been taught to sacrifice their individuality, their achievements, their emotions, and even their goals in order to comply with others. The "good girl" puts others' needs first, and she defines herself through her relationships with others. This leads to anger, resentment and powerlessness, and in some cases, to illness. In the seventies, Claude Steiner, Ph.D., a psychologist, wrote a best-seller called *Scripts People Live*. Although he did not know it, his scripts about women often described victims of the "Good Girl Syndrome." For example, he described "Mother Hubbard," the woman behind the family, who has been taught to take care of her husband and children, and gain satisfaction vicariously through their achievements. When the children grow up, she no longer has a source of satisfaction. The problem is—she never takes the time to nurture herself. In fact, she thinks she is not supposed to be powerful; she is just supposed to perceive other people's needs.

Living in a society where men are better may seem perfectly normal to you. For many women, this condition has been unavoidable; it's been the only world they've ever known. For example, think back to your childhood. When you were young, you may have been a "good" little girl who wanted only to please Mommy and Daddy. Your world was built around them. They gave you everything—including your identity and self-worth. The truth of the matter is that while they may have loved you dearly, they still wanted you to live up to their expectations.

And since they made the rules, if you didn't do what they wanted, you thought they might "take away" their approval. So the "good girl" was weaned, toilet-trained, dressed and molded to fit strict rules of society. Your clothes may or may not have been pink, your hair long or short, but your demeanor probably was deferential. You may even have been allowed to be creative or somewhat independent, but these impulses always took their rightful place—far beneath "fitting into society" and "pleasing others."

"If you do that, I won't love you anymore" or "God doesn't like bad little girls" are familiar messages to the female child growing up in our culture. I was "trapped in the name of love," said Amanda. "Every time I didn't do something my mother asked she said I was bad and didn't love her anymore." Amanda learned very quickly that following the rules of others (external control) leads to love and approval, while creating your own system to live by results in rejection and condemnation. Kay, one of the most timid women we ever set on the road to wellness, said, "When I was six, I was certain I'd go straight to hell if I ever got a spot on my party dress. No wonder I hate socializing and going to parties today!"

What's more, in the midst of learning to obey external versus internal signals, many girls often feel a strange tension growing inside them. Maybe around the age of 4, or by the time you entered the first grade, you might have noticed that little boys were allowed to make more of their own rules, break more of the external ones, and have their way far more often than you were. If you asked about it, your teacher or your parents might have just said, "Boys will be boys." In other words, "It's OK for boys to break rules, but not girls." If you wanted to do any of the same things, you couldn't. No wonder you were confused.

Doing what he wants means a boy is strong, independent. Doing what she wants means a girl is spoiled, willful and disobedient. The message is seldom this obviously stated, but the point definitely makes its mark. So strong is its effect that by the time Daddy's little girl comes of age, she is still taking cues from what an external world expects of her rather than what she may want to make of herself—that is, if she's ever even allowed herself to *think* about what she wants. Why a woman is prepared from birth for dependence while men are raised to be independent and how to change this in your life are the topics of this book. By now, you probably see that this preparation is no accident! But, as you will also learn, it is possible—and rewarding—to free yourself!

Portrait of a Typical Case

Though we didn't recognize it at the time, many of our early cases were victims of the Good Girl Syndrome. Their common complaint was *so* common it didn't seem to make them different from most other women. Basically, the women we talked with didn't feel they were getting enough out of life. In later years we discovered that what set them apart was the *chronic* and *severe* nature of this complaint. "I felt down so long, I forgot what it was like to be happy," or "I thought everybody was miserable when they got older," or "I hated my life but was just too tired to do anything about it" were common comments. Many women had had this feeling for a number of years: It went back to early childhood. And it overwhelmed others to the point where they could not bear to get up in the morning. Perhaps most self-destructive was the fact that most of these women felt their lives were filled with "I shoulds" and "I oughts" rather than "I wants."

A typical example of one of these cases was Kathy, who, at 25, was still living with her parents because they "needed" her and it "wouldn't be right to abandon them." First and most obviously, Kathy felt there was something inherently, deeply wrong with her. She believed she had a quirk or basic problem deep inside that she had caused and that she had to correct before she could ever hope to deserve happiness or fulfillment.

"I've always had feelings of inadequacy," she said, "like I'm not good enough for anyone." This worry was coupled with her belief that men were better than women: They were inherently smarter about more important topics and therefore should be obeyed by virtue of their superiority. "Who would pay any attention to a nothing like me?" were the first words we ever remember Kathy saying.

Kathy was rigid and inflexible, believing that rules were sacred, made by superior men like her father, to be followed blindly in exchange for male approval, just as she did when she was a "good little girl." Her father, a career officer in the military, left no room for discussion. Right was right and wrong was wrong. "Good girls" honored and obeyed their parents without question. "Father knows best," she answered when we asked her why she had been so unquestioning as a child. She never had learned the difference between following the regulations set forth by a parent who loved her versus someone who only wished to manipulate her. She trusted all sources of authority without question. She attended parochial school through eighth grade and learned blind devotion to the Holy Father from the Sisters. Her sense of "rightness" and "goodness" depended upon how closely she was able to follow the set of rules set forth by significant men in her life. She engaged in sexual relations but was afraid to say that she enjoyed it because she was afraid of losing the approval of her male partner and being labeled "bad." Kathy described her early sexual encounters as "disasters" because the boys called her cold and frigid for being so unresponsive. "They'd think there's something wrong with me if I got too sexy," she explained.

Her senior year in high school, she did manage to get a boyfriend, Curt, a man very much like her father who expected a woman to be unaroused by the sex act and do what she was told. The relationship left her unfulfilled, but she kept seeing him because he said she was sweet and kind and he loved her. Also, her parents wanted her to marry him. Curt came from a "good" family, worked hard and lived close enough to see them every day.

Kathy's sense of identity came not from within, but from how men saw her. Their approval was everything. To insure this approval she maintained as low a profile as possible so as not to risk rocking the boat or offending a man. Until she took the step to visit us, Kathy had kept herself from experiencing her unknown beauty inside. She had hidden it all to be "good."

In the course of our sessions, one of the exercises we used was to ask Kathy what rules she would like to make for herself—no repercussions, no strings attached. At first, Kathy seemed afraid to come up with an honest answer. She would be too guilty and worried over breaking any rules to ever risk creating one of her own. "Rules of my own? What are you talking about?" she said in total self-denial. Kathy wouldn't even allow herself to admit that she thought about what she would want in her ideal world—it would be much too selfish. Only after she came to be comfortable with us did she begin to admit that she wanted to leave her parents and her boyfriend, to get a job, and to see what the world was like on her own. These were dreams that she thought were unreasonable and that she hadn't shared with anyone before. This was the first time we had ever seen Kathy angry, but it didn't surprise us. We knew Kathy was almost always in an angry state, but she never showed it. And her thoughts of independence, fleeting as they might be, triggered an almost primordial horror. "They'd eat me alive," she shouted when we suggested that she had the strength to make it in the male-dominated business world. "Besides, who'd even hire me?"

Kathy's case may sound extreme, but it is not. In fact, it cannot begin to convey the intensity of Kathy's bottled-up emotions. It has been our experience that women initially will deny much of this picture in themselves—that is until we paint in a bit more detail, filling in the other typical problems. It is only by knowing what those problems are that you can do something about them.

Are You a "Good Girl"? A Test

Let's get started. We have to come up with a specific and

thorough program in our work with women that can clear you of every problem area that may be making you too much of a "good girl" for your own good. Your first step to independence is determining just how much of a "good girl" you really are.

There are twelve parts to our program. Each relates to a different problem area that may be giving you trouble. The more of these areas that apply to you, the "gooder" you are within the context of a male-dominated world. And the more you are satisfying the needs of others to the exclusion of your own. To help you get down to the bottom line and find your own particular programs—the ones that control your life—we ask you take this test. We have included the program number after each question to let you know what specific problem area is being tapped when you answer it.

You may believe you know for certain whether or not you are a "good girl." But this test may surprise you. It's easy. Read the following forty questions designed to measure the extent to which you or someone else controls your emotional world. Answer the questions as truthfully as possible. If the description *almost never* applies to you, rate it 0; if the behavior occurs *sometimes* (not really like you but happens on occasion), give the rating 1; and of its present *almost always* (more like you than not), rate it 2.

1) 0 1 2   You believe there might be something basically wrong with you that's making you unhappy. **(1)**

2) 0 1 2   You're afraid to ask a man for a date or initiate a phone call—he'll think you're too aggressive. **(11)**

3) 0 1 2   You feel better about yourself when you don't have sex. **(6)**

4) 0 1 2   You feel guilty whenever you have your own way, even if it's for something simple. **(10)**

5) 0 1 2   You think that you are "bad" because you think about sex too often. **(6)**

6) 0 1 2   The thought of having to support yourself fills you with terror. **(12)**

7) 0 1 2   You don't like to rock the boat, even if something doesn't seem right. **(4)**

8) 0 1 2   Ideally, you would like your man to be better than you are—taller, smarter, older, more experienced. **(9)**

9) 0 1 2   You feel guilty if you shirk a domestic duty—neglect to clean up the house or make your man cook for himself for a change. **(7)**

10) 0 1 2   You constantly seek the approval of men, whether at work or at home. **(7)**

11) 0 1 2   You feel uncomfortable discussing sex with your children even in a positive way. **(6)**

12) 0 1 2   In your heart of hearts you believe "a woman cannot have both love and career success." **(8)**

13) 0 1 2   You believe that in worldly, important topics, such as business, politics and science, men are inherently smarter. **(2)**

14) 0 1 2   It is more difficult for you to say no to a man than to a woman when he asks you to do something you'd prefer not to do, such as running an errand or doing a favor. **(3)**

15) 0 1 2   An inner voice tells you that it is the goal of a good woman to help her man succeed, even if he doesn't help her. **(5)**

16) 0 1 2   You truly believe that sacrificing for others, even if it means ignoring your wants, makes you a better person. **(5)**

17) 0 1 2   You give up men friends when you enter into an intimate relationship with a man. **(4)**

18) 0 1 2   Deep down, you worry that you are selfish for wanting independence. **(12)**

19) 0 1 2   You still seek the approval, not just the *advice*, of your parents for major decisions in your life. **(12)**

20) 0 1 2   You would be afraid to stimulate or bring yourself to orgasm during lovemaking. **(6)**

21) 0 1 2   You find yourself attending more meetings, weddings, funerals because you feel you should, not because you want to. **(4)**

22) 0 1 2   You believe you aren't allowed to show anger. **(11)**

23) 0 1 2   You respect what is old, such as work schedules, mealtimes, opening a door for a lady, and are suspicious of change. **(9)**

24) 0 1 2   You feel guilty over spending your "husband's [or lover's] money." **(5)**

25) 0 1 2   You eat like a bird when you go with a man to an expensive restaurant; even if you're hungry it wouldn't be right to eat too much. **(7)**

26) 0 1 2   You believe that the most important place for a woman to be is in the home. **(8)**

27) 0 1 2   Your mother or father comes to mind whenever you go against a rule they taught you when you were a child. **(10)**

28) 0 1 2   You make plans with friends and

family, even if you don't want to see them, and consequently resent them for causing you to have a bad time. **(5)**

29) 0 1 2   It's hard for you to accept compliments; often you think they come from only ingenuine politeness. **(1)**

30) 0 1 2   You wear fitted business clothes to work even though you hate them and would rather wear a more comfortable dress or slacks. **(2)**

31) 0 1 2   You haven't done anything really new in more than a month. **(8)**

32) 0 1 2   You use sulking or silence to get what you want and show your displeasure. **(11)**

33) 0 1 2   You are terrified at the thought of a parent or child accidentally "catching" you in the sex act. **(6)**

34) 0 1 2   You feel that rules should be followed because they are made by people whose judgment is better than yours. **(3)**

35) 0 1 2   When you break a rule you feel bad and think you should be punished. **(10)**

36) 0 1 2   You assume traditionally "feminine" roles. You do dishes, iron and clean even if you might prefer to trade off with your husband for some of his chores. **(9)**

37) 0 1 2   You feel you're not complete without a man who loves you. **(7)**

38) 0 1 2   You would do almost anything to avoid a fight or confrontation. **(12)**

39) 0 1 2   You find yourself making statements

such as: "Things have always been that way," "You can't beat the system," "You can't fight city hall," "That's only natural." **(9)**

40) 0 1 2   You feel uneasy at work because you fear the supervisor or colleagues will uncover the "real" you. **(1)**

Now tally your numbers. The following guide will show the degree to which you are a victim of the Good Girl Syndrome.

0 to 20   You are already an independent woman. You set your own rules for personal fulfillment. Read this book to validate your approach to total living or to help someone else.

21 to 50   The Good Girl Syndrome is looming on the horizon. Read the instructions outlined in the next section to determine where you need to focus your energy. There may be only a few areas that need work.

51 to 80   The Good Girl Syndrome is in full operation. You need to give your complete attention to the steps necessary for clearing each program. If you find that this book simply does not offer enough, you may want to speak with a therapist.

How to Create Your Own Design for Change

Now let's analyze your test more closely to see what your strengths and weaknesses are in the way you relate to men. This will allow you to set up your own program for using the techniques we'll outline in the upcoming chapters. You may find, as the woman in the example will show you, that you'll need only to work on a few of the programs in the book. But knowing exactly what you want to work on is the first step in working toward any solutions!

Now let's look back to the "good girl" test you just took. On a separate sheet of paper, draw three columns with the headings: *Almost Never True, Sometimes True* and *Almost Always True*. Review the test and place each description in the appropriate column. Here's how Nancy B., a 36-year-old housewife and free-lance writer, filled in this design for change:

Almost Never True

— Has nagging feeling at work that supervisor or colleagues will uncover the "real" her. **(1)**

— Has more difficulty saying no to a man than a woman. **(3)**

— Wears a suit or jacket to work when she would prefer not to. **(2)**

— Hears an inner voice saying that it is the goal of woman to help man succeed. **(5)**

— Feels less of a person without a man to love her. **(7)**

— Identity is dependent upon the approval of men. **(7)**

— Eats like a bird to be viewed by a man as feminine. **(7)**

— Believes a woman cannot have both love and success. **(8)**

— Believes that the most important place for a woman to be is in the home. **(8)**

— Feels like an ingrate when has own way over a man. **(10)**

— Worries she is selfish for wanting independence. **(12)**

— Sulks to get what she wants or show her displeasure. **(11)**

— Would do anything to avoid a confrontation. **(12)**

Sometimes True

— Believes there's something wrong with her. **(1)**

— Does things because she should rather than because she wants. **(4)**

— Assumes "feminine" roles due to cultural demand. **(9)**

— Afraid to ask a man for a date or initiate in other ways. **(11)**

— Believes sacrifice for others, to exclusion of self, makes her a better person. **(5)**

— Believes that denying sex makes her more spiritual. **(6)**

— Feels "bad" because she needs sex to keep mood up and feel attractive. **(6)**

— Would be afraid to bring herself to orgasm during lovemaking. **(6)**

— Feels guilt if she shirks a domestic duty. **(7)**

— Expresses attitudes that lock her into the past. **(9)**

— Feels guilty over spending "husband's money." **(5)**

— Mother or father comes to mind when she goes against a childhood rule. **(10)**

— Still seeks approval of parents for major decisions. **(12)**

— Makes statements to the effect that things will always be the way they are. **(9)**

Almost Always True

— Believes men are better. **(2)**

— Feels rules should be made by those who are superior. **(3)**

— Feels it's bad to break rules, even if they don't work for you. **(4)**

— Not seen alone with another man without her partner present. **(4)**

— Agrees to do activities she doesn't want to do with friends and family and then resents them because she has a bad time. **(5)**

— Seldom discusses and never talks about positive aspects of sex with her children. **(6)**

— Uncomfortable with the thought of a parent or child "catching" her in the sex act. **(6)**

— Hasn't done anything really new in more than a month. **(8)**

— Would like her man to be better than she is. **(9)**

— Feels bad and worthy of punishment when she breaks a rule. **(10)**

— Believes it unfeminine to show anger. **(11)**

— Has difficulty accepting compliments. **(1)**

— The thought of having to support herself fills her with terror. **(12)**

Now let's analyze our findings. We'll look closer at our test case so that you can get a better idea of what we do to spot your areas of GGS.

Nancy B. scored a 38 on the test. As we look at the profile of columns, we see many contradictions. For example, the thought of having to support herself fills her with terror, but she believes it unfeminine to express anger at this situation. This is not uncommon for a "good girl."

Now look at the programs that pop up most often in the *Almost Never True* column. This will reveal your *strong* points. In the above case, we see three points that reflect Program 7: "I am as men see me." Women who are victims of this program form their identities according to how men see them rather than how they see themselves. Since Nancy B. says that three of the behaviors from this program almost never occur, it is reasonable for us to say she has a good self-image. She doesn't need men to give her her sense of worth. But we see later what seems to be a contradiction. She rates the belief "Men are better" a 2. She thinks well of herself, has confidence in her own decisions, but still views men as superior.

Next, look at the most frequently occurring programs in the *Almost Always True* column. Here are your particular problem areas, your reactions that most make you a victim of the Good Girl Syndrome.

In our sample case, Program 4, "The rules are sacred," and Program 6, "Good girls don't really enjoy sex," each occur twice. Nancy B. seems to be fairly rigid in her need for absolute blacks and whites in her life. She feels she must obey, even if it means that she has to sacrifice liberty, so that she will not have to think her way out of gray areas. She would rather follow rules that don't work for her than make them herself. Along with this comes her belief that she has to deny sexual pleasure, which eliminates another common area of conflict in exchange for another freedom, sexual expression.

"I am as men see me" (**7**), "The rules are sacred" (**4**) and "Good girls don't really enjoy sex" (**6**) are most noteworthy in this profile because they show up so often, but only at one end of the rating. This allows us to draw some conclusions about Nancy B. "I am as men see me" (**7**) never appears in the *Almost Always* column, and "The rules are sacred" (**4**) and "Good girls don't really enjoy sex" (**6**) never pop up in the *Almost Never* column. We can see from this that Nancy B. has a strong sense of her own identity but still has two problems: going against rules that don't work for her and enjoying sex.

We were able to help Nancy B. using the strategies described in Chapters 4 and 7. We asked her to list all the rules she followed that did not lead to her own personal happiness.

Together we closely examined whether following these rules really made any sense, even if it did make her feel like a "good girl." Next, we taught her the exercises described in Chapter 6 for sensory expansion so that she could go beyond the logic of her sexual taboos and experience fulfillment. Today, Nancy has rid herself of her self-defeating thinking and is fully prepared to succeed in her own world, on her own terms.

You can build your own design for change as you examine your test. Notice the problems that occur more than once in the *Almost Always* column, but not at all in the *Almost Never* column. You will want to read the chapters covering these problems first and will want to begin trying some of the strategies we present in them.

Each chapter begins by telling you *where* your problem came from—the circumstances that led to your becoming a victim of it in the first place. Then, we'll carefully explain *what* your problem looks like—the everyday behavior that shows you have it. Next, you'll learn *why* you choose to hold on to your self-defeating behavior. Finally, and most importantly, we'll instruct you in *how* to get rid of your problems using proven strategies we've developed based on sound behavioral principles.

We'll give you many of these strategies at the end of each chapter. They are things that anyone can do, and we'll show you how to use them to get definite, positive results. The rewards for giving up good girldom are many. As you will soon see, the fruits of freedom are sweet.

The "Good Girl" Versus Personal Freedom: A Challenge

We created this test and design for change to make you more aware of yourself and to give you some strategies for freeing yourself. Once you know yourself—what governs you, and what you need to do—you can begin your climb to freedom.

Most of you who are reading this book have already taken

the first step. You've decided you don't want to give all your power to others. You no longer want to be generous to a fault, at the mercy of the people you serve, no matter how "good" they say you are for doing so. Your growth begins with your awareness. Self-satisfaction can come with knowledge of your powers to change yourself.

Join us in this challenge! Study the behaviors and the rewards for engaging in them that unfold as we describe the twelve programs comprising the Good Girl Syndrome. Be honest in your self-evaluation, do not be afraid to see yourself clearly, and do not be afraid to try the strategies. They're simple, effective, and at the heart of our programs. Once you make the change, you'll *feel* the difference in yourself and what's more, others will *see* it!

But don't forget to give yourself a break. Don't be too hard on yourself. Even if you're only taking one small step, imagine that you are trying to create a woman you would like to know. Think of the marvelous possibilities. Then act on them to produce a wonderful new reality. You definitely have the power to do it!

1

"There Is Something Wrong With Me"

I've been running from myself ever since I can remember . . . probably 'cause I don't like myself much.

CLAIRE S.
age 34

Claire is a housewife and mother of two children. She is happy in her marriage to Mike except for one thing: Mike has an overpowering need to dominate and thus keep Claire dependent upon him. Claire lets Mike get by with this kind of behavior because she doesn't believe she deserves anything better. "I know there must be something wrong with me to feel this way," she explains to us. "Mike is really a wonderful husband." Because she feels that being unhappy in the relationship is her fault—her defect—she has no expectations that her husband should change in any way.

In typical "good girl" fashion, she came to us to help her reduce her stress, believing there were no valid outside reasons to make her feel so tense. Using a behavioral approach, we immediately got down to specifics. We asked Claire to describe *exactly* what Mike did to squelch her independence. Claire quickly said, "He won't let me buy my own car. If I could just get out of the house once in a while, I wouldn't feel so trapped. But he says there's no place I need to go he can't take me."

"He won't let you?" we parroted. Claire was speaking as a

22

child would about her father. "Well . . ." she hesitated, "he doesn't want me to." We were rapid to point out that there's an enormous difference between not being allowed to do something and not doing it for fear of losing someone else's approval. Then we asked the all-important question, "Do you think you *deserve* a car of your own?" She hesitated a moment, then she smiled, "You're damned right I do!"

We then helped Claire to see that she was *acting* as if she didn't deserve to independently go for what she wanted whether others wanted her to have these things or not. We helped Claire to start doing some of the things she wanted to do and to let everyone else adjust to her for a change. Claire did just that. She stopped asking for permission and simply went out and bought a wonderful secondhand car to help alleviate her feeling of being trapped. Mike was upset at first, and that was OK—it was to be expected. Everybody gets upset when things don't go the way they would like. But nobody can stay mad forever, and in time he got used to the idea. He adjusted.

Like Claire, you can hold yourself back only if you *believe* you are flawed and undeserving. People who *want* to hold you back know this, and they may use it to their advantage.

Since the story of Eve tempting Adam with the apple, society has painted woman in a negative light. But we're going to help you see yourself in a better light. At the end of this chapter we'll show you a strategy for boosting your self-image and fighting off the negative things you may be believing about yourself. Your self-image *is* tremendously sensitive to outside influences, but you have the power to make things better. If you tell yourself "There is nothing wrong with me, I am all right as I am" you can open yourself up to a new world. We all begin from the same source. What you accomplish from there depends on what you believe you're capable of achieving. Believing in yourself is the key to your personal energy, and to a new, happier you!

The Universal Myth that Women Are Flawed

Where does Claire's feeling of inadequacy come from? More important, why do many women feel as inadequate as Claire does? On the surface, at least, it seems that everyone is trying to tell women that something is wrong with them.

Some women believe that their problems began with the way women were viewed in the Bible, particularly in the Garden of Eden story. Women have commented to us, "Why is it always the woman who is to blame when things go wrong? Is that what the Bible is supposed to be telling us?" or "I'm sure it was a man who wrote that God said Eve's punishment for eating the apple was that men should rule over her." From the story of Adam and Eve onward, some women have come to feel that not only must they obey men without question, but that any independent move they make will be worthless and possibly destructive.

Another problem area for women lies in our fairy tales. Nowhere is passivity in women more rewarded than in the golden classics we learned as children. Colette Dowling develops this point in *The Cinderella Complex* when she says, "Like Cinderella, women today are still waiting for something external to transform their lives." To many, the Damsel in Distress is the ideal woman: The only way she can attract Prince Charming is if she has a problem that only he can solve.

Here the message is that you must have a terrible problem, or at least be passive, to be loved by a man. Rapunzel, Snow White, Sleeping Beauty, Cinderella—all of them needed men to rescue them from situations they could not escape on their own. Through fairy tales, girls learn that being helpless is the ideal way to be appealing and to catch a man. So you grow up waiting for The Knight in Shining Armor, since you were never taught that you could save yourself.

Like so many of the myths you were taught, this idea of helplessness just doesn't seem to work. Did you ever ask, "Why didn't Rapunzel just cut off her hair herself, tie it to the windowsill, crawl down the tower and get on with her life instead of waiting for a man to do it for her? Why did Snow

White and Sleeping Beauty have to lie around forever waiting for some man's kiss? Why didn't Cinderella try to leave?" The answer to these questions is simple: The men who wrote these stories and the societies that supported them want you to believe you are lacking and can't live without them. They want you to follow their rules because it supports the system they have created.

Women have unwittingly perpetuated this myth about their worth. It may have been because they couldn't see an alternative. In any event, if women don't think they have an out, they can't teach their daughters to be free-thinking. Believing that you are too incomplete to do your own thinking naturally leads you to look for someone to do your thinking for you. So sometimes without realizing it, women come to think that they can't take care of themselves. The problem is compounded as girls learn that they should look for someone to take care of them.

Alexandra, 53, is treated like a princess by her adoring husband, Bill. From the day at age 18 when she married she has never had to do a speck of work. Cooks, maids, caterers, gardeners and poolmen do everything for her. Yet good as Bill is to her, Alex is not satisfied. "Do you know what that man does when we're out in a restaurant?" she asked us. "He refuses to order more water for me until I've drained my glass completely. He won't talk to the waiter if there's so much as a drop remaining!" Now we realize this won't seem like such a serious problem to most of our readers, but it was to Alex. We bring it up here because it so beautifully illustrates how a woman can get so locked in to her *role* of dependency that she fails to solve the simplest problem. The solution in Alex's case was to order water refills herself. "Why didn't I think of that!" she exclaimed when we proposed it to her. Why? Because she *expects* to be dependent. Movies and television, as well, promote the image of inept, childlike women. As late as 1972, Marlon Brando in *The Godfather* even says, "Carelessness is for women and children." The lesson, again, is that it is all right for women to break down; there will always be a man around to clean up after.

What This Learned Helplessness Means

So you see that many women in our society, like Alexandra, are taught to be helpless. Some even say they were taught to be masochists. In general terms, a masochist is anyone who takes pleasure in being abused or dominated. If you are one of the many women who allows herself to be dominated by a man, you may receive the pleasure of his approval and his stamp of "goodness." The label of goodness is your reward for being dominated. Some women take it one step further—they see their passive "goodness" as a way to win martyrdom and sainthood.

One of our clients, Kim R., was a vivacious 34-year-old woman who wanted very much to go back to school. "I don't feel like I'm growing unless I'm learning new things," she said. She had missed the opportunity to finish college when she married, but couldn't quite pinpoint what was holding her back. She reviewed catalogs regularly, filled out application forms, bought the appropriate texts, even paid the registration fee, but never showed up for class. She said that her husband even supported her, saying, "You can do anything you want, honey."

Yet whenever Kim made moves toward knowledge and independence, her husband Marty would slip into spells of withdrawal, which Kim interpreted as anxiety at the thought of being temporarily separated from her. "He always got so depressed whenever I was away from him," she said. She then reported feeling so sorry for him that she couldn't bear the thought of leaving him on his own for the period necessary to take classes. It wouldn't be "nice," she explained. "So I gave up school to be good to my husband." Over time we came to explain to her, "Kim, your suffering for the pleasure of being called a saint is a very small reward for your sacrifice." We then gave her an exercise. We asked Kim to make a list of all the benefits Marty was reaping from her sainthood, all the payoffs to Marty for keeping Kim out of school. The list contained what one would expect: companionship, meals on time, more money in the household kitty. But there was one surprise: a bigger ego. As Kim explained it, "I guess I just didn't realize that in spite of what he said, it made him feel smarter to keep me uneducated." She suddenly saw both herself and Marty more clearly. There was nothing saintly or commendable about staying in ignorance for any reason. She is now enrolled in a college night program and is passing her courses with flying colors.

Many men love helpless women because they don't make waves; they don't upset the system of rules. They reward this kind of suffering with approval, and women become all the more masochistic for it. Psychiatrist Natalie Shainess in her book *Sweet Suffering* observed that "the masochistic person always feels in the wrong." She continues, "When someone powerful comes along and says you are wrong and this is right, she has no capacity to fight." Shainess says that suggestibility is a hallmark of the serious masochist, a total willingness to accept the premises and arguments of another person.

In the pages that follow, we're going to show you how to fight the negative influences of others and heighten your suggestibility to the *positive* things *you* tell yourself about yourself. Because in the final analysis, the advice you give yourself is the most important. Only you know what's best for you and the only one you can depend upon to get it for you *is* you.

The Danger of Feeling You Will Always Be Taken Care Of

As you may already know, and as Kim has already shown you, believing you always will be taken care of can be dangerous. There are many reasons why, but the most basic and most important one is because it is untrue—it's as big a fairy tale as the stories of Cinderella and Rapunzel.

The problem of thinking you need to be taken care of shows itself in many ways. One of the most common is in the way women have to deal with supporting themselves—for example, in the aftermath of a divorce. In an age in which one out of two marriages ends in divorce, many middle-aged women who have been full-time homemakers for over 20 years abruptly find themselves in the midst of financial crisis.

Diedre, 32, divorced a year, is struggling to make ends meet and support her four small children. She has two jobs, almost never sees her kids because she works nights and weekends as well as a regular 9-to-5 job, and still has to rely on money from her widowed mother in order to get by. She tells us that her ex-husband, Eric, a plastic surgeon, "makes five times what I can as a receptionist, and yet he gives me less than half his income in alimony and child support."

In the early years of their marriage, when Diedre was in her 20s, she worked hard to help Eric through medical school. Once he graduated, they set about having a family. Soon after the last child was born, Eric began having repeated affairs, but Diedre believed that marriage should be "till death do us part" and resolved to stick it out. She asked Eric to join her in marriage counseling, but he refused. A little over a year ago he left her for his 22-year-old office secretary. Diedre angrily summed it up this way: "All society talks about is how great being a wife and mother is, but when the whole thing falls apart and you're out on your own with four kids to support, then where is society?" This is a common complaint we hear from women who have come to see the hard way that men will *not* always take care of them. They learned that the only way to assure that they'll always be taken care of is to know *how* to do it themselves, or know they *can* do it for themselves.

Women at Work: A Problem

As many of you know, taking a job doesn't solve the problem of being dependent. It just opens a trunkful of new problems. Not only must you buck the system, you face an even tougher opponent: yourself.

Cindy was a 60-year-old accountant with ulcers she developed and maintained with her constant fear of being fired. Cindy was compulsively exact about work—so relentless that she drove the rest of the staff crazy with her hairsplitting attention to detail. She was the first one in the office in the morning and the last one to leave, slaving into the wee hours to meet a "deadline" even if she knew it could wait. Pencils were always sharpened, stationery overstocked, entries obsessively neat, and assignments nearly perfect. Yet an hour never passed in which she didn't harbor images of losing the job she had held more than thirty years.

"I was raised to be a 'lady,'" Cindy said, "with doll houses and knitting needles, frilly dresses and china dishes." Her mother thought that her love for facts and figures was silly, and definitely not something she should consider seriously. "Stop trying to be as smart as men" was mother's advice. She did rebel against her mother, to an extent, however: She became an accountant. But the reprimanding voice of her mother stayed with her throughout her life, always telling her there was something wrong with her for choosing a career, and even worse, a career as an accountant, that she could never really make it in a man's world. "Everyone has his place," was what mother said, "and yours is not to join the ranks of men." Inevitably she would fail in the "man's business" of numbers. During all her years on the job she refrained from doing anything to reduce her stress or alleviate her ulcers because she knew the condition was hopeless; she simply was not a man and therefore had every reason to worry about competing in a male-dominated company. The payoff for this self-defeating reasoning was that Cindy did nothing to change. When we were able to help Cindy to become aware of her problem and her reasons for holding on to it, she was quick to develop strategies to change it.

A strategy that worked especially well is the mind-clearing exercise we describe in Chapter 6, for turning off the chatterbox in your head. Whenever Cindy heard the voice of her mother telling her she had no business in a "man's job," she would breathe deeply several times and do this exercise to clear the unwanted voice from her consciousness. "I never realized how really locked into the past I was," Cindy said. "I was still paying attention to things my mother told me when I was five years old!" Although there are still times when Cindy hears the inner voice of her mother trying to limit her actions, she has stopped paying attention. Other exercises we devised for Cindy included instruction to voluntarily go over deadline on certain tasks and take unscheduled time-outs for chats and walks. This served to break down the compulsiveness of her ulcer-producing behavior.

Why the Damsel in Distress
Fails on the Job

"I'll never understand men," Betty, age 25, complained to us. "They're like Jekyll and Hyde. Sometimes they make me feel like a queen and other times they treat me like the lowest thing on earth." Betty's three-year marriage to Joshua had been "made in heaven." Whenever Betty wanted something, she would roll her eyes and sweetly ask Josh to get it for her. However, when she went to work part time in Josh's clothing store, things changed drastically. He no longer thought it cute when Betty flirted with him in front of customers or asked him to do everything for her from telling her where the merchandise was to ringing up the sale. The helplessness that so enamored Josh at home turned him off totally at work.

Many a "good girl" often discovers that what pleases a man in the home does not please him in the business world. At home, a woman's helplessness may make a man feel like a king. It is here women learn they have to be helpless in order for their men to love them. But on the job this helplessness only costs him money. A damsel in distress at work puts the whole operation in distress. Women, who have been trained to get help at home by acting helpless, suddenly discover that the rules are completely different at work. At work you inspire the support of others by being competent and helping yourself.

Leslie, 34, a client of ours who was almost fired from her job as an assistant plant manager, provides a good example of how the damsel in distress fails at work and how she could change. Leslie was continually going to her supervisors, even her subordinates, throwing her hands up in despair at the seemingly insurmountable problems with her staff. "I just don't know what to do," she would complain. "It's just too, too much." In the ten years that Leslie had been married to Herb, this kind of behavior had never failed to get her what she wanted. If the faucet leaked, the light switch shorted, the piles of dishes got too high, she would just let Herb know it was more than she could bear and he'd cheerfully take care of it. So cheerfully, in fact, that Leslie would go out of her way to ask for his help. He seemed to enjoy being in the strong position so much.

Gently, we explained to Leslie, "While this kind of behavior might get you what you want at home, it's only trouble at work." Leslie had two choices. She could continue to let others do her work for her or she could learn to change; in other words, stop complaining to others when she was in distress and turn to herself for the answers. In either case, she would be choosing to be honest, admitting, "There is really nothing wrong with me."

Leslie decided to change her behavior, and with our help, she learned to counter all self-defeating statements that she made to herself with their positive opposite. Whenever work got to be too much for her, we asked her to simply repeat several times to herself "I can do this if I just put my mind to it." In time she stopped complaining, and soon not only was she believing in herself, her colleagues were believing in her as well. "I learned my lesson," Leslie smiled in her last session with us. "People at work help those who help themselves."

Some Typical Behaviors

Now that we have looked at the nature and source of this self-defeating damsel-in-distress idea, let's move on to the second step in clearing it from your way of thinking. We'll examine *how* this idea pops up in your behavior. We want you to be able to answer the question "If I had this problem, what would I *do?*" or "What would someone *see?*"

So here are just a few of the most common ways women say to others "There is something wrong with me."

- Needing your choices validated by others.
- Being unable to accept compliments.
- Denying yourself the good things in life that you love—roses, facials or whatever—because you don't believe you're worth it.

As we saw in the case of Leslie, success on the job comes from *inspiring* people to support you, not crying for it. Georgia, 43, had been five years without a promotion in a company that manufactured paper bags. Like Leslie, she emanated an aura of helplessness that did anything but inspire confidence in either the staff or the executive level. Instead of just throwing up her hands at every problem as Leslie did, Georgia showed there was something wrong with her in different ways. She never made an important work decision without first consulting male colleagues with, "That design's more efficient, don't you think, Hank?" or "Isn't that a better color, George?" or "The other guys agree. . . ." The compliments she did receive, she negated with, "Oh, anybody can do this" or "I was just lucky, I guess" or "The concept I started out with would make anybody look good." What flaws couldn't be telegraphed verbally, Georgia communicated in her lifestyle. She dressed plainly, she never wore jewelry and seldom applied makeup. Georgia let everyone in the office know that her social life was as drab as her office one—she never vacationed, never went out.

After months of working with Georgia, we finally asked her, "How many people in your office do you think would like to be you?" She immediately replied, "None, I don't even want to be me!" Then we asked, "Could you be inspired by someone you would not like to *be?*" The moment Georgia was able to see herself as others were seeing her, she knew why she had not been promoted: There was nothing in her behavior that inspired confidence in others because she had no confidence in herself. We told her that *first* she must *behave* like she had confidence and soon others would believe she did as well as herself. She started making decisions on her own, said "thank you" to *well-deserved* compliments, spruced up her appearance, and began telling staff how much fun she was having on her weekends (we laid out a special program to soup up her social life). Within months, people were wishing they could be like Georgia and were coming to her for advice. People whose advice is sought get promoted, and within a year Georgia was, with more than double her former salary!

- Meeting someone you really like and thinking, "This can't last. As soon as he discovers what kind of person I really am, it'll be over."

We found a good example of this kind of thinking in Mary,

a woman in her late 30s who claimed to want a husband and children desperately. She kept herself in shape with exercise, dressed beautifully, spoke articulately and was able to attract many desirable men. Yet whenever one told her he loved her and wanted her for his wife, Mary had an overwhelming urge to escape from the situation. She had the same problem with friends who expressed strong feelings for her. Mary wanted to return the positive feelings others extended toward her; yet every time a man said he loved her, she suffered such attacks of anxiety and colitis that she was forced to end the relationship. The words "I love you" filled Mary with unendurable guilt. They made her feel like a deceitful, unworthy temptress who was snaring her unsuspecting victim into a romantic fantasy that would surely go up in smoke as soon as he discovered what she was really like. The source of these feelings of lack came from her parents who had always wanted a boy. Her belief that she was flawed and unworthy had won Mary pity from those around her, but the price was too high. We tried to help Mary to understand that she was just fine as she was. That way, she would feel no guilt in having someone desire her, for she was an intelligent, attractive woman. We provided her with a strategy—to correct herself out loud every time a negative thought crossed her mind. In time, Mary was able to turn her behavior around. Two years ago, we were invited to her wedding.

- Feeling constantly uneasy at work because you believe the boss and your colleagues will uncover the "real you."
- Excessive apologizing for almost everything.
- Indulging yourself in self-deprecating statements.

While Mary's negative image of the "real" her ruined her personal relationships, Mandy, a 28-year-old legal secretary, was jeopardizing her job security fearing that the men she worked for would soon "be on" to her. Her mother, whose obsessive neatness reached clinical proportions when Mandy's father left for another "more passionate" woman, always called Mandy a "slob." No matter how many times the little girl cleaned her room, washed her face and changed her clothes, it was never good enough for Mommy. Now, no matter how many times the adult Mandy typed a perfect page, kept a perfect file or made a perfect call, she knew it wouldn't be enough to keep the bosses from eventually seeing the slob she "really" was. Because of this false insecurity Mandy apologized for everything. If the boss complained about the indigestion he got from the caterer, Mandy said, "I'm sorry," and truly believed she was somehow responsible for it. When she wasn't apologizing for conditions beyond her control, she was putting herself down with statements such as, "I'm so stupid" or "I'm always late" or "That's just the way I am" or "I'll just never get it together."

We worked to show her that the "real" Mandy was not what her mother or even we told her she was, but what *she* told herself she was. We instructed her to tell herself repeatedly, "I really am good. I really am competent," until she came to believe it. But *before* the change in her belief occurred we told her to change her behavior. She was to carry a small pocket notebook with her at work at all times. Whenever she found herself apologizing or putting herself down, she was to mark what she had done, the time, place and activity. *When* did it occur? *Where* did it occur? *What* was she doing at the time? For example, if while talking to a colleague at 9:30 A.M., in the lobby of the office building she said, "I'm always such a nit," she was to record this information *immediately* into her book. After a few days of recording she had a very good idea what circumstances needed the most work. In Mandy's case, she discovered she was most likely to apologize late in the day, at her desk, while on the telephone. She made a special effort to stop *acting* like there was something wrong with her under these conditions.

- Feeling defensive and always thinking you need to explain yourself ("I did it because" . . . "You'd be like that too if" . . . "I'd like to see you do any better").
- Giving too many reasons to justify your behavior.
- Being overly opinionated, taking any disagreement as a personal attack on your self-image.

Victoria, 58, is a perfect example of a "good girl" whose belief that there was something wrong with her made her defensive and opinionated to the point where she risked losing the love of Stan, the man she had been married to for nearly forty years. Victoria's five children were all grown, with families of their own, and while they were loving and saw her often, she was plagued by feelings of uselessness and unworthiness that cropped up now that her children had left the nest. Because Victoria had never really felt adequate simply to be herself, she needed the role of motherhood to justify her existence. Once that was gone, the old feelings of incompleteness came back. Stan was supportive and caring, but Victoria began reading things into his every word. If he said, "I see you got the groceries," she'd defensively snap back with, "I did it because we're out of food. You want to eat, don't you?" or "You'd go shopping too if you had nothing else to do like me" or "What'd you expect me to do all day?" Then she'd follow with a deluge of reasons to *justify* the innocuous piece of behavior Stan was referring to. She could never make a simple statement such as, "Yes, we needed some things." Instead it had to be followed by all the possible reasons why she went grocery shopping: "There was a sale on produce" or "I need to use my coupons before they expire" or "I had to go today because I'll have too much work tomorrow"—as if she were being questioned as to her competency and decision-making abilities. The final phase in her overreaction was always a form of opinionated speech. Victoria went from defensive, to justifying, to attacking, all in a few seconds: "I have every right to get groceries whenever I please. Who do you think you are? You have no right to attack me like that."

No one had attacked Victoria. She was attacking herself. The hardest part we found in helping Victoria was getting her to see what she was doing. For a long time she really couldn't comprehend that she was being defensive, overjustifying and opinionated. We began by asking her to keep a record of *every time* she found herself explaining *why* she had done something. Then, item by item, we discussed whether there really was a need to explain herself and her reasons for doing each action. Eventually she saw that there wasn't. We pointed out that it really was OK to be herself, to do what she wanted without having to explain why.

• • •

- Taking care of everyone else first, implying that you deserve to be last.
- Never expecting anyone to do you a favor or go out of his way for you.
- Always letting men take the lead in conversation when in mixed company.
- Socializing mainly with friends and acquaintances of your husband or their wives (you are not a complete enough person to merit separate friendships of your own).
- Often feeling as if you are a child when you're in the company of men.

Alice, 42, the mother of three and active in more than a dozen civic organizations, always speaks a little softer and childishly raises her voice in the company of men, yet when serving on a committee with other women, her behavior is strong and self-assured. Her entire life is devoted to keeping the men in her life happy—catering to friends of her husband, letting them speak first, arranging surprise parties, buying presents even if it's not a special occasion, setting up activities—yet she would never dream that someone might do the same for her. Why would they? She doesn't deserve it. Again, Alice, like the other women we've discussed, is getting exactly what she *expects*. The day she expects to be treated like she is a complete person, she will be on her way to independence.

Each of these women had different ways of showing it, but all of them felt that they were in some basic way unworthy. There are so many ways you can put yourself down. And, as we've been saying, you are ultimately only as "good" as you believe yourself to be, and you show it in the everyday behavior of your life. And we're going to show you how to act as if you feel good about yourself. But first let's look at:

The Rewards for
Putting Yourself Down

Why would any woman choose to go through life believing and acting as if there were something wrong with her? What a terrible waste. The heart of learning to be an effective person is comprehending your motives, gaining insight into the payoffs for behaving as you do. There is a reason for all actions, and only when you realize what you do to maintain your situation can you begin to change it.

There may be many dividends for thinking there is something wrong with you. Some you may already be aware of; others will come as a revelation; still others you may not yet be willing to face but will come to with patience and resolve. If you choose to harbor the program that there is something inherently wrong with you, you may find yourself "rewarded" with the following:

- A license to do nothing till you find *it*. Even though the "it" is the message itself!
- A ready-made excuse for why you can't get what you want in life. You do not have the *advantage* of being a man.
- A reason to avoid any of the risks that go with putting yourself in the competition. You also can skirt any failure or criticism.
- A lot of pity and attention for your "plight."
- Allowance to lean on men, as you did on your parents. You don't have to take the risk of accepting responsibility for your own life.
- You won't have to compete if others expect less of you.

These are some of the payoffs for believing you're a helpless woman. They keep the self-image so low that you have to do very little with yourself. The trouble is that while this way of thinking may be easier, the consequences are great—anger and despair.

Recently we were reviewing some of the many letters we get from women who wish to come to us for help. All these women were unhappy but we knew which ones to take seriously by one common statement, "I need to change." This is the all-important ingredient to a better life. If you've already decided to *change,* then you are halfway there! Now let's look at exactly how to do it!

How to Believe You Are All Right

The final step in getting a negative idea out of your mind is to develop a way to rid yourself of the behaviors it breeds. You now understand the what, how, and why of the first program in the Good Girl Syndrome. Now that you have come to understand *it,* and perhaps yourself, better, you can take this final, triumphant move.

The most important step to take is to challenge the idea head-on with your actions. You don't have to know all the reasons *why* you want to change, you just have to know that you want to make things different. And to start, we are suggesting a few concrete strategies for reshaping the way you think about yourself. All our suggestions revolve around the idea of trying to increase your faith in yourself. When you do begin to think better about yourself, you'll feel more in control of your life and the crazy situations that always seem to pop up. The next time you forget to dust the house you won't feel guilty, and you won't feel you have to go out with a friend just because you feel you "should." Try this strategy, and see what happens.

- The next time you find yourself saying something like "I just don't have what it takes to compete with a man," counter that statement out loud with its positive opposite. That is your strategy. *Replace the negative idea with a positive one.* Say to yourself, "I have what it takes to compete with a man. And I'm going to do it!" Your self believes what you tell it. Tell yourself that you're fine, and eventually you can come to believe it!

• • •

A wonderful example of using positive ideas to raise one's self-image is Vickie, a 15-year-old "good girl" who came to us to help her keep from failing school. Vickie believed everything that "superior" adults in her life told her, and when her math teacher said, "You're too stupid to grasp this subject, you'd better drop it," *all* of Vickie's subjects went down, even the ones in which she was getting A's. We worked with Vickie to develop some positive ideas that would counteract the destructive message her unthinking teacher had given her. She told herself, "I am bright. I have the power to do well in any subject I focus on. I will do it." Within a month, Vickie was back to getting A's in her good subjects and even her math grades were rising. Research shows that teachers have tremendous influence over their students. Students often perform more in line with their instructor's expectations than their so-called IQ. But even more important is your own expectation of yourself. If you expect to succeed, you probably will!

Another interesting example is Terri, an attractive divorced woman in her mid-30s who felt it was "unladylike" for her to approach a man she liked in order to strike up a relationship. Terri was desperately lonely but always countered with "What will he think of me?" when we encouraged her to exercise her power and make the first move. In Terri's case there was a man she always ran into in the supermarket that she was dying to meet. After some discussion, we arrived at the special set of ideas that would work for Terri. The next time she saw this attractive stranger across the tomatoes at Safeway she was to repeat softly to herself, "He will like me if I talk to him." The first time Terri tried this strategy, she chickened out, but the next time it led to her walking up and introducing herself. They made a date and he *did* like her for making the first move. He admitted, "I just didn't have the courage to come up to you. I was worried what you would think of me!"

Our strategy produced similar results with Grace, a 42-year-old housewife who thought of herself as mousy and uninteresting. Grace's behavior matched her low self-esteem. She never used makeup, kept her hair unstyled, wore baggy, unattractive clothes and shuffled around. "Why do you act like such a loser?" we asked her. "Because I am!" was her immediate reply. "Only because you *believe* you are," we shot back again. "Tell yourself that you are something else and you will *be* something else." It took some doing, but we finally got Grace to spend five minutes, three times a day, repeating to herself, "I am beautiful . . . I am beautiful . . . I am beautiful . . ." The next time we saw her she was wearing lipstick and a dress that actually revealed a waist. "I'm too beautiful not to show it off," she explained, to our delight.

A bad self-image can interfere with any phase of your life. We counseled Esther, a 52-year-old wife and mother who was so convinced of the myth that women were terrible drivers that she was afraid to drive on the freeway. In her mind there definitely was something wrong with her when she sat behind the wheel of an automobile. We worked out a whole series of exercises for Esther. She was to begin by telling herself "I am a good driver; I have total control" five minutes, three times a day, in the privacy of her home. Next she gave herself this same positive lecture while sitting in her parked car, then while driving on side streets, and finally while driving on the freeway. In three months Esther believed that there was nothing wrong with her on the freeway—and there wasn't!

Believe there is nothing wrong with you and there won't be. The only thing "wrong" is the belief that there is. You are right *as you are!*

2

"Men Are Better"

My parents always wanted a boy, so that's what I
tried to be like.

SANDY R.
patient, age 27

Sandy's parents never came right out and said, "We wish you
were a boy," but they didn't have to. The message was there
from her earliest memory, in the way they treated her two
brothers in comparison with her. If Kip or Sean got an A in
school or excelled in some extracurricular activity, Mother
cooked a special meal and Dad put a bonus on the allowance.
If Sandy did an extra good job helping Mother clean up or if
the little cake she baked tasted great, there were no celebra-
tions or financial rewards. Do you wonder that Sandy grew up
believing that only men's activities were *worth* doing? That
men must be better because what they *do* is better?

Sandy's condition is not unusual; in fact, as we've seen,
many women are taught in the subtlest ways to believe they
should be like a man. It is the logical conclusion to the mythical premise we introduce in this chapter: "Men are better."
The fallacy then compounds itself: "Since there is something
wrong with me, and men are better, I should try to be like a
man."

But women who try to be like men have the cards stacked

against them: They can't be what they are not. And what's worse, the more women try to be like men, the more power they give men. Imitation is the greatest form of flattery. It's time you stopped putting men on a pedestal by trying to be like them.

In the pages that follow, we're going to show you *exactly* how to begin treating men as equals, not superiors. You'll learn how to stop being intimidated by rules men make for you to follow. Intimidation can survive only if you believe your intimidator is better than you. By the time you finish this chapter, you'll know how to keep a man—or anyone else— from manipulating you. You'll also learn how to *behave* as an equal and eliminate all the reasons you may have had for believing in a man's superiority. You will then be equal in power with any man who comes into your life!

The History Behind the Myth that Men Are Better

As you know, there are hundreds of years and dozens of cultures supporting and promoting the idea that men are better. You have a lot of years of dogma to support your feelings of inadequacy.

In many ancient civilizations, woman—the goddess, the earth mother—was considered superior to man because she possessed the power to give life. Some modern feminists and psychologists believe that because man believed he took a secondary place in the biological world, he was prompted to usurp woman's power and make woman dependent on him. In other civilizations man was believed superior because of his greater physical power. He could wage wars and overcome woman physically.

The ancient idea of man's physical strength as "proof" of his superiority has trickled down to women today. Whenever little Sandy's brothers took one of her toys away from her, her mother would warn, "Better let them have it. They're stronger than you. No use fighting." And when Kip and Sean joined the Marines, Sandy's parents threw the biggest party the house had ever seen, while Sandy's move to teacher's college went almost unnoticed. Again, Sandy interpreted that what men did must be better: It received more attention. It was much more important to be a marine than a teacher. This message comes from the highest levels of government and is passed on from family to family. It's the woman who ends up with the short end of the stick.

While it is understandable how, over the ages, man might have come to be known as the sex that dominates physically, we see that women like Sandy believe that man not only dominates physically, but is mentally and spiritually better, too. He is stronger, smarter and closer to God.

It's interesting that psychiatry and psychology take up where religion left off in promoting the myth that men are better. However, it is not surprising when you consider that religion, philosophy, psychology, science, even the arts, have been male-dominated for centuries. It is true that there have been few famous women artists, but the most probable reason for that is not their lack of talent, but the single fact that art is a *business* and men control the marketplace. Men commission men to paint for men in men's institutions. Can you imagine a woman being commissioned to paint the Sistine Chapel?

And Freudianism, the great psychological movement of the twentieth century, casts woman as an inferior being, pining in "penis envy" to be like a man. As Sandy told us, "I went to college to study psychology but all I got was an indoctrination into male accomplishments. You'd think that not a single woman in the world had ever had an original thought." So not only religion, but "science" came to support the myth of masculine supremacy. Today, though women have made considerable strides, these myths of male supremacy still flourish in the arts, in business and, as we've seen, often at home. What we want to show you in this chapter is how to preserve your womanly values of love and kindness in the face of a masculine philosophy that insists that only its rules be followed. In the world we show you, you'll find that you don't have to follow either one set of rules or the other; you can learn to *make* the set of rules that works best for you!

How Your Family Tells You
that Men Are Better

You probably first learned about men from watching your mother and father. None of our institutions can perpetuate the myth of male supremacy so absolutely as marriage. By watching her parents, many little girls learn to model their behaviors according to the ways they see their parents' unequal marriages working.

Kelly, 24, had been married to Brian for three months when she came to us because of problems she was having making the marriage work. We soon saw that her difficulties stemmed from early family training. Her mother considered Kelly's father a "strong" man because he gave all the orders, which she unquestioningly obeyed. Mealtimes, places where they lived, clothing allowances, even their entertainment, were determined by Dad. Mom wouldn't change the brand of her laundry detergent without first consulting Dad. Since Kelly's mother labeled this behavior "strong," Kelly saw it as favorable and looked for a man having these same "positive" qualities as her father. She fell in love with Brian, but after living with him, he clearly didn't meet her expectations. He asked her what she'd like to do evenings, what she'd like to eat, how much money she needed for clothes, where and in what kind of place she'd like to live. In Kelly's eyes Brian was weak. A *man* would make these decisions for her. We helped Kelly to redefine her characterization of manhood: having the strength to let others do what works for them, even if it may not benefit you the most. Kelly finally saw that Brian was, in reality, stronger than her father. He had the strength to let the woman he loved be herself.

The model family teaches a girl to believe men are better because she sees a man making the major decisions of the household, telling her mother what to do and supporting the family financially. Victoria, a 38-year-old postal clerk, faced the painfully difficult decision of whether to permit her 14-year-old son, Eric, to live with his father. She plaintively asked us, "Isn't a boy's place with his father?" Why? Because men are better. A father can make the right decisions for Eric's future plans. A father knows about the business world and can tell Eric how to survive in it. A father can support him better. The things Victoria can give her son—love, caring, understanding, nurturing—may not be good enough to get Eric through the stresses of life. We helped Victoria to realize that she was as good as any man, and her conflict ended. She saw that what she had to give him was just as valuable as what his father had. In the end she fought to keep her son, and she won.

What the Schools and Media Do

At the age of 6 or 7, many "good girls" departed their model homes, where their father ruled, to enter another male-dominated institution: school. Though your teachers may have been women, the people responsible for what you were taught were probably men. Few superintendents, principals, and members of school boards were, or are, women, not to mention members of legislatures governing them. So it's no wonder that women, even if they were teachers, seemed to play secondary roles.

"I've been out of school nearly 25 years now," says Tracy, 42, head of her own greeting-card company, "but I can still feel its mark. Not a day goes by I don't get a flash that it's impossible to compete with men because they're better." Though presently a success in the business world, her good fortune didn't come easy. Much of her difficulty came from scars she got in school. As Tracy described it, "There was no doubt that boys were better than girls in my school. Girls couldn't run for class president. . . . Girls were never allowed to be captains of the teams. . . . Girls couldn't even be smart. I was ostracized for getting the highest grades. Boys wouldn't talk to me 'cause they were jealous. And girls ignored me for fear the boys wouldn't approve if they were my friends. It was lonely. I guess you could say I made it in spite of my education." We helped Tracy to gain peace of mind, as well as to work more efficiently, by challenging the premise of male superiority and *repeatedly* telling herself, "Men are *not* better. I am as good as anyone." She had no problem competing with an equal.

Though there have been changes, our institutions of learning still work against you in many ways. There remains a strong tendency to protect girls from strenuous disciplines that eventually would earn top dollars in the marketplace. Enrollment in home economics is still predominantly female and in some schools is still required for women. Can you imagine the stir it would cause if Home Ec. were *required* for men? (Not a bad idea actually! Everybody should know how to cook and take care of themselves.) While women have recently been allowed to play in more competitive sports, they seldom, if ever, compete against men, and girls' sports are almost never as highly regarded. They never will be in the same "league."

What's worse is that the school's influence continues to be felt long after graduation, and in many cases through a woman's entire life.

Thelma, 58, had a complete breakdown when her husband of twenty-five years, Jay, died of kidney failure due to alcoholism, leaving her penniless, with no means of support. "If only they'd pushed us in school," she cried, "instead of steering us into homemaking. If only they'd shown us how to make some money! The sad thing is that I was bright. I was good in math and the hard sciences. I just couldn't see how algebra or biology or business was going to help me raise a family." Like so many women who are Thelma's age, Thelma went back to school and started from scratch, majoring in economics. In a society whose major institutions only push men to excel, you have to push yourself in order to be better.

The idea of male supremacy runs rampant in the home, in school, in sports and in the media. When the "good girl" reaches adolescence, she may turn to rock or pop music for entertainment and for role models. But what does she hear? With few exceptions, a young girl is exposed to blatant messages of male supremacy: male needs, male desires, male visions of power and happiness. "It's degrading," said Morgan, a 15-year-old we were counseling to reduce her stress. "They make it sound like we're only good for sex and fun."

"Guys call all the shots in these songs," commented Lisa, a streetwise 12-year-old we were helping to free from cocaine addiction. "The music tells us to get high and fly with our man, but it doesn't tell us what to do when we crash. Then the guy splits."

When we first saw Lisa she was wearing a belt with a buckle that said, "boy toy," and we asked her if this was the way she wanted men to see her, as just something to play with. "It's better than nothing," she answered. Her father had treated her mother this way, using her to satisfy his needs, then deserting her when Lisa was only 3. From that time on, her mother had supported Lisa and herself through prostitution, short affairs, and other financial arrangements, all involving meeting the needs of men in exchange for favors. "Coke makes it easier," Lisa explained. "It keeps you from thinking about tomorrow . . . when they won't want you anymore . . ."

We were able to help Lisa when we learned why she thought men were better, deserving to treat women like playthings. According to her, "When you got the bread you can do anything." We therefore concentrated our efforts on getting her to experience making money honestly through her own efforts. When she landed a summer job running errands for a photographic studio, she began to think better of herself and started to tackle her cocaine problem. She was no longer afraid to think about tomorrow.

Motion pictures and television have been as guilty as the record business of painting a woman's chief aim in life as helping and supporting men. Some say that this stance makes us glorify the traditionally "male" ideas of violence. Some of our younger clients show us how true this is. Jody, for example, was a 14-year-old girl who was referred to us by the state for disciplinary problems. She had been in trouble of one kind or another ever since she was 7, when she set fire to the janitor's storeroom at school. Her parents had marital problems and fought with each other so much that they totally neglected Jody. Her pranks became more serious as she grew older, until, at the age of 13, she poked a fellow student's eye out with a pencil in a dispute over who was first in the lunch line. Jody was sent to Juvenile Hall. It was then that we met her. But it was only after a few sessions that she told us that she had been taught men were better and that she thought she should be like a man. Violence was her expression of masculinity. "I'm tough," she would say, "I don't need anybody." We tried to help Jody work at loving and accepting herself. But first we had to help her find herself. She learned that it was difficult to love yourself if you don't even know who you are, when all that meets the eye is a desperate imitation of what you think you *should* be. Our *first* step was to convince her to stop trying to be like a man.

Schools and media that create models for young people to emulate that are far from their real selves are doing a disservice. They perpetuate the myth that others are better than you. Worse yet, they keep you from liking and being yourself.

Signals from the Business World that Men Are Better

The pinnacle of power in the modern world does not reside in government, but in business. Money controls society, and corporations channel their money to serve *their* needs. Corporations rule more than money. Ultimately they affect our economy and our ways of thinking. Unfortunately, even today, the vast majority of these rulers are men.

According to a 1984 study by Catalyst, a nonprofit group working for the advancement of women in the corporate world, sixty-four percent of the largest American companies still have no women on their boards, and only eight percent have two or more. Only one company of the Fortune 1,000 has a woman chief executive, Katharine Graham of *The Washington Post*.

What's worse, at most levels of the work force women do not seem to be gaining ground. And without money or the influence to channel it, women cannot expect to truly change this system run on finance.

Since business equals money equals power, a male-dominated business world definitely implies that men are better. We've talked to women from every level of the business world, and they all face this problem. We once worked with Kate, an operations manager in a branch of a major bank, having an extremely difficult time advancing in her corporate network. Kate insisted she was better than her competition, but was never given a break by the male higher-ups in charge of promotions. We helped Kate through counseling to see that she was ruining her chances of success without realizing it. "If a male supervisor comes my way," she said, "I smile and try to catch his eye. I seem to get more attention that way." We explained that a businesslike smile and direct look would be more acceptable. Kate was getting the wrong kind of attention, the kind that comes from flirting, an activity she had learned from her mother who long ago had told her, "No man can resist a woman who gives him the eye." "If a man talks to me," she further revealed, "I agree with everything he says. If I ever do give my own opinion, I put it as a question. Even my body language is deferential." We told her, "You're setting yourself up for failure. You need to unlearn all the 'feminine' behaviors of inferiority that cater to male supremacy and think of yourself as a *person* in the company structure." Through role playing, we taught Kate to look people straight in the eye, smile evenly, lean slightly into them, keep her hands relaxed and say what was on her mind in simple, concise statements. It worked. She got a promotion!

How You Show that You Feel Inferior

Many "good girls" may not believe that they defer to men. But deference to men shows itself in many ways. You may have been doing some of these actions for so long you are not even aware that you're doing them. And you might not realize what they're doing to your self-image. Here are some of the common ways of reacting that our clients have talked about. Some of them may be familiar to you.

- Shifting your position or rephrasing your ideas because a man shows signs of disapproval.

- "*Catering*" to a man at work to make him feel comfortable in his masculine role.
- Feeling embarrassed or inferior when a male colleague disagrees with you.
- Needing permission from a man to speak, make a purchase or even order the wine because you fear making him upset.

Gail, 36, executive secretary to the president of a large skylight manufacturing company, was killing all chances of ever making more money with her defeating belief that men were better. For more than five years her boss, Chad, had promised her profit sharing and an eventual partnership in the company if she would just be "patient." In the meantime, Gail was a human doormat, catering to Chad's every demand—pouring his coffee, removing the lint from his suit, cleaning his office. She treated him with a reverence fit for royalty—seldom speaking unless called upon, blushing red if *anybody,* even the janitorial staff, disagreed with her, and immediately changing her statements to win unanimous approval. Gail was so demeaning of herself that she was setting herself up to be taken advantage of.

We helped Gail to see that the very word "partnership" implies equality. Then we asked, "Why would Chad want an inferior partner?" If Chad were ever to offer her the partnership she had waited so long for, she would have to get him to see her as an equal. She did this first of all by *taking a position.* She told Chad that if within a year's time the profit sharing and partnership had not come to pass, she would join another company. She immediately stopped all the catering that signaled her inferiority. She *expected* to lose male approval and run into disagreement. But she kept on. She said what was on her mind when she felt like it, needing permission from no one but herself. She was so impressed by the reactions her new behavior got from colleagues that in a year Gail left Chad to form a company of her own, selling porch swings. "I finally realized," she smiled, "anything he can do, *I* can do!"

- Wearing a suit or jacket to work when you would much prefer a dress or slacks.

- Phrasing your thoughts to men as questions r
  than direct statements.
- Retiring body language.

Chris, a legal aide in her mid-20s, complained that the male lawyers in her firm were not giving her enough respect. "They never pay attention to anything I say," she said. We pointed out to Chris that people are usually seen by others the way they see themselves. This is communicated by the way you act. Chris was acting as if she had no respect for her own opinions by never taking a stand on anything. She had a closetful of appropriate dresses she wanted to wear to work but instead wore dull, boxy suits because she was afraid to be herself. And her body language said that she thought everyone else was better. When she was speaking to a man, she leaned back and held her hands close to her face as if she were protecting herself from a punch, or she crossed her arms to hug herself so tightly her ribs nearly cracked. All these movements showed she regarded him as her superior. Whenever she had something to say, she put it as a question instead of a direct statement so that she could cover her tracks if she was "wrong." We showed Chris how to gain respect in the office by simply changing her behavior. We told her to trust her own judgment and wear what she felt like to work. Then we worked on getting her to use more self-respecting body language by leaning slightly into the person she was speaking to and letting her hands fall comfortably at her sides. Finally, she was to stop putting men one up by phrasing all her ideas as questions. Were they authorities on everything? Why did she have to ask? Instead of saying "It's a nice day, isn't it?" or "That was an intelligent decision, don't you think?" simple rewording: "It's a nice day" or "That was a smart decision" made Chris a person with a more independent point of view, someone worthy of respect.

- Letting the man make the decisions in your life from the neighborhood you will live in to the school for your children to the color of your house to what restaurant you will visit.
- Truly believing men are smarter than women.
- Making easy sexist remarks about other women from

incompetent women drivers to "bitchy" female supervisors.
- Being fearful of a woman President.
- Disapproving of female politicians as "unladylike" and "out of their element."

Hattie, a 48-year-old beautician, came to us because she thought she could generate more business in her shop by undergoing a "personality change." "I just know that if I had more oomph, I'd have to fight the customers off with a broom." At first we laughed, but soon we saw that there was a problem in Hattie's personality that needed correcting—her belief that men were better. We discovered this belief by routinely discussing what her interests were. We found that Hattie liked to read. But more important, when we asked what some of her favorite books were, not one of them turned out to be written by a woman. When we mentioned this to her, Hattie replied, "They don't know anything. Why should I read a book by one of them?" She went on to voice her views on how "stupid" she thought it was for women to try to "wear the pants" in government and business. Women simply weren't good enough to run the country or make the rules. We knew that if Hattie was putting down her sex to us, she was doing the same thing to her exclusively female clientele. We emphasized to Hattie that her first step toward building business should be to speak positively about women, to build the egos of her customers by relating to them as equal, not as inferior to men. We also encouraged her to read books by women to rid herself of the idea that only men are intelligent. Hattie was impressed by what she read, and now she is impressing her customers. Business is booming!

- Feeling more genuinely complimented by a man than a woman.
- Being more likely to turn to a man for help than another woman (men are experts on everything).
- In a store, seeking out salesmen because you think they know more and do their job better than saleswomen.

Caroline, a 24-year-old graduate student in archaeology, almost lost her best friend, Janet, because of her belief that men are better. The two of them had been like sisters, growing up in the same neighborhood, their parents being best friends, going to the same schools, even studying in the same field. But now their relationship was faltering and Caroline was depressed. We asked her if Janet could come in a couple of times with her so we could get a better idea of what was going on between them. In less than ten minutes the problem was evident. Janet explained it like this: "No matter what advice I give Caroline, she cross-checks it with someone else—always a man. If I say she looks good in blue, she doesn't believe it until some guy agrees. If I say she has a super smile, she looks at me like, 'Who cares what *you* think?' If a man, no matter how old or unattractive, says something nice about her, she's on cloud nine for a week. If she needs help in a class or with some everyday problem, she never turns to me for help—only a male. It makes me feel like a second-rate person. I thought friends were supposed to be important to each other." The truth had come out. Men's help and compliments *were* more important to Caroline than Janet's, because Janet was a woman. Caroline began strengthening her relationship with Janet when we helped her to challenge the premise that men are better. When she saw women as equal to men, she valued Janet's input as much as any man's.

There is no doubt that this list could go on indefinitely. It becomes dangerous when your day-to-day activities lead you to give up power and with it your well-being. Now let's look at why you continue to think you're inferior. It's the next step in changing your ways of thinking! All you have to do is trust yourself enough to be honest with yourself.

Psychological Payoffs for Choosing to Believe You Are Inferior

Let's look at the advantages to believing you are inferior. There are many reasons, some of which you may know about already. We've included only a few of the unhealthy bonuses for keeping others above you. Do any of these rationalizations sound familiar to you?

- If men are better, and have all the answers, then you never have to think for yourself.
- You can blame others for anything that goes wrong.
- If you think men are better you don't have to face the dangers and risks of change.
- You get applause from the men you "look up to" and approval from other women who think as you do.
- You have a sense of security, even though it may be illusory. Some women do not want to accept their own equality. It means that men are no better than they are at protecting them.
- You can put off growing up by looking to a superior external source for guidance.
- You can feel good in believing there is something bigger and better than yourself.
- You believe you're a better person for following someone who is "better" than you.

These are some standard reasons for keeping man where he is. These reasons may bring you rewards—but the rewards aren't *real*. It doesn't bring you real power or identity. That can come only from *you*. We also want you to remember that a man has *only* as much power as you give him. You can make that all-important decision to change, and to think of yourself as an equal. When you do, here are some wonderful strategies to gain equality!

Some Easy-to-Master Exercises for Achieving Equality

The most important way you can think that you are as good as a man is to meet your beliefs head on and challenge them. The following exercises will show you how to do this. Work on them one at a time. There's no need to rush. Do the ones you feel most comfortable with first and gradually work up to those that seem more difficult. You don't have to understand the principles behind them, just *do* them. We know you'll be amazed at what a little action in the right direction can do for you!

- Challenge the premise. Tell yourself, as we told Tracy to do to compete more effectively in the business world, "Men are *not* better. I am as good as anyone."
- Call men on their manipulative behavior. Instead of fuming when a man tries to manipulate you, try saying firmly, "I guess you don't think my opinions are worthwhile. Why do you think that?"

Though we have taught this strategy effectively to many women, we always remember a special client, Fanny K., when we describe it. Fanny was approaching 50, her children were grown and on their own, and her husband, Raymond, acted like "he doesn't even know I'm alive." "What does he do to give you this impression?" we probed, trying to get down to specifics. "He ignores every suggestion I make," she said. "Like what?" we continued. "I told him to paint the living room green. He painted it brown," she answered. When we asked Fanny what she had done about it, she said, "I told him that he never listens to me." It was apparent to us that Raymond had heard this from Fanny so many times, he was simply acting out her expectation of him. We told her, "Next time Raymond ignores your wishes, tell him what it *means* to you when he behaves like that. Then ask him why he does it." The next time we saw Fanny she was all smiles. "I told Raymond not to wear a green tie with a blue suit," she informed us. "When he didn't change the tie, I told him it made me feel like he didn't value me or my opinions when he ignored my advice. Then I asked why he ignored me. He admitted that it was the easiest way to get his own way, but if it hurt me that much he wouldn't do it anymore." Fanny applied this strategy every time she felt ignored and soon her relationship was much improved. Always tell people the consequences of their actions, how their behavior affects *you*. And if the effect is unpleasant, ask them *why* they do it. Bringing manipulative behavior out in the open usually eliminates it.

- Explain to the man how his behavior makes you feel. Rather than calling him names, let him know the consequences of his behavior. Is it rage, hurt, humiliation, despair, depression . . . what?
- Never be afraid to disagree if you believe someone is wrong.
- Use the tips we gave Kate to be more businesslike and advance in her company. Look a man straight in the eye when you talk to him. Hold your chin up and don't be afraid of an open, broad smile.
- Be firm in what you say. Make statements positively.
- Watch your body language, as we taught Chris to do to gain respect in her law firm. Stand straight or lean into the man. Let your hands rest comfortably at your sides, showing you have no fear of opening up in the presence of a "superior."
- Make a list of all the reasons you still may have for believing men are better. Then try developing some of those traits in yourself. If you look up at men for their physical strength, then exercise, lift weights, master karate, build your own muscles. If their mastery of the hard sciences impresses you, take a course or hire a tutor in chemistry, biology or mathematics. If a man's mechanical aptitude bowls you over, go to the library or bookstore and research automotive repair or mechanics. If it's man's financial wizardry that suspends you in wonder, study economics. *Anyone* can cultivate these skills. They have nothing inherently to do with sex.

Believing men are better can make your every day less than it could be. This was the case of Marissa, 32, married to Bernie, whom she labeled a "picker." "My life is a living hell," she said. "Day in and day out he picks till he gets what he wants. He doesn't beat me or yell at me, he just *picks*. I can't stand it. If he doesn't want me to go to the movies with a girlfriend some particular night, he just keeps bringing it up till he wears me down. I just don't have the same stamina as a man." Marissa was licked before she started because in her mind she was not an equal match for her husband. We gave Marissa a strategy that is fail-safe in handling any man's attempt to assert his supremacy over you. We told her to *let* Bernie pick. She was responding way too much. She needed to give herself a good talking to. Together we devised an affirmation that Marissa was to repeat to herself in order to turn Bernie's negative behavior to positive: "I love it when Bernie picks. It shows he cares." Once Marissa accepted and expected Bernie's picking, it stopped having an effect on her. When it stopped having an effect, it stopped period. There was no longer any reason for Bernie to pick. Marissa did what she wanted anyway! We are also happy to say that Bernie has become a much more likable person thanks to Marissa's help in eliminating this terrible trait from his personality.

You now have some techniques for removing your belief in male supremacy. There is nothing like action to dispel a myth. Once you take the necessary first steps you'll be amazed how easy change really is. You *know* you can do it!

3

"It Is The Right Of The Superior To Govern"

We could never have a woman President. Who'd balance the budget and fight off our enemies? Not to mention what would happen when that time of the month rolled around . . .

MARION R.
"good girl," age 27

It's incredible how many women we found who feel the same way about a woman in a position of power as Marion R. does. Marion's views are not uncommon. Marion herself is pretty average, raised by caring middle-class parents to be decent and hard-working, married in her early 20s to Harold, a stable, concerned father of their two young children and a devoted husband. Yet when we just happened to be discussing the news of the day and the subject of a woman President came up, this quiet, polite woman exploded. It seemed we had touched a nerve that began with Marion's belief that men are better. Believing that men are better leads naturally into the program to be discussed in this chapter: "It is the right of the superior to govern." If there is something wrong with you, and if men are better, it seems only logical that men should be in charge. As another of our patients, Stephanie, put it, "Who wants to be ruled by a woman? Women just don't have what it takes to make the right decisions."

Bursting the bubble of the Good Girl Syndrome will reveal a simple truth: men—or anyone you allow to rule you—have only as much power as you give them; and you probably have been "generous to a fault" toward them, giving them far too much control, including the power to make the rules.

The biggest danger in allowing someone to make the rules for you is that the results of following them will benefit the people who create them—and not you. In this chapter we'll be showing you how to take back the power you have so generously and self-defeatingly given away. You'll learn the difference between monarchy and autonomy and how to apply principles of power in order to become more independent. You'll gain an insightful understanding into the reasons why you allow yourself to be ruled by others along with solid, simple strategies for learning to trust yourself enough to make your own rules, ones that work for you!

Autonomy and Monarchy

Since one of our goals in this chapter is for you to achieve autonomy, we'd like to explain what we mean by the word so you can better understand it. As we've seen, many of you are born into a world where men make the rules. It seems only natural. Autonomy is self-government. Monarchy is undivided, supreme rule by a single other person. Which would you prefer? To have the rules governing your life made by yourself or by another person? While in primitive times man's *size* gave him power to be monarch over woman, this physical difference has no real bearing in a civilized society. Yet this ancient idea still carries down to today. Research in psychology shows that among men, the man who is tallest is given the most credibility and is most likely to be believed by a given group of people. Of course there is no *factual* basis for believing a big man is any wiser than a small one, any more than there is for believing a man is smarter than a woman. However, the myth of "big is better" is still very much alive and well. At a subconscious level, you may easily be giving men the power to rule your life just because they're bigger!

Your life is not up to what a supreme "big" other dictates.

Your life is up to you, the only one who can make it work to its fullest.

The thinking of one of our clients, Marie—an attractive woman in her early 50s—is a good example of how one's self-image is sometimes allowed to be determined by a vote of the majority, or of one other person, rather than by one's own standards. Marie was on the brink of suicide when she was fired from a job she had held for twenty years. She was a nurse, a job she had devoted her life to, the only thing she ever had wanted to do. She described her graduation day at nursing school with tears in her eyes, "We wore all white, and I carried red roses. It was like a wedding. I committed myself to healing, to helping others." She never married, seldom dated, and devoted all her energy to her cherished profession, gaining much love and satisfaction from doing so, including being given a top honor, the Florence Nightingale Award, for her superior achievement. A few months later, when a political shake-up occurred in hospital administration, hirings and firings took place. Marie, who didn't believe in office politics and thought they took valuable time away from treating the patients, was accidentally caught in the cross fire. She said, "I never want to nurse again. It ruined my life." Marie was consumed with an unrelenting sense of betrayal. "I feel like everything I ever worked for has gone down the drain. . . . everything I believed in was a mockery."

While Marie did feel betrayed, her real problem lay much deeper. Marie was allowing others she thought were better—in this case, a predominant male administration—to determine her self-worth. She was fired. So she figured she must be no good. The love and admiration of all those she had helped over the years suddenly meant nothing. The good she had done in achieving a childhood dream was canceled out. She was letting her sense of self be ruled by the supposedly democratic process, a majority vote of the board of administrators.

We asked Marie: "Who betrayed you, nursing or the administration?" When she stopped to realize all the joy she'd found in her profession, she saw that she was allowing others to determine her level of self-satisfaction. She decided not to let any administrative board take that away from her and set out to find another position in the field that meant so much to her.

To be truly autonomous you must be your own governing body, making rules that benefit you. If you let others take your power of self-direction away from you, you in essence become their slave, working for their good and not your own. We will next show you how the key to gaining autonomy is regaining your power and channeling it to get what you want.

Understanding the Principles of Power

For a time, Marie had gotten caught in the trap of believing others had the authority to govern her own sense of satisfaction. She saw her whole profession and the women in it as a mockery because she allowed one small group of people to determine her self-worth, forgetting about the thousands who looked up to her for the help she had given them. If you do not believe that you have authority, you may find it difficult to believe that other women can have authority. Authority is the power to influence or change opinions, or behavior. It is impossible to affect anyone—especially yourself—if you don't have it or if you don't believe you have it.

In a *Los Angeles Times* poll taken a month before the 1984 presidential election, forty-two percent of women polled felt men were better than women at making decisions concerning war and peace. It is also interesting that one-fifth of those polled agreed with the statement: "Women in public life just don't seem to be very ladylike." The problem in this question, of course, lies in the way we have come to define a "lady"— quiet, self-effacing and obedient; that is, far removed from the way we think of most successful politicians, male or female.

Another enlightening section of the poll revealed definite negative attitudes toward female politicians or rulemakers as a whole. Pollsters described two hypothetical candidates for governor. Candidate A, 55 years old, was born and reared in New York City, was married with two children, and had a business background. Candidate B, five years younger, was born and raised in the Midwest, had three children and a career as an attorney. One group of those polled was told A was a man and B was a woman, while in a second group, pollsters reversed the genders of the hypothetical candidates. In both groups the female candidate was defeated. Men and women polled responded similarly.

How did we come to believe this?

Women have been artfully and unfairly manipulated into believing they are "good" if they follow, rather than make, the rules, and many of them continue to pass on this idea to their children. Even worse, women have been intimidated into believing that the *reason* they should allow others to make their rules is that there is something wrong with them, and that they never could set their own rules, even if they wanted to. The result of this intimidation is not only total loss of power, but poor self-image, lack of accomplishment and depression—the hallmarks of the Good Girl Syndrome.

Milly, 32, an only child born to a professional couple late in life, had a father who did everything for her to enhance his own feelings of being strong, protective and needed. Although little Milly's helplessness was flattering to her father, it left her feeling totally inadequate and dependent on men for guidance in her adult life. This early conditioning was hurting her chances for advancement in one of the city's investment firms, where she worked as a broker. In the words of her supervisor, "You're wonderful when it comes to taking orders. We always know we can count on you for anything we ask. The problem is you seem to lack a sort of creativity . . . the talent for making and carrying out decisions on your own. In order to promote you to the next level we need to know you can function on your own . . . that we could go away for a few days and not worry what we'd find when we returned." When Milly was able to trust herself and the decisions that came from this trust, she was able to inspire trust in others as well, and get her promotion.

Giving Yourself the Power to Govern You

Like Milly, you too will learn to trust yourself enough to use the power to make your own decisions.

If others have only the power you have given them to affect you, there is only one way to break free from their hold on you. You need to know how to take back the power you have given away and how to use it to govern yourself.

Many women will say, or imply in their actions, "I'm afraid to take back the power." They worry that they will lose the security of their current relationships. This case history of a typical relationship and the crisis points the couple encountered when the woman decided to take back her power gives you a good idea of what often happens. Though Sam and Lila are fictional characters, they are not unlike many of the patients we counsel regularly.

Sam C. is 24 and Lila is 20 when they marry. He has an M.A. in business and she has a teaching credential. He is more career-minded than she. She takes a temporary job teaching part time to make ends meet until her husband is able to advance to a higher income in the corporate structure of the automobile company he works for. In the next four years they have two or three children, and she stops working to devote herself full time to raising the family. She's ambivalent about quitting but goes along with her husband, saying, "I'll really miss the satisfaction I get from being a teacher, but I guess Sam's right when he says I'll get more satisfaction out of being a full-time homemaker." Her sense of identity comes from how well she is able to help her husband advance his career and how well her children are doing. Their friends are primarily his friends and often business contacts.

Six or seven years later, Lila begins experiencing disenchantment. She calls it a sort of "is this all there is?" feeling. "I get up. I fix meals for Sam and the kids. I shop. I clean. I go to bed. I keep wondering, 'Is this all my life is ever going to be? Is this *it?*'" None of this condition makes sense because she never thought it could happen. Since she feels the way she does, there must be something even more wrong with her than she ever imagined. "I keep asking myself why I feel so dissatisfied. What's wrong with me? I feel so guilty. Sam works hard. The kids are great. The house is great. My friends are great. Why am I always so vaguely discontented? What more do I want?" She has all she "should" ever want . . .

After much soul searching, Lila starts to see the specifics of her relationship as products of her own choice. Things do not have to remain as they are. She can *put* more into her life. She can change and he can adapt. It's a glorious revelation. Though it's sometimes difficult for her, she stands her ground. And she takes a step more. She takes a course on running a business from her home, and she makes friends totally unrelated to her husband or his business. And, though she discusses her problems with him, she finds she no longer looks for his constant approval. She finds she needs more free time, more space to grow on her own, and she asks that he share in some of the household duties.

Lila is now strong enough to *accept* that she might lose some of his approval if she gets what she wants. This acceptance helps tremendously. Sam calls her an ingrate and says she doesn't appreciate all the things he's done for her. When trying to make her feel guilty fails to get him what he wants, he threatens to leave her. Lila knows that if she gives in and lets her husband have what he wants, she will find herself once again being dominated and feeling frustrated. She can no longer tolerate this as her life-style and draws strength from *accepting* the possible consequences of her independence. She loves Sam dearly and wants to keep the marriage alive, but she takes a chance. She explains that just as he needs room, so does she. Though it takes time, and compromise on both sides, they both come to follow needs of their own, and to appreciate the other's need for independence. "You cannot improve your life without taking some risk," Lila says. "I saw a chance for happiness and I took it!"

Some Typical "Pushed Around" Behavior

As you can imagine, it takes a long time to reach the state of understanding that Sam and Lila reached. Before you can do anything, you need to realize whether someone is manipulating you. If you think someone may be trying to push you around, take a look at some of these common manifestations, and see if something looks familiar. Do you find yourself:

- Running errands for a man and feeling resentment for not being able to say no?
- Being intimidated by a salesperson and buying something you don't want or feeling fear at the thought of taking it back?
- Allowing your male escort to order for you in a restaurant and being too "generous" to change his decision?

Amelia, 28, married five years to Alfonso, described how believing men had the right to tell her what to do made her feel like a "woman without a country." "It's 'his' home, 'his' money, 'his' territory. I'm just a guest. I have nothing . . . no rights . . . nothing . . . how can I refuse him anything?" Alfonso kept her running all day long with things he wanted her to do for him, not only the traditional wifely duties of cooking, cleaning, and rearing their two children, but extra chores involving the dry-cleaning store he managed, such as working odd hours, subbing for help out on sick leave, bringing him lunch when he was too busy to go out. Alfonso even dominated the recreational aspects of their lives. In a restaurant he did the ordering; on a vacation he picked the location and itinerary, including what they would and would not see. Amelia resented him terribly for governing her life but didn't protest because she believed it was his "right" as a man and "head of the household." Her father had been the supreme patriarch in her family, with no apparent resistance from her mother, and Amelia accepted this as a "natural" condition. "I can't even tell a male salesperson no if I don't want what he's selling. I feel like I *should* do what he tells me." It took a long time to get Amelia to begin changing her perspective, to see that marriage is a *mutual* contract that does not give either partner ownership or the right to tell the other what to do. We eased her into this insight by asking her to focus on one specific behavior at a time. What *one* decision would she most like to make for herself that she was presently letting Alfonso make for her? "What I do with my money," she said. While Alfonso was giving her a minimum wage for her time at the store, he was putting it into their "joint" checking account without Amelia ever seeing the check. This was an account she felt she didn't have the right to use. Amelia wanted her own account. We told her to open her own account, *then* tell Alfonso where the funds were to go. "What if he won't give me the money?" she asked. "Then don't do the work!" we answered. Amelia asserted her own right to disobey her husband's demands and told him *her* expectations. He didn't like giving up control, but he had no choice once Amelia stopped *giving* it to him.

- Losing at tennis, golf, even cards, so as not to offend your male partner?
- Continually asking men—or anyone you think is superior—for sanction and permission?
- Apologizing excessively?
- Having fear and self-recrimination at the thought of approaching a younger man?

Olivia, 30, twice divorced and owner of her own women's wear shop, was dating Bruce, 48, who had just sold a chain of clothing stores and retired. Olivia's failed marriages, both to older, dominating men, had left her insecure and feeling that she just wasn't "pleasing" people enough. She set out to remedy this with a vengeance. Bruce had asked Olivia to teach him to play tennis, and while she was good and Bruce just a beginner, he still got angry when he didn't score. Olivia played worse to please Bruce. If she accidentally beat him, she apologized, making up a million excuses for Bruce's failure— the sun was at a bad angle, she had the best side, she chose the wrong racket for him, she'd forgotten to give him some key pointers—always it was her fault if Bruce errored. On top of this, Bruce was demanding too much of her time, since he now had so much of his own, and Olivia found herself continually asking permission for the time she needed to spend in her business: "Is it OK, honey, if we don't go sailing tomorrow? I have a shipment coming in." Or "Would it be all right if I skipped a set of tennis today? I'm hiring a new clerk." Bruce would grouchily give in, and Olivia would feel guilty for not giving him what he wanted. Olivia even started seeking sanction and permission from her girlfriends for time she couldn't spend with them. The day she stayed home with the dog because he barked in disapproval when she started to leave, she knew it was time to get help.

"Why do you put up with Bruce's behavior?" we asked. Olivia surprised us with her answer when she said, "I can't get what I really want anyway, so what difference does it make?" We learned that what Olivia really wanted was to date a younger man, but she didn't feel she had the right. "*Who* says so?" we asked. Olivia was stymied by the question, so we helped her out. "Older men say women can't date younger men, and they say it for their *own* benefit!" Olivia laughed. The spell was broken. She stopped losing, stopped asking permission, stopped apologizing and stopped seeing Bruce. She is presently dating Clark, 28, a young stockbroker who is self-assured enough to appreciate a woman who's a winner. The moment Olivia *questioned* the rules that were binding her, she was on the way to freedom. When she made her rules to govern herself, she achieved it.

- Letting your husband or lover boss you around, but never considering asking him for something you want?
- Tolerating someone's ridicule, shouting, and even hitting?
- Saying things such as, "Who does he think he is?" or "He acts like he owns the world?"
- Using phrases such as, "It's OK," "I don't mind," or "Don't worry about it"?

Rosie, 27, married five years to Henry, drove friends and family crazy complaining about his mistreatment of her. "Who does he think he is?" she would start; "He bosses me around like he owns me: 'Get my dinner,' 'Make my bed,'

'Bring me a beer,' 'Make a sandwich for my friends,' 'Shut up,' 'Make yourself scarce for a while.' '' If Rosie didn't obey immediately, Henry would shout the orders, sometimes giving her a push ''to get her moving.'' These pushes sometimes turned her black and blue. But if Henry suddenly felt remorse for his actions and apologized, Rosie would say, ''It's OK, I'm all right,'' as if there was something wrong with her if she had trouble following her husband's rules. We told Rosie that the best defense was a good offense. ''Start giving Henry some orders of your own to follow and you'll be amazed how soon he stops doing the same to you.'' We call this technique ''dishing it back,'' and it almost never fails. When Henry ordered, ''I want my breakfast at six,'' Rosie retaliated, ''I want you home by 5.'' When Henry insisted, ''I don't want you wearing such a low neckline,'' Rosie replied, ''I won't go out with you unless you wear underwear.'' When he directed, ''Stop spending so much money on the house,'' she said, ''You can't afford a new boat this year.'' When Rosie started giving Henry a taste of his own medicine by making demands of her own, his demands on her ceased dramatically.

- Having frequent crying spells? (Not only is this a common reaction to being pushed around, it often functions to make the person feel he has even more power. He may feel *guilty* for a while but the lasting impression will be one of having power.)
- Finding yourself in states of apathy, lethargy and sulking? (These behaviors are passive reactions to rules that don't work for you.)
- Finding that you're often bored, and looking for ''answers'' or solace in buying things you don't need or really want? (This tells you that something isn't working and you may need to examine the way you live.)
- No longer planning vacations or special events because you know they will never come to be if your husband doesn't want to participate in them?

Sharon, 40, described her twenty-year marriage to Wayne, a real-estate developer, as ''boring and going nowhere.'' In the early years they were involved in starting their family of three children, putting down roots in a new town, building a home, making new friends, establishing Wayne in his career. But now their life-style was routine. "He pulls all the strings," she said, "and I guess he's happy, so shouldn't I be too? Isn't that what a good wife does, make her husband happy?" With this thought in mind, Sharon tried to give up expecting any more from life, to "grin and bear" it. Still, she couldn't help resenting Wayne for being so happy when she wasn't, and she began withdrawing from him, going through long sulks when she avoided or refused to talk to him. Most recently she found herself beginning to cry spontaneously when watching television, driving, shopping, even talking to friends, "for no reason at all."

We helped Sharon to see that the heart of her problem was that she had stopped making plans and rules of her own. She was blaming Wayne because his rules weren't working for her. There really wasn't any reason why they should. "What do you *want* to do?" we asked Sharon. "What do you really *feel* like doing?" All her life Sharon had wanted a trip to the South Sea Islands, a trip Wayne said they'd take someday but presently didn't have time or money for. Once when they almost had bought the tickets, Wayne informed her how the price of the vacation would pay for the new addition to the living room they had always wanted, and Sharon agreed it would be better to have "something to show" for their money. She improved her home at the expense of herself. "OK," we said to Sharon, "you have just made a new rule. You are going to start being good to yourself. You will begin following that rule by going to the South Seas. With love in your voice and a smile on your face, why don't you try having a long, serious talk with Wayne. Tell him that some of the rules aren't working for you. Tell him how you really feel about going on this vacation, what it *means* to you, how long you've wanted it. Be direct. Be positive. Take the responsibility for making this choice." When Wayne saw the *energy* and *enthusiasm* with which Sharon pitched her vacation idea, he went for it. She actually sold him on the idea that what would benefit her also would benefit him. In this case it did. They both had a wonderful time!

●   ●   ●

While allowing men to make the rules can show itself in countless ways, these examples reveal some of the most common ways this problem surfaces in your day-to-day behavior. One thing is certain: You can never know what your talents are until you look for them. You may be one of the most talented persons in the world. All you have to do is give yourself a chance to come to the surface. And you can do it if you begin to make your own rules. Once you do, your life will be vastly better!

Why You Allow Yourself to Be Ruled

A wonderful way to start building your self-esteem by creating your own self-government is to gain insight into your reasons for resisting it. Recognizing some of the "rewards" for letting others tell you what to do can lead you on the path of freedom. Here are some of the more common rewards.

- Giving people control over you makes them appear to like you. But it can't be real friendship or love, for mature love is based on reciprocity and mutual give and take.
- It fosters a sense of martyrdom and sainthood. But it seems a high price to pay for one's freedom.
- It has a feeling of "rightness" when you allow yourself to be ruled by an authority figure. This emotion is one of the most difficult and deadly components of the syndrome, because the idea of respecting "authority" is so ingrained into the minds of most "good girls."
- It frees you from the responsibility of making decisions (although there is generally a greater risk of being unhappy when someone else makes your decisions for you). In reality, you are trading lack of responsibility for greater risk, though you may not view it this way.
- It allows others to tell you what to do, reinforcing a poor self-image and continuing to allow you to do nothing.

- It produces a false sense of security that anyone you accept as an authority will in turn accept responsibility for taking care of you.
- It provides someone else to blame when things go wrong in your life.

Some Simple Strategies for Learning to Trust Yourself

Though there are valid sets of laws and real, established authorities, when you come to think about how you want to live your life, nobody knows what is good for you better than you. And nobody has more control over you than you, if you will just trust yourself to use it. Here are some wonderful ways to build your self-control and beat the old ideas that have been keeping you back. Even if you try only one or two of these suggestions, you will be amazed at what you'll discover about yourself.

- First and foremost, try to change your perspective. As we taught Marie, refuse to let others determine your criteria for satisfaction. Give yourself the chance to make the right decisions for you. Try making one or two new decisions for yourself every day, no matter how small.

Ruby, 41, described herself as "just your ordinary everyday housewife with three hungry mouths to feed and a house to keep up." She did everything her husband, Charlie, told her to do because she thought he had the "right." We got Ruby to start changing her perspective of Charlie as monarch by changing one piece of her behavior. It seemed that whenever Ruby and Charlie socialized, she talked about nothing but Charlie. "I just feel that what I do is so common and ordinary, nobody'll want to hear about it," Ruby explained, "so I talk about Charlie." Charlie's occupation as a bricklayer hardly made for scintillating conversation, but the truth of the matter was, Ruby just plain didn't think *she* was worth talking about. The more she focused on Charlie, the more she elevated him in her eyes and the more willing she was to follow his orders. Together, we devised a new rule to benefit Ruby: "Talk to others about what *you're* doing, not what your husband is doing, unless it relates directly to you." If people need to know about your spouse they can ask him. Ruby applied the rule and it came as a pleasant surprise to her to learn that friends really did care enough about her to be interested in what she was doing, no matter what it was. She was more to them than just a reflection of her "superior" mate.

- Trust yourself and the power of your own decision making process as we helped Milly to do. Question some of the ideas you've been taught that have left you uneasy, as we showed Olivia to get over her idea she "shouldn't" date younger men. Work toward understanding your mind, your values and your emotions. For many, keeping a daily journal is a useful tonic. Laws of the land may tell you how to *behave* but no one has a right to control your private thoughts!

- Realize that there is a great deal about women that men will never understand and much that you won't understand about them. But it's all right that you are different. As we explained to Sharon to help her improve her marriage to Wayne, don't expect their rules to make you happy. They can't. What you need to do is to try to make your own rules, ones that make *you* happy.

- When a man tells you what to do, try counting to ten slowly to yourself. This breaks the chain of your usual method for reacting.

- Try to delay following a rule that you resent—even putting things off for a day or two can give you a great feeling of accomplishment. Laura S., a client of ours, found it too difficult to say no to her husband's demands for exotic recipes that took days to prepare. We told her that she might try "postponing" these culinary treats ("Maybe tomorrow, honey"; "As soon as I get persimmons, dear") until one day he finally adjusted to the idea that they were never coming because it was unreasonable to expect them all the time.

There may be times when it is easier to stop following someone's orders a little at a time rather than doing it cold turkey. We recall a case where a man insisted that his wife accompany him on boring business trips. She knew there would be tremendous resistance if she flatly refused, so she began by skipping every third trip, until over the course of a year she had eliminated them from her life completely.

- Try following a rule *partially* now in an effort to eliminate it totally later. If it's an unfair rule of the house that dinner be on the table promptly at 6, put *some* of it on by 6. Next, have only the table set at the appointed hour. Eventually, you'll be able to adapt to everyone's schedule—including your own.
- When you say no to someone, indicate that there is no malice intended. Look him squarely in the eye to show you are determined and honest in your resolve to stand your ground.
- Try to have a long talk with the people in your life who try to order you around, but do it when you are all calm. Outline what most upsets you, what is most destructive to your sense of self, as Amelia did with Alfonso to get her own checking account. Maybe you can negotiate a set of rules that works for everybody.

Believing that it is the right of "better" people to tell you what to do may keep you from getting many of the things you want in life. One of our many success stories, Mammie, 43, housewife and mother of two, described how this belief almost prevented her from fulfilling a lifetime dream: to study yoga with one of the great masters of the East. She related that such a yogi, who was visiting this country for the first time, and possibly the last, was giving two weekend seminars before returning home. Enrollment was limited and the demand was high, but through sheer luck Mammie had met the man while waiting for a bus, and he offered to reserve her a space for $1,500. "I'll never forget the day I told my family," she said.

"It was me, the two boys, my husband, Lloyd, and my mother. We were at a restaurant. They all seemed mildly interested until I mentioned the money involved. Then Lloyd said, 'I think you're being extravagant.' I could tell my mother agreed. I couldn't believe it. I remember vividly the way I felt at that moment. . . . Everything in the restaurant vanished . . . in a flash. I didn't know where I was for a second. Then I just wanted to run. But I remembered what you told me about the importance of standing my ground. So instead of getting angry, as I normally would have done for assuming I wouldn't be 'allowed' to take the course, I just smiled at them all and calmly said, 'I'm sure it will be worth it.' I studied with the master, and it made me a better person all around. Like you, he didn't tell me what path to take to happiness but, rather, how to find it."

Believing that a man, or anyone else for that matter, is better than you and therefore has the right to tell you how to live, can make you unhappy. It blocks you from you, from ever becoming the beautiful person buried deep inside. Don't think that you have to follow what works for others. Find your own truth—and live by it!

4

"The Rules Are Sacred"

> Why do we have to do what men tell us just
> 'cause *they* say so? Why is what they say more
> important than what we say? What makes them
> God?
>
> GEORGINA L.
> *patient, age 40*

Georgina, who had always wanted to be a dress designer, was
resentful of her husband, Hal, a 42-year-old tax accountant,
because she felt, "He *talked* me into marrying him. I was only
nineteen at the time. I didn't know any better. When he said to
me 'All girls get married. That's the way things are. Do you
want to be an old maid?' I went right along and accepted the
rules he was giving me to live by. I think what bothers me
most was his implication that my life would be *better* with
him, that marriage would change me without my having to do
another thing. It took me twenty-three years to realize that
what I think is right for me is more important than what a man
thinks is right for me."

Many women come to us with the same complaint that
Georgina has. They're angry, they feel powerless, and they
aren't fully sure why. But the more we talk, the more we all
come to see that they have great respect for rules—the structure they create, the security they provide—even if they don't
really think the rules are helping them. "That's the way it is"
or "It's never been done any other way" or "It really doesn't

bother me" are phrases we hear often and press our clients to explore. Why, after a generation of supposed strides, do some women seem so lackadaisical? Every case has its own particularities, of course, but we always seem to come down to a common denominator: the power of rules and the power of the people who make them. This is the problem we want to explore with you in this chapter. We'll be showing you how you came to believe other people's rules were sacred and more important than your own in the first place: how men place themselves in positions of authority to make you more suggestible and more likely to do what they tell you, how many women would rather be ruled by others than tolerate ambiguity, and how following the sacred rules ties into your sense of mythical "goodness." You will learn to free yourself from your belief in the rigid absolutes, "shoulds" and hero worship that are making you captive to a set of rules designed not for you, but for the benefit of someone else. You'll see how to spot your own behaviors that make you the victim of a self-defeating belief, along with recognizing what you get from letting others tell you how to live. Most important, you'll discover how to think for yourself and make your own set of rules, ones that work to free your spirit and draw out the wonderful potential that lies within!

Let's look at how we perceive rules. Why are they sacred? Who are they supposed to serve?

For many women, rules are sacred because they are made by men, who are better. Unfortunately, they usually are made to serve the people who created them, usually men. But, as we have been saying, it is important to find out which rules only benefit the makers and try to take them out of your life. A wonderful quote by Thomas Jefferson inscribed on the Jefferson Memorial in Washington, D.C., reads to the effect that most laws will be outdated before the ink to write them is dry on the paper. Laws and rules are meant to last only while they are beneficial to the people they're made for. There is nothing sacred about a rule. It is the *consequences* of abiding by it that are important. If following a rule improves your life without taking from the quality of someone else's, you will probably want to follow it.

But when a rule becomes more important than the people

it is meant to help, the rule doesn't work. You can see this clearly in your daily life. It may be a rule of the house that lunch is at noon, but if this conflicts with the schedule of a household member, there is no valid reason not to change it. Georgina explained to us, "It seems that once I accepted Hal's first rule that all women must get married, I started accepting the hundreds of little rules that went with it. We ate when he said, went out when he said, had sex when he said. . . . Nothing we did had anything to do with *my* needs as a woman, only my need to be a good wife to Hal." Don't misunderstand us to be saying that these rules only begin with marriage. They also may determine *who* you will marry. For example, waiting for a man to ask you out might be considered a "rule" of etiquette, but if that rule keeps you from possibly opening up a new world for both of you, what's the harm in breaking it? Sometimes rules need to be broken. It may seem difficult, especially when there doesn't seem to be anyone to back you up. Your husband may not approve at first or your boyfriend may not understand, but you have to take the chance anyway. After all, it's the risks you take in life that often make the most positive impact. In fact, we've found that most of our clients say that what they've regretted most in life are the chances they *haven't* taken. So take their counsel to heart and begin to question the rules that bind you. You may discover things about yourself that you never had expected!

How Rules Became Sacred

Now that we've established the idea that for many women rules are sacred, let's examine how so many women came to believe in the sanctity of rules. In some ways it came about as we accepted the cultural idea of male superiority. But that alone was not enough. The male rules were *made* sacred. To begin with, women were told that man didn't make this system—God did. Men have quoted passages of Scripture, such as Genesis 3:16—"You shall be eager for your husband, and he shall be your master"—to show that God has put men in authority over women. You could argue against a man, but who could go against a god?

The fact is that many religions throughout history have featured female deities in powerful positions. For example, the ancient Egyptians worshipped Isis, the mother, alongside Osiris, the father, and Horus, the son. But the Judeo-Christian tradition has concentrated on male images of deity almost to the exclusion of any female image. Paul, in his letters, taught that women had a subordinate place in the family and in the church. In his Letter to the Ephesians, he says, "Wives, be subject to your husbands, as to the Lord; for the man is the head of the woman, just as Christ is the Head of the Church." His words have been used to dominate women ever since.

June, a 34-year-old bookkeeper, was the youngest child and only girl in a family of six children raised Presbyterian in a Midwest town of 1,500 people. There was no doubt in her mind that the man was the head of the woman, having been taught this by her parents, brothers and the church. "It took me my whole life to realize," she said, "that I don't have to spend the rest of my life keeping records for men. I can start my *own* business. I just never saw myself as bossing men. But that's what it takes to run a business." June is just one of many women we've seen who've denied themselves financial opportunity because they thought of themselves working for men instead of for themselves.

Why You Believe
the Rules Are Sacred

As you can see from the "rules" in your home to the various interpretations of the bases for male superiority, rules are, at heart, suggestions. They tell you that if you follow the prescribed guide, you will somehow benefit. Why else would you follow them? Rules make the strongest impression when they are given to a person who is suggestible, or easily influenced.

We are all most easily influenced by people we *perceive* to be in a position of power. As we've mentioned, power is defined as the capacity to influence, so if you create the illusion of power or authority, you can increase the suggestibility of the person you want to influence. The chances are better that you will influence him with what you say. And, in turn, you are much more likely to believe in a rule made by someone you consider an "authority" than someone you do not.

But giving power to others usually puts you in a vulnerable, dangerous position. We have a friend who is 58 years old, a housewife and mother of four children. Her husband, a wealthy and respected Beverly Hills doctor, recently left her for a younger woman. She paid little attention to the divorce proceedings because he repeatedly said, "Don't worry, I'll take care of you." Although his yearly income in the last decade was more than a quarter of a million dollars, he claimed he had very few assets when it came time for a settlement. The total community property amounted to less than $200,000. The wages were either squandered or hidden. As a result, she was forced to settle for much less than she deserved and had to move to a studio apartment with not even enough support to pay her medical expenses. Why? Because she *believed* her husband. He was a man, and a doctor. She allowed herself to be suggestible to everything he told her. "I sure learned my lesson the hard way," she told us. "The only one who you can count on to take care of you is you!"

Even more amazing is Lila, a laboratory technician who came to us for help in relieving her anxiety and upset after she ended a relationship she had with an obstetrician. She had visited him because of infertility problems. The doctor persuaded her to leave her husband and allow him, the doctor, to father her child. "We will get married," he told her as they headed for the bedroom. Once Lila was pregnant, the doctor changed his mind, wanted her to get an abortion, and went so far as to deny to friends that he was the father. Lila decided to seek help after the doctor's mother phoned her and called her a "bitch." She asked him to come to the first session. He did, but did not even offer to split the fee for the visit.

Lila also learned a lesson "the hard way." We are now

teaching her how to start a new life with her young son. She now formulates her own rules, ones that she can be *sure* work for her.

Hating Ambiguity

One of the greatest problems our clients have had to deal with in coming to believe that not all rules are sacred is fighting their own dislike of ambiguity. Most "good girls" hate ambiguity. They would rather follow black-and-white rules—most of which are made by men—even if they don't work, than deal with the gray area of creating their own rules.

A perfect example is Jackie, a client of ours who was constantly upset because her boyfriend, Clint, saw other women. Jackie was consumed with trying to figure out why. "There has to be something seriously wrong with me for him to do something like that," she said. Jackie was constantly running her self-image into the ground wondering what she could be lacking, asking herself, "Why aren't I woman enough to hold my man?" There were moments when she contemplated suicide and vacillated between rage and depression.

The real problem with Jackie was that she let her man get away with his tricks. Something inside nagged at her, telling her that she couldn't be happy with the double standard. "I know I couldn't handle Clint seeing other women," she said, "and I sure have no desire to see other men." Clint swept aside her concerns with comments such as, "What are you worried about? You're the only one I love. All guys play around a little. It doesn't mean anything." We showed Jackie how to free herself from his rules and the ambiguity of her situation by setting a rule of her own: "I will not spend my time on a man who is insensitive to my needs."

Jackie, like so many other "good girls," was a masochist. The masochist *needs* rules. She lives in a world of black and white, dominance and submission, where there can be no in-between. To maintain this distinction, the rules must remain sacred and inviolable. Psychiatrist Natalie Shainess, who has written more than ninety scholarly articles on female psychology, observes, "Few human beings find ambiguity comfortable, but for the masochistic person it is nearly unbearable."

The masochist would rather follow a rule that works for someone else and incur pain and loss than remain in a limbo of uncertainty that requires her to formulate her own rules. Giving in to the male system provides a temporary release from uncertainty, but what a high price to pay. We want you to decide to go for a better deal!

The Myth of "Goodness"

We have already talked about the myth of goodness as it applies to other problems, other ways of thinking. But let's look at it in light of a love for rules. The word "good" is most often used to mean commendable, right, or conforming to the moral order of the universe. The question is, commendable by whom? Right according to whose standards? Conforming to what morals? A girl can be "good" to the extent she is commended by, is right by and conforms to the rules of men or anyone she puts in authority.

There has to be some reward for subservience to the men you place on a pedestal, and that accolade is the label "goodness." It might sound flattering for someone to tell you, "You are good," but not when he's really saying, "You gave me what I wanted." We would like to present a new definition of good: that which benefits *you*. We think you will find this a much more satisfying way by which to live than the old definition: what benefits others only.

Nothing is more difficult than competing with a myth. It's nearly impossible to attack a myth rationally, because it has no rational basis, and, what's more, *you* do not think of it in rational terms. The myth of "goodness" is no exception. It would be irrational of you not to want to be good; yet, it is just as irrational of you to think that you can be "good" in the eyes of everyone you meet. What we are trying to do is to show you that being "good" is a relative term and that it is most important to your well-being if you strive first and foremost to be "good" for yourself.

Still, it always surprises us that so many women cling to the belief that "good" is doing for others and "bad" is doing for yourself. One of our clients gave us some surprising insights into the way women see the link between goodness and rules.

We worked with Tracy, who was 24 years old, for a number of months. She believed she was the incarnation of evil because she wanted a night out with her girlfriends once a week. "You'd think I was the devil himself just 'cause I wanted to be out on my own a couple of hours a week," she told us. Her husband, Grant, 25, objected strongly, saying it was "wrong" for a married woman to go out at night without her husband. However, nothing stopped him from bowling, poker and marathon ball games with the guys. She tried to become more "good" by doing extra things for him. She made him special desserts, gave massages, even took over some of his "duties," such as mowing the lawn and carrying out the garbage—but she never became "good" enough to deserve a night out on her own. After months of striving for sainthood, she was ten pounds underweight, couldn't sleep and was so fatigued that she could barely drag through the day. "How can being so good feel so bad?" she asked with a frown. We told Tracy that she had the wrong idea of goodness. Good activities were those that made her feel better, not worse. She had to take the risk and *do* something that would make her feel better. Tracy learned firsthand the fallacy of this supposed goodness, a "goodness" built solely on her own unrealistic expectations, and she actually began to take a night out with the other truly good girls on occasion.

Freeing Yourself from Absolutes, "Shoulds," and Hero Worship

There is no such thing as an absolute guide to happiness. All things are relative to *you* and how you react to them. There is nothing on earth that you can be absolutely certain will make you feel better *beforehand*. We wish we could say that there was, but we cannot. You can only be sure after the fact. You may spend many nights lying awake dreaming, yearning for a certain man you think will change your life. But you can never be completely positive that he will make you happy until after you have experienced him. Or, as Tracy told us, "I spent my whole life trying to be the perfect wife and I hated it." Or, in the words of Jackie, "I thought sure I'd be happy if I could just please Clint more, but pleasing him more didn't make any difference." Or, as Georgina said, "I got married and it didn't change my life a bit." These are reactions we hear all the time. Whether achieving goals is rewarding or not is something you can find out only after you get there. So it is with a rule. It is valuable only if it guides you to happiness. We trust that yours will if it springs from the deep-rooted feelings of your own soul.

As you may already know, the problem with believing in sacred rules is that you will abide by them whether they benefit you or not, simply because you believe they are right. Nothing is right that doesn't work. For example, science has seen the fall of many rules when it became apparent that they were untrue (the earth is flat; matter can be destroyed; we are the center of the universe).

A further problem of believing in these "sacred" rules is that you may develop a "should" mentality. If being president of a big company, having money, a large house or a new car is absolutely good, then you might think everyone "should" strive for these things, even though you may know that these goals might not be what is best for everyone.

A good example of the "should" mentality was Joan, a 29-year-old travel agent, married to Philip, a man who firmly believed "He shall rule over you" was an absolute rule. Joan's life was full of "shoulds." "Whenever Philip wants something," Joan said, "he begins with 'Women should . . .' It drives me crazy!" Men *should* rule over women. Women *should* give men whatever they ask. There was no need for Joan to examine whether following Philip's rules made her feel good. That was immaterial. "Because I say so" was the only explanation she needed. We taught Joan to make a list of all the things she did simply because Philip said so. We then asked her to stop doing the things that she thought were unnecessary. At first Philip was shocked, but Joan held her ground and waited it out. In time he stopped giving orders, and they've accepted the idea that each of them has to live by what he or she thinks is best for him- or herself.

Another problem comes up: In a world where rules are sacred and "should" be followed by you because they are so absolutely good, there tends to be a hero and hero worship. *Somebody* makes these absolutely good rules. Naturally, it has to be somebody who is absolutely the best. In the Good Girl Syndrome it is often the men who fit this bill.

But most superiority is imaginary, a power you give to others out of fear of taking the power yourself. So many heroes are scapegoats. They give you an escape from responsibility by giving it to someone better.

"How could my husband be wrong?" asked Joan in one of our sessions. "I just can't believe I could be so taken in. I worshipped him. I believed everything he said." But the real problem of looking to a "higher" source for a sacred set of rules means that you lose the freedom to make rules for yourself. "I lived so much for him, I forgot to do any growing of my own," said Pam, a 28-year-old woman who felt totally helpless when her husband left her for a more exciting, assertive mate. You cannot afford to worship rules or the ones who make them; the price is just too high.

Some Typical "Rules Are Sacred" Behavior

We have already talked about how easy it is to come to live by other people's rules and what problems doing so may bring. Now we need to look more closely at how you may reveal your belief in the idea that "rules are sacred." Some of the ways you show you believe in this idea are conscious, some unconscious. They may not be pleasant, either, but you have to face them. For only by recognizing them can you start to act upon them. Use this guide as a checklist. Do you find yourself?

- Blaming men, circumstances and the world in general for your present situation?
- Shifting responsibility for your emotions onto men?
- Worshipping people—especially men—you know as heroes?

Ana, 22, a clerk in a cosmetic department of a major department store, blamed God, the elements, her family and especially men for the fact that she still wasn't married. She was so angry because men weren't asking her out that she went through periods when if a man even spoke to her, she'd snap his head off or not answer. When we asked Ana why she didn't go for what she wanted and at least tell a man she'd like to see him sometime, she was outraged we'd suggest such a thing. "It just isn't done," she said. "If a guy wants to see you, he'll ask you." "Really?" we answered. "Where is that rule written?" After some thought, Ana said, "Someone told me that Tom Selleck *hates* women who come on to him." Ana was taking her cues from idols, following the rules *they* thought were appropriate. We told Ana that she needed to take responsibility for her anger and poor social life and do something about it—stop worshipping the rules of her heroes and make some of her own. The first rule Ana made was "If I see a man I like, I'll let him know." This one extra effort led to several men picking up on her positive signal and asking her out.

- Relying on the "shoulds" of etiquette, fashion and tradition to give you security and to tell others who you are?
- Doing things because you "should" rather than because you "want"?
- Following orders from "superiors"—men, bosses and even religious officials?
- Needing a new dress for every occasion and agonizing with, "What should I wear?" because you feel you

have to keep up with fashion?
- Attending societies, conventions, meetings, weddings, showers and funerals not because you want to but because you are supposed to?

Lydia, 32, was taking 20 mg of Valium a day in order to cope with the life-style of her husband, Tony, the director of new accounts for a large advertising firm. She and Tony went to social functions at least three times a week, and Lydia needed a new wardrobe for almost every one—by the "right" designer, in the most fashionable color, to match what Tony was wearing. Their life had gone on at this rigid pace for five years when an argument erupted that made them see how much they were in need of counseling. One evening Lydia refused to accompany Tony to an awards banquet even though the boss expected his staff always to bring their wives to complete the image of success he was trying to build around his employees. "*All* good wives help their husbands," Tony stormed angrily, trying to get his way by making Lydia feel guilty. "But where does it end?" Lydia cried back. "There has to be a limit!" In couples counseling, we helped both Tony and Lydia to see that she had overextended her limits. We told Lydia to ask herself, "Why do I care *so* much if others think I'm good?" Following someone else's rules, even if they were from your husband's boss, was not worth it if you needed to be on medication to do so. We all agreed that Lydia needed a rest. For a year she put away the fashion books, stopped going places she didn't want to go and really did nothing. This change went against the Puritan work ethic instilled in her from childhood that every moment of the day should be filled. But in time she adjusted to a new set of rules, a set not dependent on someone else's judgment for their worth or one she needed Valium to follow.

- Assuming "feminine" roles in daily living because you feel you have to?
- Feeling you need to follow old household rules, such as everyone eating at the same time or in the same room, even if your schedules and needs are completely different?

- Often having sex when you're not in the mood, because you feel you shouldn't say no?

"How many men does it take to clean a toilet?" Beth, 28, a delightful woman attending one of our seminars, joked to the group. When no one could supply the answer to the riddle, she laughed, "None. It's women's work." This was just one of the "sacred" duties Beth was tired of performing. "Where is it written," she complained, "that a woman *has* to do dishes, iron, clean? I'd much rather trade these duties off with my husband, Louie, for the gardening, mowing or even fixing the electrical and plumbing." Beth, like so many women today, was looking for someone to give her feelings validation, to say "Right on! Do what's right for you." The group supportively gave her permission to set up a more workable system for her life that included her trimming the hedge and leaving waxing the kitchen floor to Louie. Louie came around when he saw that Beth was not going to have it any other way.

- Never asking a man for a date, calling him or paying his bill?
- Giving up your male friends when you enter into a romantic relationship because you think people will talk?
- Never being seen anywhere without your partner, even though there may be many activities you would both love doing on your own?

Irma, a 29-year-old screenwriter, was upset because she felt she had to choose between the wishes of her new husband, Brad, and her best friend of twenty years, Martin. She and Martin had grown up together like sister and brother, with many things in common—art, theater, metaphysics. They had great times going to galleries and plays, discussing ghosts, demons, and UFOs. Brad, however, was into basketball, sports-car racing and computers. He refused to partake of art and drama with Irma and Martin, and when they discussed topics that Brad wasn't interested in, he clammed up, making it too uncomfortable to pursue the topic further. Martin was the only friend Irma had whose interests were in these areas, and giving up Martin would be giving up her special interests as well. Irma was afraid Brad would object if she went out with Martin in public without him. Her mother had never gone anywhere with a man other than her father, and she was pretty sure Brad would expect her to follow the same sacred rules. "How could I put it to him?" Irma asked us; "How is he ever going to go for this idea?" "You don't have to explain yourself," we told her. "It's OK to do something because you want to." One day Brad came home to find a note from Irma, "Gone to see the Calder exhibition with Martin. Be back at 6:00. Love, Irma." When Irma returned, Brad said, "Thank God you didn't ask me to go." The sacred rules Irma felt so trapped by weren't those of her husband at all. They were left-over relics from early childhood conditioning.

These are only a few examples of letting "superior" others tell you how to live. We're certain you could think of a lot more. But before you make a list of your own, ask yourself why you would choose to trust another source to dictate what is best for you. This is a hard realization to face, and it may take time, but it is extremely important for freeing yourself of your constraints. As you come to see that only you truly know what is best for you, we're certain you'll stop letting other people tell you how to run your life.

What We Get from Following Rules

Here are some common payoffs for letting men lead you around by the nose. You can use these tips as signs to watch out for in your own life.

- You have a feeling of "rightness" that comes with being a "good girl."
- You can blame your problems on the faulty rules. You don't have to bear the pressure of making rules of your own.

- Rules that are sacred and absolute let you manipulate others. By telling someone that something is the law, no one can refute you. Rules *make* you right. But it is illusory rightness.
- You get great approval from the people and institutions whose rules you are following. With this goes a lovely, but potentially lethal, sense of belonging and doing what you "should."
- Rules provide a marvelous ladder to self-appointed sainthood.
- As long as you concentrate on what works for others, you don't have to worry about what works for you. You can exist through all your rules rather than taking a chance and really living.

Feeling good and right and saintly is not worth the price of happiness. Neither is finding a scapegoat for your problems and a chance to manipulate others. *Nothing* feels better than directing your own destiny!

Some Techniques for Freeing Yourself

Believing the myths of sacred rules is something you learn to do. But making rules that work for you *also* can be learned. That is the wonderful thing we are going to show you how to do. That is a true education. Author Muriel Spark defined it this way in her strong book about a school teacher finding herself, *The Prime of Miss Jean Brodie:*

> To me education is a leading out of what is already there in the pupil's soul. . . . It is [not] a putting in of something that is not there. . . . That is not what I call education, I call it intrusion . . .

Rules that are external, fixed and "sacred" can be an intrusion upon your free spirit. They are the opposite of learning to think for yourself. And the best way to begin to free that spirit within is to start now! Here is a brief list of some of our favorite suggestions for leading out what lies dormant within you—the seeds of self-esteem. The important thing is to take action, *doing*—even if it's only a step or two at a time.

- You cannot be courageous unless you do something you are afraid of. Break the rules. Take a risk. Be like our client Tracy, who braved taking a night out on her own, and *do* something! Even if it is something small —visiting a town you've never seen, reading a new kind of book, even brushing up on old piano lessons! Think of any new activity as an adventure and a triumph!

- Do like Joan did to free herself from Philip's domination and compile a list of all the rules you follow that do not seem right for you. Try to pinpoint why you give them credence. Keep a journal about them for a week or so. You may be surprised at what you learn about yourself.

- Create your own "rules to live by," as Jackie did when she decided not to spend time with insensitive men, or Ana did when she resolved to let men know if she liked them, or as Beth did when she took over Louie's "male" chore of hedge-trimming and left the kitchen floor for him to wax. Write down these rules even if you don't think you can follow them.

- Put one of your self-made rules into action. Resolve to face the consequences of this one behavior with calmness and equanimity. For example, if you've always believed it was inappropriate for a woman to invite a man to her place and you meet a man in a social situation that you really like, ask him out to lunch or to a party. Take small steps—and watch the wonderful reactions!

- Remind yourself that a rule is really only a rule if you follow it. When catching yourself doing something because you think you should, do as Lydia did in breaking free of the demands of her husband and his boss by asking yourself, "Why do I care *so* much if others think I'm "good"?

- Ask questions. When someone wonders why you don't

jump at their command, ask questions such as "Why should I?" "Can you see why I wouldn't want to do this?"

Ida, 62, ran a bed and breakfast establishment with the help of her husband, Homer, 68. Ida cooked and cleaned for the guests and Homer made repairs, handled the finances and was in charge of promotion. Both roles were equally demanding, but Ida complained, "Homer treats me like I don't have a thing in the world to do but look after him. 'Get this. Do that' is all I hear from morning to night." We suggested to Ida that the next time Homer made an unreasonable demand for something he could just as easily do himself, she was to respond, "Why should I?" After his answer, she was to say next, "Can't you see why I wouldn't want to do this?" It didn't take long for an incident to arise. One evening Homer told Ida to get him his pipe while she was in the middle of baking bread for the morning guests. When she asked why she should, Homer answered immediately with, "Because you're my wife." As we directed, Ida answered back with, "Can't you see why I wouldn't want to do this?" "Because it takes too much effort," Homer snapped. "That's right," Ida agreed, "and *because you're my husband,* I'd expect you to want to save me as much effort as possible." Ida had just issued a new set of rules, a system in which a "good" husband does all the things previously reserved for a "good" wife.

- Negotiate. Show others your problems with their self-centered systems.

Suzanne B., a client of ours, was married to Dean, a high-powered businessman with a staff of more than 400 beneath him, who made it a rule of the house that she always retire when he did. If she didn't, he flew into a rage. He said it was because he had trouble sleeping alone. She knew what the trouble really was. He plain liked having things his own way. Finally she decided to negotiate the issue. She told him, "The way I see it, I'm giving up freedom, television, reading and a lot of other things I like to do in exchange for your not yelling at me." It didn't seem like a fair exchange, not much inducement to follow the rule. He offered to assume the weekly laundry duties if she continued to join him in bed. She agreed. The balance of trade was equalized.

- Beware of letting others' opinions become too important to you. Try saying, "I don't care what other people think" when you begin setting new rules.
- Remind yourself that you don't have to explain yourself. Like Irma did when she went to the art exhibition with her friend Martin without first explaining it to her husband, you can do something simply because you want to.
- Refrain from falling into the trap yourself of *expecting* others, men and women alike, to follow your rules just because they work for you. Remember, the only way you can be free is to let others be free.

These are the actions of women who think for themselves. These actions will most likely clash with the lessons you've learned growing up as a "good girl," when you were trying to be the epitome of obedience to someone else's rules. Now it is time to believe in the beauty and sanctity of your own. Our client, Suzanne B., put it better than we ever could: "The system that works best is the one you make for yourself!"

5

"Self-Sacrifice Is A Virtue"

I gave everything I had for my husband. He loved it . . . but there was nothing left for me.

CINDY
patient, age 37

Cindy's husband, Roger, a 42-year-old dentist, was always calling her "selfish." "I just can't understand it," she said to us. "I gave up the job I loved as a dance instructor to be able to spend more time with him. . . . I quit my needlepoint class so I could be with him on Wednesday nights. . . . I always keep my weekends free. . . . I bake from scratch. . . . The house is immaculate. . . . Still he keeps calling me selfish." It wasn't until we told Cindy to ask Roger *exactly* what he meant by selfish that Cindy started to see the light. She explained, "I now see that selfish means different things to Roger at different times. But in all cases, I discovered, it means he isn't getting what he wants. So no matter how much I do for him, as soon as there's something else he wants that I'm not providing, I'm selfish."

We've all been taught that it's more blessed to give than receive, that the meek shall inherit the earth. Yet far more women than men harm themselves with this idea. Why is this? Catering to the needs of others, to the *exclusion* of yourself, is a very popular idea. If you look closely, however, you'll discover that it has been *made* popular by those who receive the catering. The reward for doing this catering is that you'll be labeled "virtuous." Who wouldn't want to be thought of as virtuous? The only problem is that you may let your desire for it go too far; you may end up believing it is better to be saintly than satisfied.

We don't mean to paint an ugly picture of beneficence. What is true, though, is that the inheritors of the earth have been those who satisfied, not sacrificed, themselves. If you sacrifice because you believe it is the only way you can feel self-worth, and in the process avoid doing some of the things you really want to do, you'll probably end up unhappy and powerless. Too many women have been disenchanted with their belief in the "paradise" where everyone lives only for the joys they can bestow upon their fellows. Unfortunately, such an idyllic system can succeed only when everyone follows that philosophy. Such is sadly not the case; yet many women may have allowed themselves to continue to follow it because they *want* to believe the myth, and so they do, at the sacrifice of truth and personal freedom.

Women sacrifice career, achievement, independence, identity, their name in marriage—but where is the paradise, the promised reward? It appears that your only real reward for this earthbound sainthood is suffering. Martyrdom plays well in the Hollywood epic, but it won't sit so well with you in life. There is no salary and no fringe or retirement benefits. Setting yourself up for self-sacrifice on earth doesn't lead to ecstasy; it takes you only to misery and bitterness. Only satisfaction with yourself can lead to joy—for yourself and for others.

Self-sacrifice promises paradise. But women who sacrifice all for their husbands' careers are not always acknowledging their own wishes. Giving up your own education so that your husband may finish medical school and then never returning to school is not thinking about your needs or about what might happen if you are not "taken care of."

Brenda, 35, always had wanted to study costume design, and she had several friends in the industry who were willing to help her get work if she would develop her skills. However, her husband, Brian, a 38-year-old cameraman, said he didn't want his wife getting involved in "a dirty racket like the movie business." "He says it's beneath my dignity," Brenda explained. We asked Brenda, "What's the worst thing that could happen if you become a costume designer?" After a moment's thought, she answered, "Brian would think me undignified." Then we asked, "What's the worst thing that could happen if you don't become a designer?" Brenda shrugged her shoulders, "I never really thought about it." "Think!" we prodded immediately. Suddenly she gasped. "Brian could leave me and I'd starve to death because there's not a thing in the world I'm qualified to do for a living." Then we asked Brenda, "Which situation do you consider the most undignified—Brian's disapproval or starvation?" Brenda is now a highly paid costume designer and it was not at all beneath Brian's dignity to share the wealth from her career. He adjusted beautifully!

Without money, or at least the authority to generate it, you cannot expect to support yourself. In the real world of flesh and blood, autonomy and dignity, as well as concern for others, should be your criteria for success. We want to help you achieve these aims. The greatest virtue is being kind to yourself. If you can do this, all else will follow. In this chapter we'll show you how to gauge your worth in terms of what you make of yourself, instead of what you have or haven't done for men. We'll set about creating strategies for constructive independence. You'll eliminate self-sacrificing habits and learn how to help the men in your life to adjust to your changes.

Women Give, Men Take—Has it Always been That Way?

Through the ages, as we've already mentioned, women's ability to carry children and men's superior physical strength were the main differences between the sexes. Women raised the next generation; men protected them and guarded them—sometimes by fighting and taking other lives. So it began: the woman gives life and the man takes life.

This concept of giving women and taking men is still with us today. But man's right to take, to expect the sacrifice of others, doesn't work in our civilized society, so he has substituted economic strength. And again, despite the gains women have made over the years, many people still think that since men are the ones who do most of the "important" work, earn the most money, and make most of the rules, it's only "fair" that women should do something in return: "support" them.

One of our patients, Jennifer, a 28-year-old housewife, found herself in this Catch-22 situation: "My husband, Ivan, expects me to do everything he says because he makes the money, . . . but he won't let me get a job and make money of my own!" This situation was especially frustrating to Jennifer because she had graduated with honors from one of the country's best secretarial schools and could easily have landed a job making more than Ivan, 26, a courier for Federal Express. "That's just the problem," Jennifer said. "He's intimidated by my earning potential so he makes sure I don't work. It's the only way he can stay the boss."

Even women who have successful careers sometimes face this problem. Eva, a 54-year-old attorney, found herself continually giving emotional support to her husband, Herb, a 54-year-old plastic surgeon, and getting relatively little in return. "I walk in dog-tired from overtime at the office," she said, "and I never get what I give to Herb . . . Dinner on the table? . . . A warm greeting or 'How was your day?' . . . Forget it! He doesn't give me as much as a smile. But when *he* gets home he expects the adoration and attention of a lap-dog. And if I don't give it, he says I'm selfish. It's not that I mind being adoring . . . I just want some adoration back once in a while." We told Eva that it was time to turn the tables on Herb, to tell him that he was just as selfish for expecting her sacrificial support as she was for not giving it. Either they would both give or there would be nothing for Herb to take. Eva would stop the one-way sacrificing Herb expected in their marriage. With a little additional help from us in counseling, Herb was able to see things more from Eva's point of view and stop being only a taker.

It seems that even in our supposedly enlightened age women believe that they won't get the help from their husbands that they give to them—but that "it's to be expected" that the man needs more support than they do. It's the myth of "goodness" all over again. Many women echo the words of Eva in her first session with us when she said, "I'm so tired of always being the one to help and then never getting any help in return." The time has come for you to make sacrificing a two-way street!

"Virtue": A Label Used to Manipulate

Remember Sandy whose family coerced her into doing everything for them just by saying, "Be a dear and . . ." or "Be nice and . . ." How many times have you felt manipulated by someone who says, "Be an angel and . . ."? The sentence always finishes with something they want you to do for them. In other words, you are good and angelic to the extent you give them what they want. Does this sound familiar to you? Men have been using this criterion for goodness on women for a very long time.

As we've mentioned, your training in "goodness" may have begun early in life. You may have been taught that you are good in proportion to how well you please mommy and daddy, and follow their rules. "Don't be naughty. Pick up your clothes." "Be a good girl and do your chores." "Help your mother with the dishes. That's a good girl." As you grew older, there was the educational system to contend with, full of new rules: "Follow the dress code" and "Never argue with the teacher." Then, all too often, you, as a young woman, are good to the extent you please your husband. "She's a perfect wife, she's always home, she's a great cook," or "You're such a lady. You never get angry in public." All in all, we see a simple progression from sacrificing for daddy, to teacher, to husband—all in order to be virtuous in the eyes of men and to reap the reward of their favor.

Sophie, 39, the eldest of four girls born to a carpenter who hated his job, learned as a little girl that it was "good" not to want much. She described a Christmas when her father kissed her on the cheek and said, "We knew you wouldn't mind not getting a present this Christmas so that your younger sisters can get something. God will bless you." Sophie extended this pattern in school, giving other children her lunch money, school supplies and even books so she could be further blessed. She told us, "My husband, Edward, married me because he said I was the sweetest girl he'd ever met . . . an old-fashioned one like his mother." Through the early married years of homemaking and child-rearing, Sophie continued her childhood program of not wanting for things in order to be good. However, one day Sophie had a revelation. "I guess I was about 37 when it happened," she told us. "I woke up one morning and realized that as long as I kept never wanting, always sacrificing, I was never going to have anything for myself. . . . I was never going to see any of the wonderful places I'd read about in books and seen in movies. . . . I was never going to wear any of the fashions I'd followed so many years in my favorite magazines. . . . I was never even going to eat in my hometown restaurants I'd heard all my friends talk about and seen featured in the papers. . . . Suddenly I started to cry. . . . It really surprised me. . . . I never even realized I wanted any of those things. But I guess I must have, or I wouldn't have spent so much time dreaming about them. The thing is, I was dreaming my life away. And what was the point if none of it was ever going to come true?" We all reach points in our lives when we realize we have to get what we want, when the dream just isn't enough anymore. Sophie had reached such a point. We asked Sophie to make a list of all the things she envisioned having or doing in her wildest dreams, to pretend she could have *anything* she wanted for a month. As we usually discover when we examine such a list, most of the items were within her reach, things Sophie could have if she'd just allow herself the satisfaction. We started with the most attainable item on the list: the most expensive course on the menu at the best restaurant in town. We told Sophie that if she didn't start being good to herself now, she probably never would. All her dreams would remain dreams forever. With our support, Sophie rose to the challenge. Sophie and Edward went dining that week. She only had to allow herself to do it.

The problem with self-sacrifice is that it does everyone good but you. The greatest virtue is being kind to yourself. If you can do this, all else will follow.

How Women Sacrifice Achievement for Beauty and Satisfaction for Sainthood

"All men seem to care about is what I look like," complained Nanette, a 25-year-old executive secretary in a firm dealing with government contracts. "I know I only get the job 'cause I'm cute and dress nice. I suppose that's OK for now. But what happens when I'm not so cute anymore?" Psychiatrist Natalie Shainess, in her excellent book *Sweet Suffering*, points to culture's "emphasis on a woman's beauty rather than her achievement" as one of two major causes of self-punishment or masochism in women. A woman's beauty is a payoff to the men who behold her; a woman's achievement is a reward to herself. Accomplishment is a "virtue" that only men are supposed to enjoy for themselves.

The decision to suffer—or to change—rests solely with you. You can continue to saddle your potential so that you can please others or you can see that a greater beauty lies in taking back the power you have given away. You have nothing to regain but the everlasting beauty of dignity and self-determination.

Serving others as saint, Girl Friday, wife, mom or whatever can be a real trap if *all* you get out of it is the approval of those you serve.

One of our clients, an attractive 30-year-old woman named Susan, found that she was trading her own satisfaction for what she thought was sainthood. Susan complained about her unhappy marriage of seven years. Her real-estate-salesman husband, Roy, never let her have any fun. "He never lets me out of the house," she said. She scrubbed, cooked, washed and tended the two small children while he spent much of his time lunching with prospective buyers and golfing with the boss. Susan's life was one long list of resentments. One day in a counseling session, we handed her a clean sheet of white paper and asked her to write down all the sacrifices she believed she was currently making for her husband. The list was a long one, but we singled out one item: "I sit with the children so he can be with his pals." We asked Susan, "Does this really make you virtuous?" Susan laughed at the ridiculousness of the idea.

Then we asked her why she didn't get a sitter for such occasions. She seemed taken aback, as though the idea was out of the question. In Susan's mind, a "good" mother never left her children with a sitter to do something out of the house unless it was with her husband. It was no wonder she was hurt and resentful most of the time: she was locked into her own idea of martyrdom, a concept that stemmed from what she was taught long ago by her mother who repeatedly told her, "A good mother puts her husband and children first *always*." She set herself up to be victimized. Once Susan examined the reasons behind the way she acted, she chose to change the definition of a "good" mother to "one who looks out for the welfare of *both* herself and her family." Then she felt some freedom in her life. "It took me a long time to realize I could be good to my family and good to myself as well," she said.

"The Woman Behind the Man"

Former First Lady Pat Nixon was once quoted as saying, "I have sacrificed everything in my life that I consider precious in order to advance the political career of my husband." Such total sacrifice to the complete exclusion of one's personal satisfaction is sad but, unfortunately, it is not uncommon.

Another woman, a client of ours, Katey, 32, was furious because her husband wanted a divorce. She was incensed at the fact that she had "sacrificed everything" for him and now he was leaving her. Once Katey had been an accomplished student of business and economics, but she never pursued a career after marriage; instead she devoted all her time to social functions, entertaining and accompanying her husband to society meetings in the service of his career. Katey's thinking, which led to her own unhappiness and possibly, in part, to the breakup of her marriage, is colored by the resentment she harbors from believing self-sacrifice is a virtue. She is the quintessential woman behind the man, but at the same time she is using her ideas as a rationale for avoiding something she has been afraid to try for a long time—succeeding in the outside world on her own. We asked Katey the all-important question: "Can you see any advantage to living solely for your husband?" "It keeps me from having to live for myself," she said. "I find that possibility terrifying. What if I can't make it out there?" As we helped Katey to recognize that her self-sacrificing was really masking her fear of failure, she came to confront her fear of the outside world with positive action. She is considering either a part-time job or a position in consulting—a decision that can lead to the satisfaction she has too long denied herself. We are certain Katey now will be successful in whatever she decides to do.

Why You Must Lose to Be Loved

Inga saw her mother constantly fail around her father. "Mom would act totally inept around Dad." She recalled, "There were many times she could have won an argument by bringing up certain important points, but she never did. It was like this in everything they did together. She even let him win at cards. I guess losing was her way of getting him to love her."

This idea may sound strange, but the belief that loss and sacrifice bring benefit runs deep, and for many women begins early in life. Loss and sacrifice are so ingrained into a young girl's mind that they have become synonymous with femininity. "Don't fight," "Keep your voice down," "Let your brother have what he wants," "Be quiet" are all messages that imply a good little girl sinks into the background so others can get what *they* want out of life. This is why so many women—highly talented, self-motivated women—are terrified of winning at work or even of being good at play. To maintain their role of sacrificing, giving and losing, some women manifest (consciously or unconsciously) a host of typically female behaviors: they turn their ankles on hikes, break their legs on ski trips, capsize their canoes, lose the matches on campouts, or hit the ball over the fence in tennis. These are only a few of the marvelously "feminine" things that make women "good" in the eyes of many men. They can take many forms and present themselves in the most subtle ways.

Sonia, a smart, motivated 31-year-old gynecologist, was subconsciously sabotaging herself to lose. At 21, she was president of her college sorority and elected Snow Queen of the campus. Everybody adored Sonia. She was pretty but not threateningly so, bright but not too bright, friendly but not aggressive, active but not competitive—an all-around likable gal who was enjoyed by everybody and intimidated no one. Sonia's popularity continued all through medical school, and she looked forward to setting up a thriving private practice with lots of referrals generated through her charm and good qualities. The dream never materialized. After three years struggling in vain to build a business, Sonia was forced to go on salary in a public hospital, a job in which she was ''underpaid, overworked and given no freedom to try new treatment methods.''

Why wasn't the sorority queen who'd generated the votes of over 30,000 men on campus able to inspire votes of confidence from her professional colleagues? The answer was simple: The sorority had taught Sonia to win by losing. Here it was the girls who couldn't pound the nails for the homecoming float, get a higher grade-point average than the fraternity jocks, or stay adrift as long as the men when tubing the rapids that were sought after. However, when it came to inspiring confidence in her professional colleagues, the criteria for success were different. But Sonia wasn't able to see this until we pointed it out to her. She was still trying to win by losing in social situations with other doctors, and this behavior was turning them off. Though a good athlete, she would intentionally hold back in her medical society's softball games. If asked to play tennis or golf at the club she had purposely joined to make professional contacts, she would not try as hard as she could to win so as not to offend her opponent. Even at the pool, she found herself letting people win at cards or backgammon, hoping they would like her better for it. The result, of course, was the reverse. These professionals admired only one thing in people they referred their patients to: excellence. While it was true that Sonia was making lots of friends, being invited to parties and private homes, she did not inspire enough confidence in her colleagues to get them to trust her with their patients. We told Sonia that not only must she stop holding back, she needed to launch an all-out attack on improving *all* her skills from Chinese checkers to scuba diving. If her professional friends saw her winning at tennis, they could envision her winning in the office as well. Our advice worked. When Sonia stopped losing to be loved and started winning to be respected, she began getting referrals and was able to go back into a successful private practice.

Naturally, people reward sacrificial behavior with compliments, gifts and invitations to see you again. This is a means to power. Only when you value yourself over an artificial, manipulating love can you begin to be happy. A love that requires you to fail is no love at all. Mature love includes respect both for the rights of another and for your own rights to be the best you can be. Make excellence, not self-sacrifice, a virtue in your life!

Signals at Work: Don't Compete, Hold Back, Help the Man Succeed

We ran into Sonia recently at a social function and started talking about the success of her new life. "What amazes me, looking back," she said, "is how I equated being successful with being liked. Of course it's nice to be liked, but it sure doesn't guarantee advancement at work. All those things I was doing to be popular—holding back, not competing, letting others beat me, being 'good' to everyone—were taking me straight to the poorhouse!"

How can a woman who is conditioned to be giving, saintly and supporting succeed at work, where incomes and promotions depend upon beating the competition and valuing your self-worth? This is a question with as many facets to it as there are answers proposed, and we can outline only a few of them here.

Women face a tremendous double bind in the business world. If they hold back from competing against their male colleagues, they lose, and stay on the lower end of the social-and-economic totem pole. On the other hand, if they stop sacrificing themselves to men—at least in the world of business—and for the same rewards of power and wealth, they risk losing the love and approval of the men against whom they are struggling. It sounds like a no-win situation. But is it possible that women have only *been made to believe* they can't beat city hall, that maybe they really can have both of the things they want: economic power and the love of their men?

The answer is unequivocally yes. It is possible to have both love and power. Men have had it for centuries. Many women even love men *because* they are rich and powerful. Why couldn't a man love and respect a woman for the same reasons? He might, if she would only rise to that position and find out. The fact of the matter is that men will *always* love women. But they will also always love power and control and will do anything to hold onto it. So what can you do?

You can change your behavior *in spite* of the way men are. Then when you've changed you can help them adapt. But don't expect them to change without your help; they like things the way they are. First, take the responsibility for change on yourself.

A client of ours, Doris, 27, is a fabulous example. She suffered desperately as she sacrificed her dreams for the approval of men. She was a fully licensed broker in a large real estate firm, kept herself beautifully, had a warm, inviting personality, and was bright and articulate. Yet whenever the firm had staff meetings, Doris shrank into the woodwork and as a result missed out on many good listing opportunities that were gobbled up by her male co-workers. They may have loved the fact that they were able to intimidate her out of business, but they certainly didn't love or respect her personally for being a shrinking violet. In Doris's words, "They like me, but they don't respect me."

Doris is the typical victim of inner signals she learned when she was young—from ages 2 to 6, the critical years that shape a child's personality. During this time, Doris's mother was constantly complaining to her father that he was always telling her "what to do . . . 'Make my dinner,' 'Shut up,' 'Go to bed' " . . . , behavior he insisted he had a perfect right to do because he "brought home the bacon." Doris had seen her mother sacrifice autonomy for financial security, and even though she was now in a position to bring home her own bacon, something inside her said that women should sacrifice for men. Since the men in the office were the most important ones in her life, they received the attention. Like her mother before her, Doris was getting a payoff for her sacrifice—pity and attention from other women around her in similar circumstances.

Finally we asked Doris, "Which would you rather be—a likable failure or a guilty success?" Doris decided to change her behavior *first* and deal with any feelings of guilt that might arise! She spoke up at staff meetings, called people she'd been afraid to phone before, and competed against men for property listings and time on the floor. At first Doris did feel guilty for taking from the men, but when we asked "Would you rather they take from you?" she saw that this alternative was totally self-defeating and stopped punishing herself for giving to herself. Doris is still a loving and caring person, perhaps even more now than ever before, because now she gives freely and willingly. And she continues to work on her new way of life every day, learning to jump in and go for new accounts and territories just as the men do, without thinking "Do I have the right?" Because now she knows she has the right to be happy! In Doris's own words, "I now realize that giving to others is not enough. You also have to give to yourself in order to be happy."

Flirting, Crying and Using Emotion: The Ultimate Concession

Just as Doris learned that she had a right to be happy, so can you. When you really believe "a man can take what he wants but I can't," you may find yourself resorting to flirting, crying, and using emotions to express your frustration and hidden wants. While these tactics may work for you in a personal relationship, they are devastating in business.

A prime example that comes to mind was Thelma, a former "good girl." Thelma was a production assistant in a large design firm who wanted to break out of her clerical duties and be given real responsibility. But she didn't know how to ask for it, so she showed her displeasure by crying every time her boss gave her additional secretarial duties. This inappropriate response worked once in a while, so Thelma continued with it. However, after years at the same job, she still hadn't received a promotion or a decent raise. We taught her to simply say, "You're giving me too much work" rather than to cry every time the load got too heavy. With fewer clerical duties, Thelma had a chance to work on the other projects she had been wanting to do. Six months later Thelma got her raise and six months after that she had a new title. Her boss didn't expect Thelma to do everything, but he did expect her to show self-control. Whenever you *use* your emotions to get what you want, the price is most often not worth the return on your emotional involvement. Thelma told us, "I don't know what ever made me think I could get a promotion by acting weak. It might have served to lessen my workload, but it sure never led to me getting a more demanding job."

Being good and knowing how to handle what you do are the only true criteria for success at work. We know that beauty cannot substitute for achievement. Neither can tears nor torrid emotions. They might make you feel better, but only for a moment—until you realize how self-defeating they really are. The machinations of business spring from logic and laws, not from emotion, and in the work world emotions are seen as a sign of weakness. Self-sacrifice that can only be motivated out of "love" is frowned upon in finance. No one would run the Federal Reserve Board or banking system on the basis of self-sacrifice is a virtue. Yet women are taught from childhood that "it's all right to express emotions." Displaying emotions is important, but not at all times, particularly not in business and in government. However, you may never have been taught when showing emotions is and is not appropriate. It's good to be open with your emotions in your close personal relationships, but in more formal situations like business, it may be considered a sign of weakness or inadequacy. Jacqueline Kennedy Onassis was probably closest to the truth when she said that the key to her success was to smile and never let anyone know what was going on in her head. Even though not everyone could be—or would want to be—as cool as Jackie Onassis, you might want to think about the real cost of showing too many emotions, what it means to your job and to who you are.

The Virtue of Self-Satisfaction at Work: Nurturing in High Places

Of course, we don't want to say that emotions have no positive effects in the business world. You just have to learn how to use them. You can be nurturing, helping and supportive at work without being too emotional. Many women worry that if they begin taking and competing they will lose the positive aspects of being female: the mothering and nurturing elements that are truly good in women. But *giving* per se is not an issue here. No one would argue that kindness is not a positive attribute; it is only when you give to others to the *exclusion* of yourself that the balance tips, when you are generous to a fault.

One of our clients, a 38-year-old secretary named Marie, was insistent about the promise that in a utopian world everyone sacrificed for the good of everyone else. Marie hated her menial secretarial duties and the cold insensitivity of the orders that came down to her from above, but she refused to attempt to rise in the company. She bolted outright at the idea of joining the "self-seeking suckers of success." She described her mother as "a martyr who never stopped complaining about the suffering she had done for her family." Mother was too good to show anger or assertiveness when she needed to change her situation. Both Marie and her mother were rewarded for this thinking by feeling they were more virtuous than the people who told them what to do.

We worked with Marie for a long time, guiding her toward seeing her sin of omission: She didn't have to let herself be used the way her mother was. We then asked her, "How would you like to work for someone like yourself? Someone warm and caring and nurturing?" When Marie nodded "yes" we told her, "The only way a company can be nurturing is if the people who run the organization are giving and caring. You owe it to both yourself and the people in your company to rise to a position where everyone can benefit from your caring.''

From then on Marie began to look for ways to advance herself within the business, and when she learned of a position that required certain executive skills, Marie took classes to learn them. A year later she was hired for the position. She's still a nurturing, caring person, but now she has a larger sphere of influence, can help more people, and has a higher sense of self-worth. "It's wonderful," she said, "to be in a position where the fact that you care can make a difference.''

As a woman, you, like Marie, have the marvelous chance to make your business a more nurturing, caring place. You can help to replace self-defeating sacrifice with self-directed satisfaction. You can elevate others *through* the elevation of yourself.

How We Sacrifice Ourselves

Awareness is half the battle to resolving any problem. You can increase your awareness by examining how "self-sacrifice is a virtue" pops up in your behavior. We've already talked with you about some of the things you do to sacrifice for others to the exclusion of yourself. Now we'll help you to work on some of the specifics: your emphasis on giving versus taking, your focus on beauty and "goodness" instead of personal achievement and satisfaction, and finally, your resorting to emotionalizing on the job. Here is a checklist of the most common manifestations of these problems. Do you find yourself:

- Holding back or deferring in conversation with men for fear they will view you as competitive, abrasive and unfeminine, even though you know your concerns deserve to be heard?
- Flirting with men in business situations or using your looks in ways you would not even consider with other women?
- Crying or becoming emotional at work?

and to try looking hard at her *need* to be a saint coupled with an inability to tell loved ones what was appropriate for her. The first step to being good to yourself is giving up your need to be a martyr. We are happy to say that Bonnie is now allowing people to sacrifice some for her and even, at times, asking for it.

- Playing the "if I can't have it, then neither can he or she" game? This is the practice of hating others for not making the same sacrifices you have decided to make for yourself. At work, you may be angry at mothers who are lobbying for a day-care center because you have decided to sacrifice children for career. At home, you may resent other homemakers who are also out in the business world for "neglecting" their children while you sacrifice career for family.

- Growing angry because people fail to meet your expectations? Many women falsely believe that if they sacrifice for a man's satisfaction, the man will return the gesture. Since this usually doesn't happen, these perfectionists inevitably feel cheated or unloved. To avoid this pitfall, you need to learn to sacrifice for yourself *before* you do so for others. Psychologist Wayne Dyer defines this kind of self-love well in *Your Erroneous Zones:* "The ability and willingness to allow those that you care for to be what they choose for themselves, without any insistence that they satisfy you." Begin to satisfy yourself and suddenly you're able to satisfy and give to others without the sense of deprivation, strings and manipulation so often associated with sacrifice.

- Neglecting your body?

- Living your life based on events you "should" be doing for the satisfaction of others rather than activities you want and need to do?

Aurora, 34, felt it was selfish for a wife and mother to pay too much attention to herself, so she focused her life totally on her husband, Ben, their two children and four cats. In the process, she neglected herself, putting on about five pounds a year. After fifteen years of marriage, Aurora, who weighed 110 pounds in her wedding gown, now weighed 185! She was mortified by her appearance and tried not to think about it by sacrificing even more for her family. This only made things worse and she went on tranquilizers which, she soon discovered, numbed her poor self-image more if she added a shot of scotch.

When we first saw Aurora, she was an alcoholic and heavily drug dependent. She was able to turn her condition around when we helped her to realize that self-*satisfaction* is a virtue. Growth comes through *mastering,* not sacrificing, your body. We immediately set out to get Aurora to begin a reducing plan in order to regain a positive self-image and sense of control over herself. We had her record when and what she was eating (time, date, specific food), where she was eating (kitchen, restaurant, car, etc.), activities she was pairing with eating (phoning, watching TV, driving), and record it *before* she ate the food in order to help break the pattern. Based on her record keeping, we gave Aurora hypnotic suggestions to eliminate specific undesirable foods. She started losing weight immediately and began feeling better about herself. Aurora's family caught these positive feelings, and now they feel better too. The day Aurora began helping rather than sacrificing herself, her life started to come together again.

These are only a few examples of the defeating behavior that comes from believing self-sacrifice is a virtue. Now make your own list. Challenge the items that keep you from happiness. Change the sacrifice to gifts you give to you. Be true first to yourself!

Rewards for Sacrificing Yourself

A major step to your coming up with strategies for eliminating self-sacrificing behavior is understanding *why* you continue your self-defeating activities. Why would you choose to go through life denying yourself those things that could make you happy? What a terrible waste. At the heart of learning to be a complete person is understanding your motives, gaining insight into the payoffs for behaving as you do. There is a reason for all actions, and once you realize what you do that keeps your myth of self-sacrifice alive, you can begin your work on the behaviors that spring from it.

There are many dividends for self-sacrifice. Some you may already be aware of; others will be a revelation to you; still others you may not yet be willing to face, but they will emerge with patience and will begin to resolve themselves when you decide to change. Here are some common rewards that keep you from self-satisfaction:

- Sacrificing yourself allows you to focus on the possibility of a dream world in which everybody sacrifices for the other. The feeling behind this usually is: "I don't care about reality. I just know I don't want to live in a world where people don't make sacrifices for other people." The faulty conclusion is that if you sacrifice for others, they will sacrifice for you.
- You feel virtuous for being so wonderful. It may be a way to make yourself feel better than others.
- You have a built-in excuse for failure: You are too good to do the things it takes to succeed in the material world.
- Self-sacrifice gains you attention, self-pity. You can spend so much time winning pity and feeling sorry for yourself that you have no time to think about what you really want to do with your life.
- You can control others by reminding them how much you have sacrificed for them and how much they *owe* you.
- You can justify your unhappiness because you have "given your life" for nothing.

Believing that self-sacrifice leads to sainthood can be a dangerous illusion because it often results in a sense of emptiness rather than fulfillment. If you give all that you have without taking something as a balance, inevitably you will be living in an emotional vacuum. Now that you have some insight into the rewards for self-sacrifice, you can begin the final step of taking action. Here are some strategies for throwing away this type of thinking to clear your path to total self-satisfaction.

How to Turn Self-Defeat into Self-Worth

A sense of self-worth comes from building yourself as well as others.

- Do as Susan did to stop from totally sacrificing herself for Roy and write a list of all the sacrifices you believe you currently are making for others. This will be a blueprint for change. Ask yourself the crucial question, "Do these sacrifices truly make me virtuous?" In most cases the answer will be no. Try to think about how you could eliminate the behaviors you have mistaken for virtues.

- Work on changing your view of the world. Realize, as Aurora did when she stopped neglecting her body, that self-*satisfaction* is a virtue. Happy, satisfied people make other people happy and satisfied. People can "catch" your joy.

- Next time your husband or boyfriend asks if there is any particular restaurant you would like to go to for dinner, be good to yourself and suggest the place you've always wanted to visit. If he hesitates or refuses, stand your ground and ask: "Do you think this place is too good for me?" Regardless of his response, finish with, "This is where I deserve to go," and settle for nothing else. Many women have an imaginary list of elegant eating spots they believe are beyond their own worth. Choose one, get dressed up and chow down.

- Have a party. Take a breather on saving for the new washing machine, for remade crowns or for your IRA account and enjoy yourself for a change. Your ability to experience pleasure makes you a more well-rounded person. People want to be around people who can enjoy life—it's contagious!

- Try to stop having to justify everything you do in terms of goodness. If people call you selfish, like Roger was doing to Cindy, find out exactly what they mean by the term. You may discover that they're being defensive and either want you to do more for them or are upset because they're not as forthright as you are.

- Do as Eva did with Herb when he expected her to provide all the emotional support in the relationship. Turn the tables on someone who calls you selfish or stingy for not giving him what he wants, point out that he or she is just as selfish for expecting the sacrifice.

- Break childhood patterns of not wanting for yourself the Way Sophie did. Create a heaven on earth in your mind where your wildest dreams are realized. For example, you might imagine you can have anything you want without the limitations of money or others' rules for the next month. You might envision yourself sleeping late every morning, lounging on satin sheets, not dressing till midday, having a manicurist, hairdresser or masseuse to your home, having a party catered. You'll discover you can achieve some of your dreams. You're not wishing for the impossible, just things you can obtain if you try to get them.

- Whenever you find yourself in a situation where you resent giving, do as Brenda did when deciding whether to sacrifice becoming a costume designer, and ask yourself, "What's the worst thing that could happen to me if I don't make this sacrifice?" You'll most likely discover that your fears of being "bad" are out of proportion to the reality of the consequences. Then ask yourself, "What's the worst thing that could happen if I do make this sacrifice?" Weigh the answers. Then make an intelligent decision.

- Remind yourself that a sense of failure often comes from not playing by someone else's rules, not meeting *their* expectations. Whenever you meet with someone's disapproval, ask yourself, "*Why* exactly are they so upset?" The answer invariably is not that you are a bad person, but that someone else simply didn't get what *he* or *she* wanted. That's too bad, but it needn't be your problem. Relax and allow others to set their own standards that have nothing to do with you. As soon as you begin measuring success in your own terms you will be much nicer to yourself.

• Do something you've been wanting to do for a long time.

For forty years a client of ours had wanted to travel and see the world. She had put off fulfilling this desire in order to raise her family, telling herself that when the children were grown she would pursue her intellectual and spiritual development (just as adults in India gave their post-child-rearing years for developing their souls). Unfortunately, these plans did not materialize. No sooner was the youngest son out of the home than the eldest daughter was back with her two small children, newly divorced, expecting Mother to take her in indefinitely. When Helen talked about traveling, Helen's husband did not understand her needs; he wanted her to stay at home. When Helen's son's wife left him and he came home to roost with his children, too, Helen did the unexpected. She took a vacation. She enlisted a friend, and the two of them went off to China together for six weeks. At last, out of experience, Helen learned a valuable lesson: "The people in my life can survive without my sacrificing. I can go anywhere and do anything and they'll still be there when I come back." Six weeks' satisfaction in China did more to make Helen's behavior "good" than did an entire lifetime of self-denial.

The above suggestions are just some of the constructive ideas that will help you to be happier. They will help to clear your need for self-defeating sacrifice just as they did for Helen. You are now ready to deal calmly with the marvelous consequences of your new behavior—your new-found power and control. If people growl or put up a fight at first, hold your ground without hostility. You'll triumph, and you'll win some unexpected respect now that they see you're a truly satisfied woman!

6

"Good Girls Don't Really Enjoy Sex"

> I hated sex because it always seemed a duty, and
> nobody enjoys doing what they have to . . .
> besides, if I enjoyed it, that would be even worse.
> I don't really know why, but it would.
>
> MARY
> *patient, age 33*

"Self-sacrifice is a virtue" reaches its peak when you deny your innermost self—your sexual self—to live out someone else's idea of goodness. Mary, a 34-year-old actress, described her sexual dilemma with her live-in lover, Russ, a 30-year-old designer, this way: "I knew I had to put out in order to hold on to him. Yet I also felt that he'd think I was cheap for doing so. I guess I thought I could resolve the problem by giving him what he wanted but not appearing to enjoy it. That way he'd respect me for satisfying his needs but not hate me for being cheap."

Mary's case is typical. Her father, the owner of a small-town newspaper, and her mother, who did the editing to help her husband, raised her for the traditional role of marriage. In that role sex was to be initiated by the husband. Mary quoted her mother as saying, "If you get to enjoying sex too much, you'll start asking for it. That's no good. The husband should be the master everywhere but in the kitchen."

While it is true that some women don't have good sex because they don't have a good relationship in general and

117

that bad sex is symptomatic of something bigger that's going wrong, we usually find that the reason for lack of sexual fulfillment stems from women's early childhood conditioning that sex is a duty to the male, not to be enjoyed. Women are usually very uncertain as to why they aren't supposed to enjoy sex. But if we look closely at the words of Mary's mother, we see the implicit message that when a woman is demanding, sexually or otherwise, she is overstepping the bounds of virtuous dependency. Because of this, even in this age of supposed sexual enlightenment, many women still have hang-ups about physical intimacy and enjoying themselves.

Alva, a 50-year-old wife and mother who had been married more than thirty years said, "I still feel uncomfortable in bed with my husband. I never know how he's going to react. When he wants it he seems to enjoy my pleasure, but when he's not in the mood he acts like I'm weird for being sexy." We told Alva that her sexual desire was "weird" only when her husband didn't share it and felt a pressure to do something to satisfy Alva. Many people label other people's behavior "weird" because it's different from their own at the moment or it interferes with what they want. Don't be fooled by it. "Weird" is in the eyes of the beholder. It usually has little to do with you. Beatrice said, "Men . . . they want you up on a pedestal *and* flat on your back . . . at the same time!" We found that the solution to both Alva and Beatrice's problems was for them to simply *be* sexual, regardless of what other people expected of them.

Our goals in this chapter are for you to discover that true goodness is sharing your sexual happiness with your partner, achieving sexual gratification *now,* and experiencing the full range of your true sexual self. We'll show you how to stop being intimidated by your "duties" as wife and/or lover, how to expand your senses to get physically and spiritually closer to your partner, and how to experience a rapturous sexual union based on intimacy and equality. *Everyone* is sexual. You'll come to see that it's just a question of understanding and accepting this fact and working things out with the one you are loving.

The Ultimate Self-Sacrifice

It might seem that we have run the idea of sexual freedom into the ground. Nowadays there appears to be so much talk about sexual expression, sexual revolution, sex and your emotions that we sometimes forget to look at ourselves to examine whether we really have changed our ideas about sexuality and have accepted them in ourselves. Often when we do look inward, we find that the answer is no.

Why is this, a decade after the so-called sexual revolution? Why do many women still not understand their feelings about sex? One reason is the confusing variety of ideas that many of you still carry about sex.

Many "good girls" were raised to believe that sex was a duty—something to be given to, not *shared* with, someone else. Others may not have even been taught how to think of sex as adults; they knew only what they were taught as children—that sex was bad, something they shouldn't think about. The past couple of decades have changed some of that, but only *some*. In many cases, what's happened is that women don't know what to think. It's a no-win situation.

Lucille, a 34-year-old divorced hairdresser, supporting two small children without benefit of alimony or child-support, told us, "Ten years ago I thought I was the most sexually liberated woman who ever lived. I read *all* the books during the sex revolution and tried everything they suggested. I was sexually aggressive, said no when I didn't want it, went to porno movies, subscribed to *Playgirl*. And my husband, Luther, left me. He said I was too dominating and made him feel pressured. Frankly I think I just wore the poor guy out! Now I don't know *what* to do." Lucille is currently in a relationship with Rory, a 35-year-old baker, and she isn't sure how to handle it sexually. "Right now," she told us, "I'm just going along and doing what he wants. I'm not crazy about the idea, but I don't want to scare him off by coming on too strong either."

We told Lucille that a good way to prevent Rory from feeling any pressure from her sexual advances was to tell him up front that it was perfectly OK for him to say no if he wasn't in the mood. If more lovers would give each other this permission outright, it would save a lot of relationships. You can enjoy sex fully without putting pressure on your mate as long as he knows he doesn't *always* have to feel the same passion when you do. When Lucille relieved Rory of this pressure by doing as we just suggested, she was delighted to discover that he was no longer threatened by her sexuality and did not make her feel guilty for expressing it.

Lucille's problem is not uncommon. Sometimes there are real sexual problems between men and women, most of them stemming from feeling that they can't be themselves or express their desires, even to their partner. Some men feel they can't be themselves when they're having sex. They're put in a position of having to "perform" just as women have been. The real answer lies not in either person seeing sex as a power play, but in being sensitive to each other's needs and not demanding what the other doesn't want to give. This is true sexual equality, a situation in which both parties can express their true sexual feelings without fear of pressuring the other.

Why Sexual Equality Is Still a Threat

But examples of sexual equality between partners are rare. One of the reasons, we think, is that women still don't know how to ask for equality. In our work with women over the years, we've come to see that women know what sex is, but not what sexual fulfillment is. Ever since they were little girls, they've been told that it's OK to have "lawful" sex, but it's still not all right to admit that you enjoy it. A 36-year-old, Lorraine T., one of our clients, saw her generation's dilemma best when she told us, "Before, nobody talked about sex. Now, everybody talks about it. That's the only difference. None of us are really any better at it."

Part of the problem lies in the idea that if the woman expresses too much sexual pleasure, the man feels he is losing control of her and the situation. "I had an orgasm once," laughed Maria L. "It scared the hell out of my husband. He didn't know what to do. It was the first time I was ever louder than him. . . . I don't think he liked it. Anyway I never did it again."

It is much safer for some men if women don't reciprocate. But this keeps you from experiencing your feelings and your love fully. A recent client, Helen R., an energetic 33-year-old interior designer, swore her boyfriend would leave her if he ever caught her enjoying their lovemaking: "He'll think I'm a whore," she worried. Each time they were together she worked at hiding her physical feelings. She believed that if he saw her experiencing passion he would be repelled by her. She would be no different from any of the other girls he used to hang around with before her. We suggested to Helen that she test herself, that she show her true feelings just to see what would happen. Nothing could be as bad as the horrible images she had formed in her mind. We also suggested that if her lover in any way seemed to disapprove, she should ask him openly why her pleasure bothered him. The next time they made love she let herself go. The man lost his erection for a few minutes, but later recovered and eventually came to appreciate her more than he ever had before. "I had no idea he'd actually start encouraging me," she smiled. "We've both come a long way."

The Fake "Goodness"

As Helen taught us so vividly, there is nothing good about denying one of your basic drives. It denies both you *and* your mate future intimacy that you both deserve. What's worse, it can also lead to other problems.

Susan was a middle-aged woman who claimed to love her husband and children devoutly. To express her love she became the perfect homemaker, kept the house immaculate and spent hours cooking and baking special treats. "My whole life was spent keeping busy around the house," she said. A holiday never passed that she didn't have the home decorated appropriately down to the last painted egg or strip of ribbon.

Yet, perfect as her life was, Susan suffered from agonizing cluster headaches, a condition even more severe than migraine.

Together we discovered that Susan was having trouble expressing her love sexually. Devoted and caring as she was, she had tremendous difficulty letting her husband, Rudy, see her become sexually aroused. "What'll he think of me?" she asked. "How can a decent wife and mother show lust?" It didn't match her image of herself as a good girl. In Susan's mind her sexual enjoyment was an animalistic, selfish response that would disgust her husband. More important, her sexual repression was crucial to her positive self-worth. Being sexually responsive was too great a risk for Susan, for Rudy might disapprove and her entire value system would be in question.

We told Susan to ask herself in the privacy of her home, "What is the worst thing that could happen to me if I allowed myself to enjoy sex?" She was to write the answer down and bring it in for us to read at her next session. "Rudy will think I'm a tramp" is what she wrote. We knew from the sessions we already had had with Rudy that this probably would not be the case and that Susan's beliefs were distorted. We asked them both to be present for the next session and brought the issue into the open by inquiring of Rudy what he would think of a wife who was totally expressive of her sexuality during lovemaking. "What a turn on!" Rudy exclaimed, much to Susan's joy and amazement. Once Susan had Rudy's permission to free her sexual emotions, her headaches went away. "What a fool I was to hold so much inside," she confided to us. "I see now I needed the release that sex could give me. Without it, I got headaches."

Susan's sex life was based on false goodness, a belief that Rudy would think more of her if she denied part of herself. When she learned it was better to be her whole self, which included sex, he also benefited more.

Goodness Is Really Sharing Your Happiness with Another

The more of yourself you express, the more you have to give. And the greatest gift you can give another person is you. For giving to be genuine, though, your gift must be from the heart. It can come only if you are happy with yourself. We both have plaques in our offices that read, "A happy you makes others happy too." This is sound advice.

Shelley, 23, married two years to Tommy, a carpet salesman, was afraid to tell him that she wasn't being sexually satisfied. "There are certain things we both could do to make it better," she confided, "but women aren't supposed to make such a big deal about sex, are they? I thought it was only guys who were supposed to be crazed in that department." When we asked Shelley what she thought would improve their sex, she said, "I'd like to touch my private parts, to stimulate myself during lovemaking. But I'm afraid Tommy will be insulted that he's not doing enough himself or, even worse, think I'm some kind of narcissist."

Whenever fears such as these exist, it's best to test reality and see if you are reading your partner accurately. We saw Tommy and Shelly together and asked Tommy how he'd feel if Shelly stimulated herself during lovemaking. "Great!" he exclaimed. "I always feel she's holding back when we make love. I want her to give her all. I love seeing her excited." Once Shelley gave herself permission to give herself freely to Tommy sexually, he was able to give more too and sex became much more enjoyable for them both.

With a truly loving couple, there is nothing more sexually arousing than seeing your partner aroused. A true sexual union is one of satisfied giving, freely offering yourself—your excitement, your passion—to your lover. If your man has problems reversing the stereotypes he learned—and, as you've seen, it's not only women who are saddled with myths—you two will need to work things out together. We hope that the strategies at the end of this chapter will help you to recognize a potential sexual concern and to deal with it.

Why We Delay Sexual Gratification: Procrastination at Its Height

We once worked months with Clara, a woman in her early 30s, who had been married more than ten years and still hadn't had a climax with her husband, Stuart. She always had some excuse. "Things will get better when we work out our money problems" or "I need to work out my feelings with my father first" or "Stuart needs to learn some new techniques." One day, in exasperation, one of us said, "Clara, putting off your sexual fulfillment is procrastination at its height."

The truth of that realization still rings in our heads. Your most intense positive physical sensations should be the last things in the world you keep from the person closest to you. And this delay can be doubly destructive as well: It can reflect procrastination in other important areas of your life.

We remember a 27-year-old woman, Rose, whose life had come to a virtual standstill because she had put everything off to be done tomorrow. Rose was unemployed, but wasn't looking for work because she intended to go back to school first. She hadn't enrolled for classes because she believed she needed to brush up on her typing skills. However, she couldn't do that until she could purchase a new typewriter. This had to wait till she saved more money. But then getting more money depended on getting a job. . . . Round and round went her reasoning in every area of life from finding employment to buying new wallpaper. Whatever the problem, the solution was always the same, "I'll do it when . . ." In attempting to find a starting point, an area to focus on doing *today,* we discovered that although Rose had a four-year relationship that included sex at least three times a week, she never had reached a climax with her partner. She giggled when first questioned about it, "Sex isn't that important to nice girls." We had found the place to begin. When Rose was able to accept the importance of sexual enjoyment, she found herself wanting to go after some of her other goals.

Procrastination is a habit. So is not enjoying sex. Begin enjoying this beautiful, natural drive and soon you will be finding pleasure in many other areas of your life as well. Not enjoying a natural drive is putting off living. Begin to live today by starting to achieve satisfaction in one of the most powerful areas of life—Sex!

Do You Deny Your Sexual Self?

We want to help you turn your life around. Here are some areas to watch out for if you are in the habit of not enjoying sex. Of course, these attitudes can reflect other problems besides the Good Girl Syndrome, but if you find that many of them are familiar in the ways we've described, you may be denying sex to achieve an unreasonable ideal of the "good girl." Do you find yourself:

- Suspending action and finding yourself paralyzed in many areas of life?
- Fantasizing that your life will get better by itself? (This leads to your putting off the best part of existence until tomorrow. "If I wait long enough, things will get better. In time I'll be able to reach a climax, attain sexual fulfillment, enjoy sex, etc." Unfortunately, the fantasy paradise of a better sex life never materializes. It can't—unless you *do* something about it.)
- Retreating to escapism in which our *happiest* moments are when absorbed in a book, watching television, or viewing a movie?

Connie, 24, grew up as an only child in a religious lower-middle-class family. She was the apple of her parents' eye and they focused all the hopes and aspirations they had never achieved onto Connie. They created a Disney, Technicolor world for her. Her bedroom was pink and purple, with heaps of stuffed animals on the canopied bed, papered walls depicting smiling lions and laughing tigers, cutouts of talking flowers and singing brooks. On Sunday her parents took her to church, where she learned of heavenly angels, pearly-gated paradises and love everlasting. Connie's was a world of pure fantasy, completely out of touch with reality and completely nonsexual.

It was not surprising that Connie continued to live in a fantasy world as a young adult. Sex was an ugly word in her vocabulary. She much preferred the word "romance," a term that conjured to Connie's mind castles and dragons and princes and eternal adoration. In Connie's magical world of fantasy, wonderful things just happened. If she wished hard enough, a wonderful fairy godmother would grant the wish without her ever having to do another thing. To keep her fantasies alive Connie spent much of her time reading romance novels or watching soaps on television.

Connie came to us because she was having spells of depression that made no sense to her. "The only thing I can think of that might be wrong in my life," she told us, "is I still haven't found the right man. But I'm sure that will happen when the time is right." We learned that one thing wrong (among many others) with the men Connie had dated was a lack of sexual chemistry. She never had reached a climax or been aroused by any of them. Still, she wasn't concerned enough to do anything about it, preferring instead to wait for the magical moment when it would all happen by itself, upon the appearance of the "right" man. Magical thinking such as this leads to suspended action in all areas of life. In Connie's case, she was still also waiting to "discover" the right career, right place to live and right group of friends—all the time living at home with her parents.

We told Connie that she could *make* sexual feelings happen using the technique of sensory expansion that we describe at the end of this chapter. Connie responded beautifully to our methods and was able to physically enjoy a man for the first time in her life. "The best thing about it," she told us, "is that now that I have control over my sexual feelings and don't have to wait for a prince to bring them out in me, I can pick men for other things. I can *create* romance with a nice guy. I can *make* him Prince Charming, if I choose to respond to him in that way!"

- Deluding yourself? (This can show up in many forms. One of the most common, and troubling, is convincing

yourself that you are something you are not: spiritual because you deprive yourself of your sexual feelings.)
- Being overwhelmingly bored?
- Hanging onto a sexually unsatisfactory relationship because you think that sex isn't important enough to end a love affair?

Julia, a 28-year-old horticulturist, was deluding herself into believing she was being a good person for "hanging in there" in her marriage to Jeff, a 30-year-old newspaper columnist, even though their sex had dwindled down to less than twice a month. In our first session together she said, "I love him and that should be enough. I don't want to leave him." "Who said anything about leaving?" we answered. "Why don't you just make your sex life better?" Instead of smiling with enthusiasm at our suggestion, Julia blushed. "I guess I never thought of it," she stammered. Julia was making the same mistake we see so many other women making who have lackluster sexual relationships, virtuously deciding to stay in their relationships *in spite* of the bad sex, never ever considering making it better. We learned that the worst thing about Julia's lovemaking with Jeff was that it wasn't often enough. When we asked who initiated sex most often, she reddened again. "Why Jeff of course," she gulped. "It wouldn't be proper for me to." We told Julia that any good relationship is a fifty/fifty proposition and that included the sexual portion of it. It was just as important for her to start the lovemaking as it was for Jeff. Julia followed our advice and was amazed to discover that when she initiated more, Jeff initiated more. "He told me he thought I wasn't interested anymore," she told us, "or I would have come on to him more. Isn't that crazy? There we both were, wanting to make love, thinking the other one didn't." A truly good girl lets her mate know when she's in the mood.

- Believing there is something terribly wrong with you because sex is important in making you happy and allowing you to feel like a woman?
- Avoiding confrontation with a lover about your sexual needs because you're ashamed for needing or placing

importance on something so "bad"?
• Refusing to praise or even discuss the joys of intimacy with your children?

As a child, Louise, a 30-year-old housewife, worshipped her father—a handsome, dignified, respected surgeon. Though Louise knew he very much loved her mother, a quiet, sweet, self-effacing woman who dutifully ran the household, she never saw her parents show any physical affection. She vividly recalled the one fight her parents had ever had. "I remember it like it was this morning," she said. "Dad was furious at mother for what he called her 'outrageous public display of affection.'" It seems that mother had kissed him on the mouth in front of friends while they were waiting in line to enter a theater. Mother didn't defend herself. She just cried." Louise never forgot that episode. And when she reached puberty, she equated showing her sexual feelings with male disapproval. Now she felt guilty for *needing* sex from her husband, Allan, and was afraid to let him see that she had these feelings, thinking he would disapprove of her in the same way her father had of her mother. She was raising a 9-year-old daughter, Adrian, in the same fashion, never letting the child see her mother kiss or be physically intimate with her father.

The first major step we outlined for Louise to help her move toward enjoying sex, was to work at showing physical signs of affection out of the bedroom, especially around Adrian— pecks on the cheek, hugs, a hand on the shoulder, squeeze of the hand, even a playful swat on the behind—all showed that it was OK for two adults to enjoy physical contact. Louise's next big step was to *admit* to Allan that she had sexual feelings and that she enjoyed them. A simple comment such as "I like the way you touch me," or "It feels so good when you hold me" were major hurdles for Louise. Once her sexuality was out in the open, once she was able to admit to being a sexual being, she was able to enjoy it.

• Being tired or sleepy whenever your husband or lover approaches you, a defense against the conflict raging within?
• Actually getting sick when it's time to make love,

which allows you to avoid something that makes you uncomfortable?

- Keeping yourself on a treadmill of constant activity so that there is always an excuse for not having sex, saying such things as, "I don't have time" or "It'll make me late"?
- Living in terror that the children might discover you're a sexual being?

Allison, 29, had a near breakdown from taking on too many extracurricular activities in addition to caring for her husband, Rick, and their four children. "I don't know what possesses me," she sighed, "I just can't say no to anything . . . PTA, Brownies, Cub Scouts, Neighborhood Watch, Security Patrol, Ladies Aid, Eastern Star. . . . I'm active in all of them. Don't ask me why, but I am." A few pointed questions that we've learned to ask over the years yielded a gold mine of information. Allison was running herself ragged, filling every moment, being constantly tired in order to have an excuse for not having sex with Rick. The problem wasn't that she didn't enjoy sex *sometimes,* it was that she didn't enjoy it *all* the time. In Allison's mind a "good" wife *never* said no to a husband's advances. We told Allison, "It's OK to say no to a sexual advance. You're not always in the mood for ice cream, are you? Then why would you always be in the mood for Rick? You can love something madly and not want it *all* the time." When Allison was able to say no to sex on occasions it didn't appeal to her, she no longer needed the avalanche of activities she was using as a substitute. She told Rick, "I love you and I desire you . . . but not *all* the time. 'No' this morning doesn't mean 'no' this evening." Rick got the message, and Allison was able to relax. And the relaxation made her feel like saying yes a whole lot more often.

When you begin acting as if sex was good you will like yourself and feel good about yourself for experiencing it. A real good girl is a sexual being.

Payoffs for Not Enjoying Sex

Even sexual frustration has its rewards. Most women deny their sexuality either to be "better" people or because they don't want to face the reality of the commitment of a sexual relationship. Here are the rewards we find most often— rewards that keep you in a state of sexual frustration.

- The delusion of being a saint or a "better" person.
- Escape from reality. Sex is a very basic part of life, and life has its problems. Without an outside world, we live only from within—in a much smaller, less satisfying, world.
- Having something to blame for your state of unhappiness. You can say, "I'm miserable because I'm not sexually satisfied."
- Avoiding all chances of not living up to your hidden sexual expectations.
- Playing the role of martyr.
- Avoiding the adult responsibility that comes with being sexual.

Learning about these whys of sexual repression will give you a strong weapon for combating them. When you think deeply about why you keep yourself from sexual happiness, you'll be able to deal directly with these blocks to make them fast fade away!

Strategies for Becoming a Sexual Being

Once you give yourself permission, finding sexual fulfillment can be surprisingly easy. Just remember, sex is a natural part of an intimate relationship and you and your partner deserve it. Here are some ideas for both of you:

• • •

- Why not initiate sex whenever *you* want it?
- Refuse to be intimidated by the rules about your "duties" as wife or lover. Don't be afraid to say no when you are not in the mood.
- Like Shelley, why not stimulate yourself or bring yourself to orgasm if your lover cannot or will not. If this is a real problem for you, discuss it with your partner. You may find that your partner would be aroused at seeing you become excited!
- *Tell* your partner that you enjoy having sex with him, both during and between the encounters.
- During lovemaking, decide to live one second at a time. Concentrate on your feelings. Don't think about past memories or current expectations—just share the time with your partner. You're very lucky—you're living in a world that just the two of you have created.
- Practice the technique of sensory expansion to get physically close with your partner. Lie comfortably flat and focus your total concentration on a spot on the ceiling directly above the level of your eyes. Tell yourself, "My lids are getting very, very heavy . . . very, very tired . . . heavier and heavier. It would feel so good to close my eyes." When you actually feel the heaviness in your eyelids, close your eyes *tightly* shut and let your eyeballs roll up in the back of your head for thirty seconds. Say to yourself, "My lids are locked so tight, I doubt very much that I can open them. My lids shut *tighter* and *tighter,* and as my lids lock *tight,* I begin to feel a rhythmic wave of relaxation starting in my toes, washing through my legs . . . arms . . . stomach . . . chest . . . neck . . . around my jaws . . . eyes . . . scalp . . . till from head to toe, every fiber, every muscle in my body, is totally, completely, relaxed." Take ten minutes to do this exercise before you have sex and you will find your senses vastly expanded. Profound relaxation lowers your sensory thresholds, makes you more sensitive in all five senses. It also blocks negative thoughts.

- Ask yourself, as Susan did in learning to express her sexual feelings to Rudy, "What is the worst thing that could happen to me if I allowed myself to enjoy sex?" The answer may jar you into action. Confronting the fear dispels it.
- Keep a journal about the ways your reactions to the world change as you become more of a sexual being. After a period of sexual fulfillment, write a paragraph or two about the way you feel at that time. I think you may be surprised at how positively you see the world after sharing yourself with someone!

Sex is your natural expression of love. We want you, like all the other marvelous people we've helped, to experience the wondrous rapture of that expression. As our client Louise said when she began enjoying sex with Allan, "I don't know how I could have gone so many years without it. Sex puts a glow in the whole world. It's wonderful. It makes me feel alive, charged and beautiful!" Let those wonderful feelings within you come out to enrich both yourself and the source of its inspiration—your lover.

7

"I Am
As Men See Me"

> I could never "find myself" because I looked in
> all the wrong places . . . in the eyes of men.
>   MARGARET B.
>   *patient, age 25*

"My whole life has been spent preparing to be the perfect
wife," Margaret told us in our first session together. "My
parents thought of nothing else but marrying me off and used
to push me on all their friends who had eligible sons. My
mother would coo, 'She's such a good cook, so neat, so
clean.' My dad would chime in, 'And such a good worker
too.' When my husband, Sly, proposed, they were happier
than I was! The problem is, now I am what Sly and my parents
think is the perfect wife, but I have no sense of myself. I can't
believe that cooking, cleaning and raising children is *me*. It's
what I do. But it's not *me*." We told Margaret that she was
what she *wanted* to do. Those natural impulses were her true
self. "Next time you're obediently peeling potatoes in your
role of the perfect wife and you get a desire to do something
else, act on it. See what it is like to follow your own expectations once in a while." The next week Margaret reported, "I
did what you said. I was in the middle of drying dishes and I
got a sudden impulse to run. So I did. I dropped what I was
doing and went jogging. It was wonderful!" Naturally, you

can't act out your impulses all the time, but most women don't give them free enough rein because they think their men would disapprove if they did.

We've looked at what can happen if you think there's something wrong with you . . . or if you believe men are better than you. Our client Margaret, a disenchanted housewife, sums up the consequences of these early programs when she says that she looks to validate herself as a person through the eyes of men. The problem translates into one basic idea: "I am as men see me." If you do not feel you can create an image of yourself from your own ideas—what you do and believe in —you may find yourself turning to someone else to set the standards for you. Often that means turning to the man in your life.

Unfortunately, when you don't let your natural impulses out, when you let others decide who you are, you lose your sense of self. It's not surprising that this problem eventually reveals itself in women who no longer know who they are. Many feel lost—"My husband seems to have a much better idea of who I am than I do," said Charlotte, with a laugh. "But he should. He made me."

In this chapter we'll show you why you let a man's approval become your measure of self-worth and how this problem is more pervasive than you might expect. You'll see the subtle ways it crops up in your everyday life and learn that "I am as I see me" is the only fair way to know who you truly are. With our help, you'll achieve wonderful new energy by redefining yourself through the power of self-creation.

Why You Want Approval

You know that some of the reasons why women want to have men approve of them are very natural and healthy. You may want to have a healthy romance or marriage—and you can do that if you listen to what your partner thinks about you. Or you know that *part* of your identity—your public self—comes from the way others see you. But the problems arise if you think that the *only* way you can be seen is through other people's eyes. If you don't think that you are an important part of the decision, it could be that you think there may be something wrong with you. And that takes us back to the first chapter of the book.

As Reverend Terry Cole-Whittaker explains, "The need for approval only arises when you believe you are lacking. If you believe you are lacking, you are then waiting for someone to give you the thing you don't have before you go do the thing you want to do. We wait before we live." You can avoid this dilemma by doing the things you were going to do *if* you got the approval. Poor Eve ate the apple without permission. Her punishment was to never do anything without permission again. You can avoid Eve's dilemma by doing the things you were going to do *if* you got the approval.

Trena, a 23-year-old bank teller, was a perfect example of a woman who was waiting to live. She felt that she "didn't amount to anything" and that her marriage to Brock, a 32-year-old systems analyst, was in jeopardy, because, as she put it, "He thinks less and less of me every day because I have no goals. Neither of us wants children . . . so I can't get my identity by being a mother. Yet cooking, cleaning, and making the best cookies in town didn't do it for me either. That's why I got a job. But that didn't help either. Anybody could do what I'm doing. I want to do something great." We therefore set out to discover just exactly what "great" thing she would have to do to feel good about herself. We asked, "Do you want to be rich?" "No," she said, "that doesn't make you a great person." "Famous?" Again she nodded no. Then she answered, "I want to help people." "But you *are* helping people, both as a wife and a teller," we answered. "I want to help people in a *big* way," she said. "Like Eleanor Roosevelt?" we asked. "Yea, but I hate politics." "Like Albert Einstein?" "Yea, but I'm no good at math." No matter how many questions we asked Trena, we were never able to find what she could do to give her a positive identity. Finally, we gave her our conclusion: "It appears to us," we said, "that your sense of identity currently has nothing to do with what you do or what you want to do. Your whole self-image presently rests totally on your husband's approval. You're putting your entire life on hold, waiting for Brock to tell you that you're a worthwhile person. Until you set your own standards for self-worth, *nothing* you do will make you feel good about yourself."

Stop waiting for others to give you permission to feel good about yourself. You're the only person who can decide for you. You don't need anyone's approval to tell you it's all right to be yourself. You don't have to hold yourself back with worries like, "Who'll disapprove of me?" or "What will people think?" or "I don't have the right." Don't give your rights to someone else. They're much too valuable, and you're much too special.

We once worked with an attractive woman, May N., an office administrator for a plumbing company, divorced, 56 years old, who complained that she didn't know how to act around men. "I'm just too nervous to get out there where I might meet someone," she said. Understandably, this condition only leads to more loneliness and feelings of unworthiness. She was waiting for a knight in shining armor to draw her out, to give her the signal that she was all right and that he would take care of her. In counseling, we asked May, "Do you think you're attractive?" "Good grief, no," she stated. "I'm much too old and wrinkled." "No wonder you're having trouble with men," we both said at the same time. "They're reacting to you the way you *expect* them to react . . . like you're undesirable. Change your perception of yourself and you will also change the response you get from men." What May really needed to think about was how she thought of herself. For without self-approval, no one else could ever really appreciate her. We told May to forget about thinking she had to be physically perfect for a man to find her attractive. The most beautiful women in the world radiate beauty from within because their thoughts are beautiful. We suggested she try some PR on herself and repeat to herself, "I am beautiful" for five minutes, three times a day. Repetition is the key to all learning, and in time she would come to believe what she had told herself *often* enough. May followed our advice, and as she came to gain more confidence in herself, she was willing to try more new experiences that once would have scared her. She approached attractive men in social situations; she dressed as if she were beautiful, wearing fashionable clothes that previously she would have considered herself too old for; and she was no longer afraid to flirt for fear men would think her, as she told us earlier in her therapy, "an old, desperate fool." With her newfound acceptance of herself, she had overcome that paralyzing fear that comes with needing approval: the fear of not being "perfect."

As you can see, self-love comes from within; it does not depend on external approval. As Dr. Wayne Dyer says in *Your Erroneous Zones:*

> Self-worth cannot be verified by others. You are worthy because you say it is so. Don't let others determine your value. Tell yourself that you are good. And you will be!

We are happy to say that May found a man who thinks she's perfect as she is: "Something that could have happened only when I let myself be me!"

The Myth that You're Nobody Until a Man Loves You

Everybody wants to be loved. To have this need is only normal. However, problems arise if you, like many women we see, equate love with approval. You can meet every expectation in the book, follow every rule laid down, and while your man may approve, that doesn't guarantee he'll love you. If only it were that simple. On the other hand, you may be pleased to discover that if you stop trying so hard to please and develop your own identity based on your own standards, you will suddenly be a whole lot more likable—both to yourself and to others.

For years Valerie, 35, a casting director for TV game shows, believed she was a nobody because she wasn't loved by a man. Then she met Greg, a 22-year-old lighting technician, and they fell madly in love. Now Valerie worried that she was nobody because she wasn't loved by the "right" man. Greg was too young, too inexperienced and too poor to be considered by her friends as a "good catch." We told Valerie that the truth of the matter was that she was nobody until she loved herself enough to do what was right for *her*. "Do you love him?" we asked. "Yes," she answered. "Does he make you happy?" "Yes," again. "Then stop judging him by other people's expectations," we smiled. "Create your own values and love yourself enough to abide by them." Whether single or with the "wrong" partner, Valerie could not be happy until she accepted herself and the necessity for meeting her own needs, regardless of what society said "should" make her happy.

Studies we've done show that in spite of the women's movement and the fight for independence people still regard single women less highly than single men. We've come to see that there are a number of reasons for this imbalance, but all of them boil down to one idea: maintaining the status quo. Women continue to sacrifice and mother their men, as well as hold back from competing in the work force, in hopes of being loved in return. What they get instead is approval. Anyone who truly loved them would not allow them to engage in such totally self-defeating behavior. Love is letting your partner be satisfied. Love is letting your partner succeed!

While things are not as cut and dried as they used to be, few men look to marriage as a primary source of fulfillment, as many women do. Men most frequently get their greatest sense of worth from their work. So a man is rarely thought to be "missing something" if he is not married. But a woman who wishes to remain single is seen as a threat. This is especially true if you not only say no to a man's romantic overtures but compete with him in the job market, as many women do today. Surprisingly, some men still feel threatened by "too many women" in the workplace. It affects their sense of self. How can a man do the same work as you, and still retain his sense of self? If sense of self is based on one-upmanship, he can't. That you should get equal pay for equal work is a threat to a man's identity and the key to yours.

Vivian, 28, and Angelo, 26, were biotechnicians in the same lab, where part of their duties included working with tissue and blood samples. Angelo was continually taking over some of Vivian's assignments with statements such as, "I know women don't have the stomach for this" or "We don't want you to break a nail, do we?'' While Angelo may have meant well, his comments were denigrating to Vivian and implied she couldn't do her work as well as a man, even though in this case they were receiving equal pay. We suggested to Vivian that the next time Angelo make a comment that reflected his belief in male superiority, she was to calmly tell him how his behavior made her feel. She agreed to try this, and when Angelo volunteered to draw blood specimens for her, she replied, ''I know you mean well, but when you offer to do my work for me, it makes me feel like you think you can do it better. And that makes me feel incompetent. And I hate that feeling!'' Angelo apologized, saying that this was not his intention. Whether it was or not, bringing his behavior, and the emotional consequences it produced in Vivian, out into the open brought it to a halt. Angelo no longer deals with the threat of a woman doing the same work as he by doing part of her work for her, and Vivian feels equal in worth.

As with anything in life, not everybody will be on your side, but don't let that stop you. Clarence Pendleton, Jr., head of the U.S. Commission on Civil Rights, was reported in the newspaper of the business world, the *Daily Commerce,* to have stated that the idea of equal pay for comparable work is ''probably the looniest idea since *Looney Tunes* came on the screen.'' The idea of comparable worth is that people in different jobs but with comparable skills should be paid equivalent salaries. This same paper reported the largest sex-based wage discrimination suit in the country's history concerning the ''controversial theory'' of equalizing pay in jobs in comparable worth. The suit was filed in November 1984 by the California State Employees Association against the administration of Governor George Deukmejian, and it involved discriminatory pay practices toward more than 37,000 then-current state workers.

We'd like to revise the myth to read, ''You're nobody till a man pays you.'' As long as you believe it is approval you're supposed to get from the system, and not money, men are safe. You are ''good'' and the man is rich. Ever think you might be making the wrong choice?

It is our goal for you in this book to have you come to think of yourself as somebody without the need for someone else's approval. When you attain this kind of self-love, others will love you, too.

Internal Versus External Standards for Identity: The "Choosers" and the "Chosen"

Like our patient Margaret B., who tried to find herself only in the eyes of men, you too may be looking in all the wrong places if you are looking outside of yourself. How can you be *outside* of you? Your identity can only be found within. Psychologist Leo Buscaglia, in *Living, Loving and Learning,* makes the beautiful point that to achieve true identity we must become who we are, not who others want us to be.

> So many people are trying to make us what they want us to be, and after a while we just give up and decide that maybe this is what is called "adjustment." *Heaven forbid!* Occasionally, someone will rebel and say, "No! I will not become what you want me to be. I am, and I will remain. I want to become who I am."

Internal standards involve following rules you make to satisfy you. External standards involve following rules someone else makes to satisfy them. If you follow the rules of another it will lead to a terrible loss of identity. Discovering and making rules that work for you take effort and persistence, but your reward of a strong and lovable identity is worth it.

Writer and columnist Eda Le Shan, in *How to Survive Parenthood*, describes how each woman will have to define her own identity on the path to independence.

> We are learning that there are no longer any simple patterns or easy definitions. Each of us has to discover who and what we are, and our own special qualities, what

makes us feel womanly. Passivity and weakness do not describe the feminine woman; devotion to kitchen or nursery serves us no better as a definition—where and what is the indefinable something our feminist grandmothers were so eager to give up and we are so anxious to recapture?

As you may already well know, it is impossible to discover who and what you really are in the context of the Good Girl Syndrome. The external conditioning that the syndrome is based on totally blocks any attempt of self-expression. If you're a "good girl," you can never know who you really are —only what others see.

In our studies we've come to see that women fall into two categories for determining their identities. Women who primarily abide by man-made, external standards of identity fall into the category we call "Chosen." They go through life thirsting for approval from men and anyone else in authority, yearning to be chosen. They belong to the Pie in the Sky Club, the Great Rescue Chapter, whose members long to be developed and appreciated by the "right" man. "If only Mr. Right would come along," they sigh. They see themselves as diamonds in the rough, awaiting the proper male hand to fashion them into the glittering gems they truly are. They are always waiting, always hoping, eternally complaining about how no man completely appreciates them. Waiting to be chosen becomes an addiction, a life-style, a reason for being. The thrill of the fantasy of being unveiled by someone who can bring out the "real" woman keeps these women from ever drawing themselves out. Unfortunately, no mortal man can create the identities these women long for, and often a succession of disappointing relationships follows instead.

Isabell, a 32-year-old production assistant in the television and motion picture industry, went through an unending chain of broken affairs, speaking in childish glee of how wonderful her next man was going to be. To preserve the "romance" of each new encounter, she would leave their meeting to accident. "If it happens, it happens," was Isabell's philosophy. Things were "happening" all the time, but her new lovers never made her happy for long. Finally we asked the crucial question, "Why don't you stop leaving things to chance? Why don't you search for the man you want and then go for it?" "Me?" she gasped. "Me, throw myself at a man? I'd die first!" We're sorry to say that Isabell was so appalled by our suggestion that we never saw her again. The intrigue of being discovered was obviously more important to her than finding a man she could relate to honestly and equally. As long as Isabell continues her Pygmalion fantasy, yearning to be chosen by a Henry Higgins who'll transform her into a "fair lady," she will be lost. You cannot find yourself in the eyes of another, no matter how many times you are chosen.

The other group we call "Choosers." Rather than yearning to be chosen, these women desire to choose. They are seekers, adventurers, not waiting for some man to come into their lives in order to make a change. They go for what they want. They pick up their partners, their careers and their life-styles. They make themselves in their own positive images and act accordingly.

We once worked with a depressed woman, Bunny, 59, living off alimony and state disability for a chronic lung condition, who moved from being one of the chosen to one of the choosers. Bunny was an inveterate name-dropper, qualifying each important person who was mentioned with a brief biographical sketch to insure that the people with whom she was speaking would know whom she was talking about. Twenty to thirty names an hour would blithely trip off her tongue, most of them people she had never met and most of them men. "I know the most divinely fabulous people in the world," she would say. "They all love me so much . . . they are all so wonderful!" Whenever she encountered approval she doubled her efforts. "Many of them wanted to marry me at one time, you know. Imagine! All those important men choosing me!" All her energy went into raising her self-worth by mentioning all the important men she claimed to know. The implication was that since these male celebrities had chosen her as their buddy she must be well worth knowing. We knew that there was a woman beneath the facade, even if one could see only the impressive people she spoke incessantly about who gave her her identity. One day we asked the question that served to give us a glimpse of the real Bunny: "If you have so many wonderful friends, why are you so unhappy?" At first the question surprised her. Then she began to cry. "I *hate* those people," she sobbed. "They don't give a damn about me." Then we asked, "Do you think people who don't care about others are nice people?" "No," she answered. "Are you a nice person?" we asked. Bunny nodded yes, smiling as she saw what we were driving at. "I guess those people aren't really so great after all, are they?" she said. In that moment of insight Bunny realized she was really better than nearly all the people on the list of names she'd been dropping all those years. From that point on she decided to choose a new group of friends, ones equal to her own identity as a caring person.

When you change your criteria for self-worth, as Bunny did the day she put more importance on her human traits of loving and caring than the celebrity status of the names in her address book, you will be shifting the standards for your identity from the external world of approval by others to the internal world of approval by self. And that shift makes all the difference. For you have then assumed the power of self-creation.

Your Self-Image as a Source of Energy: The Power of Self-Creation

Everybody has the power of self-creation, the power to create their own identity. In the sections that follow, we're going to help you to strengthen that power and use it to be the best person you can be. There'll be more of you to give as a result!

In order to give to others, you should be the most incredibly powerful, positive, fabulous person you can be. The more you have, the more you have to give! Since your self-image is the regulator of the infinite energy that is available to you, you want to have a strong, positive sense of self in order to possess something worth giving to another. That's what we're trying to help you to achieve here!

In a classic study in social psychology, children were shown a film in which one person showered another with many gifts. At the movie's conclusion, the children were asked which person they would prefer to be. Much to the researchers' surprise, the children overwhelmingly chose to be the one who *gave* the gifts rather than the one who received them. Power goes to the dispenser of the reward. This is the person who makes the rules. Women who believe they are queens on a pedestal because they have men who support them are, in reality, in powerless positions. Without power there is little energy with which to create your own identity.

The story of one of our friends gives you a good example of how beautiful the pedestal can be. Gloria W., a 35-year-old "house pet," found herself talking a lot about her marriage—a marriage that was "too good to get out of." Her husband, Clem, did everything for her. He hired a live-in maid to keep the house, recruited a permanent sitter for the children, gave her unlimited expense accounts, bought her fabulous clothes and jewels and insisted she take long, expensive vacations in exotic places. "Why is it I can't stand another minute of it?" she asked us. It was clear to us that her husband was taking away her power to make choices. He was robbing her of her power of self-creation. He was treating her like a bird in a gilded cage, and she was finally seeing herself as trapped. Finally she balked, insisting she wanted to make some money of her own. One of her girlfriends was starting a new business and was taken enough by our friend's poise and charm to offer her a job as a receptionist. Her husband was incensed. He told Gloria, "This isn't the way I want my wife. My father never let my mother work and I certainly don't want this for my wife either." Our friend's attempted search for identity was conflicting with her husband's sense of his own identity. She had to break away from her husband's definition of her and they separated. "I can't believe how much more energy I have now," she told us recently. "When I started living my own life instead of being Clem's pet, I got a whole new wonderful sense of self."

Only you can see you. Don't let someone else define you for you. Author Carson McCullers, in her book *The Member of the Wedding,* astutely addresses the subjectivity of reality, how the way the world looks depends on *who* is looking at it.

I see a green tree. And to me it is green. And you would call the tree green also. And we would agree on this. But is the colour you see as green as the same colour I see as green? Or say we both call a colour black. But how do we know that what you see as black is the same colour I see as black?

You can apply this to the way you may be viewed. A man sees you. And to him you are a woman. And you would call yourself a woman also. But is the woman you see as you the same woman as the man sees? If it is, you may want to think about who you really want to be.

You have the power to make you whatever you wish to be, to see yourself in any fashion that pleases you. First, ask yourself questions like the ones we've listed in the next section to determine how much is really you. Then follow the strategies we've provided at the end of this chapter to create your own identity—one that is not a reflection of another person's expectations, but one that comes from within!

How to Know You Are Relying on Men for Your Identity

Many women are not aware that much of who they are may come from what others want them to be. To get a clear picture of your present source of identity, you need to do some careful self-examination. What do you see when you look at yourself? Are you channeling your energy into self-creation? Or do you still see yourself in the eyes of men? Here is a brief list to help you answer these questions. Do you find yourself:

- Feeling terrific about yourself when others give you compliments and being crushed when they don't?

- Incorporating male-directed references in conversation? ("My boyfriend thinks" . . ."My husband feels" . . ."Marvin always used to say" . . .)
- Constantly turning to others for validation? ("Don't you agree?" . . . "Correct me if I'm wrong, John, but" . . . "What do you think?")

Delores's mother died giving birth to Delores. Her father was a powerful, charismatic, opinionated Methodist minister. Delores took his word as gospel. As an adult of 26 she expects the same judgmental tyranny from other men in her life and looks to them to validate her worth as a human being. Her marriage of a year to Derrick is now in trouble because he is tired of her "clinging, clawing, dependency." As he put it in couples counseling, "I feel like I'm suffocating. She can't go to the bathroom without asking me first. I'm her husband not her daddy." "Derrick never used to feel that way," said Delores, directing the conversation to her man. "Did you, sweetheart?" she asked, looking for validation. The microcosm mirrors the macrocosm and we were certain that how Delores was acting in our office was the same way she acted at home—continually referring to her husband and asking for validation. "I thought you were pretty terrific in the beginning," Derrick answered. Delores broke into tears. We could almost read her mind: "If Derrick thought I was great then, I must have been. If he doesn't think I'm so special now, I must not be."

Delores had no identity independent of Derrick. We told her that in order for her to get a sense of self she had to stop thinking in terms of Derrick. She was to stop herself whenever she found herself using Derrick as a reference point or source of validation. She was instead to speak for *herself* as if her feelings were validation enough for the statements she made. Most of all, she was to recognize that she was only as good as *she* thought she was. She could begin feeling better right now, simply by telling herself, "I'm a pretty terrific person!" Delores stopped turning to Derrick for her own identity and grew as her own person. She laughed when she told us, "I guess that's what you call giving someone their own space.

When you take your own instead of glomming onto theirs, it gives them more room to grow too!''

- Ordering a light entree when a man takes you out even though you would prefer the complete meal?
- Acting "kittenish" in the bedroom?
- Being overwhelmed with guilt if you shirk a domestic duty?

Frances, 41, complained to us that she felt like she was a "nobody." "When Ken and I were first married, some twenty years ago," she said, "I felt that being a wife was *something*. But lately I've come to see that I'm only something in *relation* to others. I'm nothing by myself. Everything I do is for Ken and the kids. If suddenly they were all to die in a car wreck, what would *I* be?" "What would you want to be?" we asked Frances. "My own person," she answered. "Someone who orders what they want when they eat out, does what they enjoy sexually, isn't chained to the stove, doesn't have to act cute and dumb to get attention . . ." Frances's list was a long one, and when she had finished we asked her what was keeping her from being all these things now. Her answer was simple and immediate. "Ken," she said. "He expects me to be the way I am." "In other words," we said, "he expects you to see yourself the way he does." Frances smiled. "I never thought of it like that before," she said.

Armed with this new perspective we asked her to record every time she did something to meet Ken's expectations rather than her own, along with the associated place and activity. We soon discovered that Frances was most likely to see herself as Ken saw her at 6 P.M., in the kitchen, fixing his dinner. "He treats me like a short-order cook in this situation," she said. "Give me *what* I want, *when* I want and make it snappy!" We told Frances to assert herself in these situations and feed her husband what *she* decided, even if it was *her* favorite dish or a TV dinner. Even better, let him cook for himself on occasion. Then he could experience how it felt to see himself as he was seeing his wife!

• • •

- Feeling worthless if the man in your life fails to compliment you or give you gifts?
- Always waiting for permission to do something you deserve to do in the first place?
- Believing labels that men have pinned on you, such as "Just like a woman" or "Women don't deserve to drive"?

Marjorie, who at 37 still madly believed she was only as men saw her, revealed, "My father died before I was born, and there was no real man in the house for me to relate to. So I had to make up a fantasy father from movies, what friends told me and most of all what the Catholic church informed me that the greatest of all fathers, God, was like. To me, God, fathers, all men actually . . . were benevolent dictators, loving if I obeyed, but filled with wrath and fury if I didn't. My sole purpose on earth was to please them." As a result, Marjorie had such faith in the judgment of men she would believe anything they said. "If a man says I'm lazy, I believe it, no matter how hard I work. If he says I can't afford a new dress, I believe that, regardless of my bank account. If a man says I'm a loser, I get sucked into that, too, regardless of how intelligent, accomplished, loving or attractive I know I am."

We told Marjorie to start making her own labels in order to get men to see her the way she saw herself, the way she wanted to be seen. We asked Marjorie what label men pinned on her that she found most offensive and misrepresentative of the real her. "Dumb," Marjorie answered. "If I don't act the way they expect, men are always calling me stupid, airhead, space cadet . . ." Marjorie's first exercise was to *advertise* the real her by telling men outright she was smart, couching the message tastefully in comments such as, "I'm really good at figures" or "I'm an excellent judge of character" or "I've always been smart when it comes to important things." It didn't take long for her to get the hang of it, and when she changed her license plate to HIGH IQ, we know we'd gotten through to her.

- Being overly compulsive about housekeeping?
- Being afraid that a man won't approve of you if you

get a baby-sitter once in a while?
- Always asking your husband or lover, "What should I wear"?
- Staying home if you're single because you're afraid of what people will think if you live alone?

When Rebecca, 28, was single she met few eligible men because she was worried about what they might think if they knew she was living alone. "I just knew they'd think I lived alone 'cause nobody wanted to be with me," she confided. "So rather than risk being labeled 'weird' I didn't go out." Because she limited her selection, Rebecca ended up marrying Willie, a traveling salesman whom she called "a nice guy, but not someone I loved." Now, Rebecca is still worrying what people must think of her, turning her home into a prison for fear Willie will think she's "no good" if she gets a sitter and goes out once in a while when he is away on his long business trips. So she fills her days obsessively cleaning house, rushing to catch a leaf before it hits the sidewalk or waxing the finish right off the furniture. Rebecca is denying herself the right to go where she pleases, when she pleases, because she considers this right unfeminine.

As we proceed with so many of our cases, we simply asked Rebecca what she would *like* to do. "Go to a movie by myself and not feel I'm a terrible person because of it," she replied. We made this her No. 1 priority, giving her permission, saying *we* would see and admire her as independent if she accomplished this behavior. We are happy to say that Rebecca achieved this priority and then set and accomplished many more, all lending to a greater sense of her own identity and self-approval.

If any of the above behaviors sound like you, you may need to direct more of your energies to establishing a more independent identity. Your energy will soar as you begin seeing yourself in your own eyes, rather than the eyes of others.

Why Women Look to Men to Define Themselves

But first let's examine why you might allow men to tell you who you are. Even giving up your identity has some payoff, and we've listed here a few of the reasons. Do any of these sound familiar to you?

- You can give men total responsibility for your self-image.
- You never have to risk change or lose the security you already have.
- You can live vicariously through the eyes of the men whose opinions you believe.
- It's always easier to listen to others than think for yourself.
- You feel wonderful when someone you think is superior smiles down upon you.
- You don't have to worry about the consequences of your behavior as long as you have someone else's permission. It's his fault if something goes wrong.

We recall the case of Sally, a woman in her early 50s who still called long distance to her father whenever she needed to make even the smallest decision, from repositioning her bed to the paint color for the bathroom. She didn't really want advice; she wanted *approval*. She knew what she was going to do before she called, but her father's blessing made it all right to be wrong. If she moved the bed and got a cold because it was too close to a window, then it was his fault because he gave her permission. The system worked for a while until her father gave her permission to make an investment that later went sour. After she had lost her money she found that it didn't really matter whose fault it was.

- When you accept someone else's beliefs, you feel that you belong to something bigger than yourself.

As we've just described, there are many reasons for letting

others determine who we are. Laziness and not wanting to take responsibility figure prominently among them, along with getting the approval from those whose expectations we meet. However, we hope we've shown you that these rewards are worth far less than the wonderful feeling of self-direction that comes from creating your own identity!

Building Your Own Self-Image

In this section we're going to show you *how* to experience the terrific feeling that comes from seeing yourself through your own eyes rather than in the way others want you to be. You'll begin committing to your own identity by controlling your reactions and rising above the negative influence of others. Here are some designs to get you started.

- Do as Frances did to achieve an independent identity from Ken. Keep a journal. Whenever you feel your sense of identity being influenced by a man's opinion of what you are or should be, jot the occurrence down in a small pocket notebook. Write the event, the date, time of day, place and what you were doing at the time. You may discover after a few days' journaling that a pattern emerges: you may be more vulnerable to suggestions at the height of your sexual cycle, in the evening, at work or while making love. It's important to fortify yourself at these times with self-enhancing statements such as, "I am as I decide to be," or "I am as I see me." These statements give you the power of self-creation, a power you possessed all along, but gave to someone else.
- Stop denying yourself things because you consider your desire for them unfeminine. If, like Gloria W., you wish to make your own money, even though your husband sees no need for you to work, break away from his definition of you and take a job. Order whatever and as much as you want in a restaurant. Let

the dishes go—make the men do them while you rest.

- Forget your identity as the perfect wife as Margaret B. did, and skip drying the dishes or whatever other household duty you are performing to go jogging, for a walk, to a movie, or watch television. It will get you out of the role in which you've let men cast you.

- Cultivate friends and join groups that will see you the way you want to be seen. Great movement and social change have sprung from the joining of like-minded people.

- Don't worry about what men will think of you if they see you alone in public. View it as Rebecca did and see it as an act of admirable independence to go to a movie by yourself. Tell yourself it's great fun to go out on your own—men do it all the time. Assert yourself. Be yourself.

- Ignore people's expectation that women "should" be shy, demure and passive. It's all right to let people know if you want something. You might even try running an item in the personals of journals like *Intro Magazine* or tell friends you're available for dating.

- Tell yourself, as May did to feel more attractive to men, "I am beautiful." You don't have to be 18 to be attractive. Only recently has the media presented women in their 40s, 50s and 60s as vital, beautiful, sexual beings. And suddenly men are going for older women, not because of biology, but plain old PR. Believe you are beautiful, expect to be reacted to as beautiful and the results will be amazing.

- Refuse to worry about whether you or your partner is the "right" age to be in a relationship together. Learn, as Valerie did, that love and the ability of each to satisfy the other's needs are the most important factors in a good relationship. In the past, men have been judged by the youthful beauty of their wives while women were judged by the economic achievement of their husbands. Men are supposed to go for beauty in their partners while women seek out money. A woman who instigates a different value system, who chooses a man on the basis of his beauty or sensitivity, presents a definite challenge to the old system founded on power and control embodied in money.

- Try the strategy Vivian used on Angelo to be seen as an equal. Whenever a man makes a statement that shows he has prejudged you on the basis of his definition of women rather than you as a person ("You'll never have the stomach for this," or "This is a man's job," or "We need an analytical mind here"), call him on his behavior. Tell him that you think he may be making a judgment here without knowing the full story, and tell him how his behavior makes you feel. There's no need to hurl insults or fly into a rage. Calmly point out the consequences of his behavior with statements such as, "When you say I can't do a job without your even letting me attempt it first, it makes me think there's no point in even trying," or "When you say you need an analytical mind in this situation, it makes me feel stupid and inept." Even if this was the man's intention, there is no way he can publicly own up to it.

- Try what Marjorie did to get men to see her as intelligent. Make your own labels, positive ones that suggest the way you want to be viewed by others, and display them publicly. A friend of ours has the license plate MASTER on her sports car. She gets a lot of ribbing but reports people show her more respect now that she shows respect for herself. Just as you have to blow your own horn if you want attention, you also have to let people know how you wish to be treated.

Be what you want to be. Meet your own expectations. Refuse to live through someone else. Make yourself in any image you choose. You are as you see yourself. And you are beautiful! Your energy is infinite. Believe "I am as I see myself," and use this energy to create the best person you can be!

8

"A Woman's Place Is In The Home"

What I hated most about staying at home was I
never got to see the rest of life . . . and it
never got to see me.

BETTY A.
patient, age 43

"Once I got married," Betty explained to us, "I felt that staying in the house as much as possible was one of my duties. But
I got so sick of those four walls I nearly went stir crazy."
What was worse, when Betty first came to us for counseling
she was considering divorcing her husband, Donald, even
though she still loved him. It was the only way she thought she
could get out of the house. Our first strategy for Betty was for
her to go away by herself for two weeks just to experience the
reality of "home" as any place you *are*. Home is a state of
mind. It is anywhere you feel comfortable, truly anywhere
your heart is. It can be how you feel in a relationship, a warm
feeling you create on the job, or a place in mind where you feel
you belong. Home need not be a geographic place, it is rather,
any situation in which you *let* yourself feel good. If you feel it
is more important to be in a definite physical spot rather than
in your own prescribed mental space, you are a victim of this
program. If being in the right house is more important to you
than being in the right frame of mind, please read on.

No idea in this book has become so embedded in our culture

than that of "A woman's place is in the home," and it shows itself in many ways.

Whether you're a mother who is postponing her work plans, a homemaker who feels that her family doesn't understand—much less appreciate—her constant work around the house, or a career woman who feels guilty because her demanding lifestyle doesn't seem half as tidy or simple as it does on the TV commercials, you're affected by the powerful pull of this time-honored concept.

You know that being at home is not a *bad* thing. But it can be harmful if it's the only choice you feel you have. And for a long time it has been. This way of life was designed largely by men to keep women away from the outside world. And since money *is* power, as long as you work at home, you won't have any direct power or influence.

In this chapter we'll show you how to maintain a "high profile," whether at home or at work, married or single, in order to achieve independence and exert influence on those around you. You'll see how belief in the myth of "your place" may keep you in a bad relationship. Ultimately you'll learn that your place is anywhere you *are*. You belong wherever you want to be and can have *power* at home, at work, at play just by showing people you're with that you yourself are important.

The "Virtue" of the Low Versus High Profile

Any time you make people *aware* of your presence, you have a "high profile." On the other hand, whenever you melt unobtrusively into the woodwork, you are exhibiting a "low profile." Any management consultant will tell you that the key to success in getting what you want is maintaining a high profile, or good visibility. To effect direct change, you need to openly deal with the issues at hand, to actively create your place in the scheme of things. Whether at home or in the work world, it is imperative that you let people know you have worth if you are to be treated with value. You do this by *acting* as if you are a valuable person, not hesitating to state what your needs are or what it takes to satisfy them.

In a modern world where the value of a product is determined by advertising that renders it highly visible, it is no use to you to hide your wares under a bushel. The tremendous amount of work you may be doing every year in household labor or raising your family has great value. However, it brings you no money because these services are provided in the low-profile privacy of "home" rather than on the open market. One can now begin to see why some men may consider women virtuous for staying in the home. Program 8 benefits men in two ways: (1) they receive an abundance of free labor; (2) since the labor is restricted to the private sphere, it is eliminated as a competitive threat. The same work that commands nothing in private is worth a goodly amount in public. Keep women's work private and men's public and again the result is "good" women and rich men.

Tina, 35, and Nettie, 38, came into therapy together, both complaining that their husbands, Wilfred, 36, and Gene, 37, workers in the same meatpacking plant, spent all their money on themselves and only gave their wives enough for groceries and minor household expenses. "Wilfred thinks he's entitled to a bigger share of his wages because he's the one who earns them," Tina complained. "But I do twice as much work as he does." "That's right," Nettie agreed. "A man may work from sun to sun, but a woman's work is never done. If I got paid by the hour like Gene does, I'd be rich!" "Me too," Tina rejoined. "Why can't men appreciate us more for what we do?" "Because," we answered, "you don't make them *aware* enough of your worth. You need to raise your profiles." We then suggested that Tina and Nettie make their husbands hire someone to do their housework. "How are they going to pay for it?" Nettie asked. "They don't have that much money." "Guess you'll have to get jobs to supplement their incomes," we answered. "Doing what?" they said simultaneously. "Housework!" we laughed. "Nettie can do Tina's and Tina, you can do Nettie's." While at first the trade may have looked ridiculous, it did one all-important thing. It put Tina's and Nettie's services on the open market and made their husbands aware of the value of their wives' work. In a society where money determines value, Tina and Nettie raised theirs immeasurably in the eyes of their husbands by charging for their services. Once this awareness was instilled in Wilfred and Gene, they were more than happy to share their wages equally with their wives in exchange for the "valuable" services these two women provided.

You can change your world by changing the way you look at yourself. When you see yourself as having value, the world will respond appropriately. In the sections that follow, you'll learn how to make the outside world aware of your increased sense of self, raise your profile and broaden your personal horizons to include any place you wish to be!

How This Myth Keeps Women in Bad Relationships

As Betty A. showed you, freedom is putting yourself in any place you wish to be. Believing that her place is in the home has kept millions of women trapped in troubled marriages and relationships. After all, a home is not a home without a man. "Home" to many women refers more to a feeling than a location. It extends to *taking care of a man, needing a man.* This is the real reason women—married or not—stay in unsatisfactory relationships, we think. Women give their lives meaning according to how good their relationships are. The relationship, then, becomes an important part of a woman's identity. Often patients tell us that they feel as if they have a home when they're in a relationship. It gives them a sense of family. However, when the price becomes too high, when the minuses of this relationship outweigh the pluses, it is important not to stay in this "home" because you believe it is "your place" and you "should." Many women often find that their relationships make them not only menial laborers but wet nurses to boot. American diplomat and congresswoman Clare Boothe Luce put it this way: "A man's home may seem to be his castle on the outside; inside, it is more often his nursery." As Tina told us, "My baby-sitting fees for Wilfred alone amounted to more than he was bringing home from the plant!"

A man often marries a woman to replace his mother. He wants someone to nurture him, to cook his meals, clean up after him and give him constant support. Unfortunately for the poor woman he marries, such a man continues to expect the same self-sacrificing and unconditional positive regard as he received from the saintly woman who gave him life. Although love of a parent for a child is unconditional—you love the child no matter how much you may sometimes disapprove of her or his behavior—it is truly unreasonable for a man to expect this same kind of love from his wife or lover. Adults are accountable to each other, and it is only natural that each of you expects something from the other. Of course the fact of the matter is that a man often does expect too much. Many men absolutely believe that it is a woman's duty to love them unconditionally—that is, no matter what they do. Women who accept their places as mothers to their men are setting their own traps, ones that almost inevitably lead to misery in a marriage.

One woman we know feels it is her obligation as a wife and mother to her husband to always be home when her man gets in from work. In his entire life, he has never come home to an empty house; either his mother or his wife was there to cater to his every desire. While most of the time Donna, a youthful 39, is happy to be the welcome wagon, there are times she resents the prison of the routine and would like to be doing things out of the house with friends or organizations. When we asked "Why do you let him get by with that?" she replied with "It's the least that I can do." Why? "Because I should be home anyway." Donna's rationale for her self-entrapment is a woman's place is in the home.

We were able to help Donna free herself from her self-erected prison by teaching her that it was all right to leave her home when she wanted. It was fine to stay at home, but it did not have to be the *only* place she felt comfortable. She discovered that her husband expected her always to be there when he got home only because she always was. She changed her behavior, and now he has new expectations: that sometimes his wife won't always be there when he arrives. Just as we were able to help Donna feel comfortable wherever she chose to be, we will do the same for you.

Learning that Your Place Is Anywhere You Are

Writer Polly Adler, in her book *A House Is Not a Home,* said, "My home is in whatever town I'm booked." What a terrific spirit to live by! "Private" and "public" spheres are artificial divisions. What's real is only life. Embrace all of it. Make your home any place you are, including work and the places you play.

We'd been working with a client, Heidi, who was 66 years old and wanted very much to move from the city to the desert. But Heidi's husband, Arthur, who recently retired, wanted to stay in his familiar surroundings, reliving the past. "I just can't get him out of the house anymore," Heidi complained. Guilt over neglecting her husband and doubt about her right to "leave home" without him scared Heidi. "How can I go against his wishes when he's given his whole life to me?" she asked. "If I could just get away once in a while, I'd be happy, but Arthur wants me home with him *all* the time." Finally we were able to help Heidi summon up enough courage to rent a small desert condo on her own without her husband's permission, using money from her social security checks. It was a place where she could go when she needed to get away from what she called "the rut of too familiar surroundings." "I have so much more energy when I change my living quarters," she explained. "Home is nice, but it pulls me down after a while and I need to get away to recharge." At first Arthur was indignant at Heidi's decision to buy the condo and refused to visit it with her. We advised her to go alone, which she did. In less than a year Arthur gave in to his curiosity as to what the attraction was and started to join her. When friends asked, "Don't you miss your home when you're way out there in the desert?" She responds, "When I'm out there, the desert *is* my home."

Another client of ours, Becky H., considered herself a fortunate woman. She had a nice home and family with no financial worries. When we first saw her in our office she complained of narcolepsy, a condition in which the victim has trouble staying awake throughout the day. Becky would doze off making the grocery list, dusting the furniture, polishing the silver, even talking to friends on the phone. "When I fell asleep behind the wheel and totaled my car against a divide, I knew it was time to get help," she told us. After ruling out any organic causes and making certain Becky was taking care of herself properly and getting enough sleep, we asked her, "Can you think of *any* reason why a person in good health, with no physical problems, would continually fall asleep?" Becky said she couldn't. We tried again. "What would you think if, while you were talking to me, I kept dozing off?" She smiled, "I'd think I was boring you to death." "Exactly!" we clapped. "Which is precisely what's happening. Only in your case, your whole life is boring you to death." Through counseling we were able to help her see that this constant drowsiness was really a defense against boredom. Her subconscious would rather go to sleep than endure the humdrum of her daily routine. She needed the stimulation of a new experience out of the house to wake her up. Although Becky's husband wanted her to stay at home, he gave in to her taking a part-time job clerking in a department store when he understood that her health was at stake. The time out of the house restored Becky's wakefulness along with a powerful realization that a woman's place is where she feels best. She had accepted the old rule until illness forced her to seek a better alternative. "Now that I've got something to be awake for, dozing off is no longer a problem," she recounted enthusiastically. "I've got more energy than I know what to do with!"

As we've mentioned earlier, we are not saying that staying in the home is the problem. Many women have been establishing successful careers along with balancing home and career for many years now. However, you shouldn't feel forced into a career any more than you should feel forced to stay at home. It's the "shoulds" we're helping you get rid of! What we *are* saying is that wherever you presently are there might be a better place to be and that you have the freedom to seek it out.

That is how you grow. Twenty years ago, in *Sex and the Single Girl*, Helen Gurley Brown addressed the necessity of continuing to grow, even within the imagined safety of the "home." Her words still ring true today:

> You may marry or you may not. In today's world that is no longer the big question for women, [but] those who . . . never have to reach, stretch, learn, grow, face dragons or make a living again are the ones to be pitied. They, in my opinion, are the unfulfilled ones.

You are entitled to life, liberty and the pursuit of happiness—without being blocked by anyone. It is your right to embrace the private, the public or both spheres of life. You belong wherever you put yourself!

How to Know if You're "Housebound"

The term "housebound" refers to a state of mind. It does not just mean staying in the house. It means thinking of yourself as *having* to stay at home. Choice makes all the difference. You can use the following listing to determine how much you believe in the virtue of maintaining a low profile. If you ascribe to enough of the items on the list you may be nearly invisible. You may need to ask yourself, "How do I know I exist at all?", so that you can begin to break your habits and start listening to yourself. Do any of these ideas sound familiar?

- Do you resist new experiences?
- Are you upset when something disrupts your daily routine?
- Do you need to plan every detail of the day's activities?
- Do you feel you *must* have a dreamhouse with fancy furniture and cars and life-insurance and pension plans to cover several families?

• • •

Although Peggy, 31, mother of three grade-schoolers, married to Zach, a wealthy movie director, complained that she was bored out of her mind, she resisted all our efforts to get her launched into new activities. Everything we suggested seemed to make her mad. "Why do I have to do anything new?" she snapped. "I've done what I'm supposed to. I got the husband, the kids, the beautiful house, a Mercedes and station wagon for backup. There's enough coverage in insurance and pension plans to make several people rich if Zach dies. I'm sick of the struggle. I should be happy by now!"

As well off as Peggy was financially, she had a housebound mentality. A good talking to got her out of her rut. Here is what we told her: "Nobody is responsible for your boredom but you," we began. "The only way to dispel it is to do something *new*. If you're sick of your mansion in Bel Air, then get out of it once in a while. *Change* your role. Stop behaving the way Zach and your rich friends expect." Peggy did just that. She got a job training horses three days a week. Anything that got her out of her gilded cage was worth the effort to Peggy.

- Do you ever feel anxiety when you think about the "outside" world where people work for a living?
- Are you staying in a bad marriage because you don't know where you would turn if you were on your own?
- Do you feel you're stagnating with your current group of friends?

Judith, 48, described her husband, Abe, as a "blah." "He never has anything to say, never thinks of anything we can do together, never asks me how I am. It's not really a relationship, just a convenient arrangement. It puts food in my stomach." When we asked Judith why she didn't leave Abe and earn her own money, she said, "I don't know what I'd do if I left home. Although I've never tried to get a job, I just have a feeling I wouldn't be able to. The thought of having to survive on my own in the outside world terrifies me." Judith's mother had been the same way, "scared of her own shadow."

Whenever young Judith had spoken eagerly to her mother of the exciting careers she was going to pursue when she grew up, her mother would only frown and say, "You don't know what it's like out there." After a few years, "out there" became a place in Judith's mind too dangerous too venture, and she married Abe directly out of high school to avoid ever having to experience it.

The first inroad we made with Judith was getting her to invite someone new into her familiar territory. She may not have been ready to leave home, but she could start rearranging it a little. Since she almost never went out, we had to draw our prospects from people she knew by phone. She had struck up a nice long-distance relationship with Ruth, one of the women on her answering service, and we suggested she invite the woman over. "Into my home?" Judith gasped at first. Judith not only could not conceive of getting out, she couldn't imagine bringing others in either. Her imaginary barriers were powerful. With our encouragement, she invited Ruth over one afternoon. They became better friends, and when Ruth told Judith about a job opening on the service, she took it. As soon as she got "out there" she was no longer afraid. She separated from Abe and is now happy among friends.

- Do you have certain times that you absolutely *must* be in the house? Many women hate themselves if they are not at home when their husband comes in or the kids get home. Another example is: "good girls" should never be out of the house alone after 8 P.M. on weeknights and 10 P.M. on weekends. We know of a friend who was "allowed" to attend parties alone since her husband worked late, but she was not allowed to stay till the end. When coaxed to stay on she would moan, "My husband will kill me if I'm not home by midnight." As long as your loved ones know how to reach you, don't you think it's all right to not always have to be home at certain times?
- Do you feel guilty and out of place if away from the house very long?
- Are you uneasy if the food isn't ready when your hus-

band arrives home from work even though it's OK when you have the food ready and your spouse is hours late?

Belle, 32, used to drive her friends crazy because every time she visited them without her husband, Arnold, she wouldn't be there 30 minutes without stating, "I really should be going. Arnold might be trying to reach me," or "I've got to get home in case Arnold calls" or "I never know what time Arnold will get home. I've got to run." When one of her friends suggested she get a beeper, Belle realized she was going overboard on her need to be "in the home." "It's like a bad habit with me," Belle laughed. "I know I'm making myself a prisoner, but I just can't seem to kick it." We told Belle that to break the habit, she would have to make a *voluntary, concentrated* effort. To get her going we asked her what time Arnold usually got home from work. Learning that it was 6:30, we suggested she deliberately be gone from 6:30 to 7. She could take a walk, visit the neighbors, anything to get her out of the house then. This half hour was designed to be short enough not to cause Arnold any real inconvenience, while giving him the message that Belle's place was anywhere she decided to be. It wasn't to hurt him, only to get him out of the habit of expecting her in "her place" whenever he wanted. At first he showed some irritation and wanted to know where she was. Belle was told to smile and vaguely say, "Out." The beautiful thing was that once Belle and Arnold both adjusted to this procedure, Belle felt much more comfortable having "unaccounted time out" when she really wanted it. Naturally, it was then no longer necessary for her to be out between 6:30 and 7.

- Is your closet stuffed with dingy old clothes that still have a "lot of wear" in them and few, if any, new and exciting garments in style and fashion? (Maybe it's because all you need is stuff to wear to work or around the house. In other words, you never go anywhere that requires anything else.)
- Are you afraid to drive an automobile? (And where would you go anyway that your husband or your family couldn't take you?)

• • •

Lena, a 34-year-old housewife, came to us needing to get over a fear of driving, a problem that was especially bad because her husband, Milton, never took her anywhere. Just the thought of getting behind the wheel sent Lena into a panic attack. We gave Lena exercises to practice in which she was to pair deep relaxation, which we taught her how to do, with the thought and image of her driving comfortably out of her driveway and down the road in front of her home. Week after week Lena would come in with a different excuse as to why she wasn't doing the exercise. Finally the truth came out when she blurted, "What difference would it make? Where do I have to go anyway?" Lena's driving fear was helping her to avoid her real fear: standing up to Milt's decree that she not leave the house without him. It was much easier to blame being housebound on a driving phobia than a dominating spouse.

We tried a cure that works surprisingly well in a lot of cases. Without telling her why, we instructed Lena to buy three of the most beautiful new outfits she could find. Lena followed our suggestion, but seemed anything but happy about it. "Where am I going to wear these gorgeous things?" she pouted at us. Trying to keep a straight face, we suggested, "How about around the house?" Lena laughed, "Not on your life!" Lena drove twelve miles to her sister's in her new clothes the very next day. The driving fear was gone. The thrill of showing off the new wardrobe canceled any apprehension she had over Milton's disapproval. In Lena's words, "It was worth it!"

- Do you become angry when anything is out of place? For example, you may be furious to find the cap left off the toothpaste, the kids' shoes in the middle of the living room, the garbage can too close to the door, dishes left on the counter, clothes draped over chairbacks instead of in the closet, food returned to the wrong cupboards, utensils in inappropriate drawers, books left in the bedroom, towels in the hall . . . The subconscious message here is that since you are in your place, so too should the rest of the world be in its place.

• • •

We're certain you could come up with many more behaviors that contribute to your making your home your trap. If you work on changing these behaviors soon as you think of them, you'll be on your way to freedom. It's easy if you begin today! Soon you'll discover that your home is in any situation you feel comfortable.

Why You Stay at "Home"

Naturally, many reasons exist why you'd choose to be in one place when you'd rather be in another. There are rewards for believing you have to stay at home. Here are the classic payoffs that prevent you from breaking free to go any place you choose.

- You feel safe. But this sensation is only illusory, as any victim of divorce knows only too well.
- There is little pressure to change. Once the routine is set, you know pretty much what each day holds.
- There is a sense of belonging. If you've done what is expected, you may feel that things are as they should be. That is why feelings of malaise are so perplexing: "I have everything in the world I'm supposed to have . . . a beautiful home, a loving husband, a wonderful family. . . . Why aren't I happy?" The truth is you may be only a bird in a gilded cage, sacrificing growth, evolution and freedom for the old trap of security.
- Staying at home keeps the unknown at bay.
- You believe you are being "mature" and "adult" by denying any natural spirit of adventure or thirst for knowledge you may possess and by remaining firmly planted in your "real" world.
- As always, you can feel superior for being such a "good girl," having followed the rules so completely.
- You can feel that you are indispensable. The thought of her family being able to get along without her even

for a little time is so terrifying to many a woman that she never gives loved ones a chance to try.

How to "Step Out of the House"— Even if You're Staying In

Even if you only try one or two of the strategies we've outlined for you below, we hope it will help you discover that your home lies within *you*.

- Make specific efforts to do new things out of the house, even if they seem "pointless" or too "far out," as Peggy did when she started training horses three days a week even though it went against Zach's expectations of her role as a wealthy matron. For example, take a class in the art of stained glass at a neighboring school. It would get you out of the house and you might have a good time.
- Begin rearranging your home territory by inviting someone new over, as Judith did to get used to the idea of change. Next, you might invite a completely different *group* of people over to your house to liven up things. For one evening throw predictability to the wind.
- Take risks to get you out from routinely being in "your place." Leave the house spontaneously and at "bizarre" times, such as right before dinner when your husband is expected home from work (as Belle did) or in the evening. Why? To get yourself used to the idea that your house is anywhere you *want* to be.
- Go away for at least a week, as Betty A. did, even if it causes considerable upheaval. It doesn't have to be far, but it should be a place you've always wanted to go, and for long enough to realize your place is anywhere you *are*.
- Think about taking a job if you want, as Becky did to end the drowsiness of her humdrum routine. Don't

worry about the nature of the work or how your family reacts. Let them help you with the housework—after all, their place is now in the home!

- Buy some exciting new clothes that are too good to be worn around the house. As in Lena's case, this will force you out of your home in order to show them off!

- Arrange, as Heidi did, to take a separate place to be used as a spot to get away, a second home. If money's a problem, try what another patient of ours, Alisa, did. Alisa combined forces with her other housebound friends to rent a condo in a resort area. They all shared expenses and cooperatively created schedules where each had her own time alone there.

- Try the strategy we suggested for Tina and Nettie and exchange household duties with friends. You needn't even charge one another. Sometimes it is just a pleasant change to work in someone else's home. Clean her living room while she cleans yours or offer to cook for her family every Tuesday night if she'll cook for yours on Thursday. It's usually easier to make one big meal than two medium sized ones. This way, you not only accomplish the same amount of housework, you add two social occasions a week to your itinerary, one of which gets you out of the house.

- Meet your husband at his work on specially scheduled evenings and go to dinner from there. It saves time and makes it nearly impossible for him to say no.

- Force yourself to read the Calendar section of the Sunday paper every week to learn what is going on about town. Commit yourself to attending one of those events regularly, with or without your partner.

- When you do propel yourself out of the house, be aware. Work at observing every exciting facet of your new reality. The opportunity for happiness is everywhere. What most people lack is the sensitivity to see it. Study the world and you will discover more and more ways to enjoy it. Teresa, 20, was so conditioned to believe her place was at home that her parents were unable to get her to leave their house. "You need to make a home of your own now," her mother kept telling her, but Teresa would answer with, "I already have a home with you and Daddy. And I like it here. Why should I leave?" The problem with Teresa was that she was focusing so much on the home of her childhood, she was unable to notice the exciting possibilities that awaited outside. We helped Teresa to appreciate other realities by giving her exercises in which she was to go to a new place each day—a beach, café, club, park, store—and to record in a journal every exciting thing that place had to offer that she could not experience at home. As the days progressed, Teresa came to see how much she would be missing if she continued to limit her space as she'd been doing. Heightened awareness of the outside led her to move out into her own apartment. She is able to enjoy her new home now that she has *developed* an appreciation for it.

- If the man in your life says that he feels neglected because of time you spend outside the home, whether it be for career, pleasure or whatever, tell him that he is the most important thing in the world to you but that while he is *necessary* to your happiness, he is not *sufficient*. You need the freedom to satisfy other needs as well. Ask him outright, "Do you want me to be happy?" When he answers "yes," take some time to really sit down with him and explain how you truly need space outside the home in which to grow. That doesn't mean you need or love him any less. It means you love yourself as well.

It is definitely possible to have both love and success, to take what you want from the world and still hold your man. But remember, you have to work on changing both your mind *and* his. Be firm but gentle. Tell your partner what you intend to do positively, and without doubt that your intentions will be carried out in action. Make these statements of intent often. In time he will believe your affirmations: that you love him, that you need him, that you love yourself too, that you need time out of the house, that he is going to show his love for you by helping you achieve this goal.

Lisa, 43, was a successful designer when, at 25, she married

Philippe, an antiques dealer ten years her senior. She gave up her career to help Philippe with the business and have two children. "Now the business is thriving and the kids are old enough to be more on their own," Lisa explained to us, "but Philippe wants me to continue being by his side in the house, twenty-four hours a day. All I want is to work part time, two days a week in a design shop, but he's opposed. I guess he's gotten used to the idea of a specially prepared meal every night and my always being there when he needs me. He says I get too tired when I work." "Too tired for what?" we asked. "Too tired to wait on him," she laughed. We told Lisa that it was only natural that Philippe would know a good thing when he saw it and would keep on wanting it. However, she would have to be gentle but direct with him. "Tell him," we said, "that you love him, that you appreciate his needing you, but that you know he loves you enough to do what you need, too, and at the moment that is *working two days a week out of the house*. Be *specific* and *repeat* it often so that he gets used to the idea. Many women are afraid to keep bringing up an issue if their husbands get angry the first time. But don't be afraid of your partner's anger. It will subside." Lisa followed our advice and happily reported that while Philippe objected at first, he gave in as she lovingly, but repeatedly, voiced her intent.

Like Lisa, you can free yourself most easily from any situation by stating your objective *directly* and *repeatedly*. Do it with love and your partner will come around. The entire world is your home—you only have to move in.

9

"Give Me That Old-Time Religion"

> I could kill a man who explains everything with
> "... because that's the way it's always been."
>
> CAROL P.
> *patient, age 40*

Carol was forced to take a job as a waitress when her husband,
Artie, a psychiatric technician, had his salary reduced by cut-
backs in government spending. To help ease her workload at
home, she asked her 15- and 14-year-old daughters to do the
household laundry. As Carol described it, "It was fine with
the girls, but Artie hit the roof. 'It was *your* job to keep the
clothes clean for me and the kids!' he shouted. 'That's the
least a wife can do.' Why do men insist on keeping us locked
into these old roles? How can we ever learn to think for
ourselves if the rules are already laid out before we're born?"
"Who do you think made these ancient rules?" we asked with
a knowing smile. "*That's* what I'd like to know!" Carol
stormed. "Let's put it this way," we continued. "Who
benefits from them?" After this question, it didn't take Carol
long to see that Artie's "old is best" mentality was just
another way of preserving a system that worked for him. Unfortunately, as Carol pointed out, being the victim of such a
system keeps you from acquiring the adaptability necessary
for handling situations on your own without needing to ask
someone else what to do.

171

A question we always asked women in all our research and interviews was, "what primary quality do men exhibit in contrast to women that gets them ahead?" There was an overriding common answer to this question: "adaptability." Chapter 10's theme, reverence for the past, found in the program "Give me that old time religion," is another "virtue" that is simply a guise for asking you to maintain the status quo, to stay in a world of others' rules. True adaptability is not conforming to someone else's rules, but rather being able to make rules of your own to fit each new situation. That's what you'll learn how to do in these pages.

Things change, and nothing should be revered just because it's old. What was good enough for Moses or your grandfather or father may not be right for you. How could you ever progress or grow—how could the world ever progress—with a belief like this? In intelligent beings, the past only explains the present; it doesn't determine it. *You* determine the present by what you choose to be today. That's what we want to present to you in this chapter.

Take from the past what works for you. The rules of time gone by are but a bridge to a better future. There's nothing on earth more exciting than moving forward to new and more rewarding experiences. We'll show you how to become adaptable, how to adjust positively to each new event that arises in your life by thinking for yourself. You'll learn to avoid confusing what is "natural" with what is old and to eliminate the trap of viewing yourself in terms of the past. Most important, you'll learn the art of combining the best of the old and the new, to free yourself to become you, a you that is truly natural because it comes from within.

The Main Reason Why Women Fail at Work: Lack of Adaptability

Women have always had to adjust to others' rules. But that doesn't make them adaptable. It only makes them obedient. As we've pointed out, adaptability is the ability to adjust to *circumstances,* to make your own rules in the face of each new event rather than needing to ask someone else for guidance.

"Everything changes so fast," gasped Norma, 32, a client of ours who had just landed a job as a processor in an insurance firm after ten years as a housewife. "You just get in the routine of things and there's a new routine. Home was hectic, but at least there I knew what to expect most of the time." A few weeks later, Norma complained of her first low performance report. "I can't understand it," she said. "I do everything they tell me to." "Maybe that's the problem," we answered. "You may not be doing enough things they *don't* tell you." We then posed a hypothetical situation to see if we were correct in our assessment. "What would you do," we asked Norma, "if, for example, you found that one of the insurance forms didn't provide enough space for adequate information?" "I'd tell my boss about it immediately," Norma said without hesitation. "Why not instead," we suggested, "modify or make up a new form on your own and save your boss the time and effort?" "That just isn't like me," she answered. We asked Norma to try a new strategy and deliberately act differently than before. "Just to see what it's like," we told her. The results were amazing. "I couldn't believe it," Norma told us in her next session. "Yesterday morning, I was about to ask my boss whether he wanted coffee. Then I remembered what you said, to deliberately act different—so instead of asking, 'cause I always do, I just brought him a cup. He was delighted. I had no idea he'd be so pleased at me doing things on my own." Norma had learned the valuable lesson of how much management appreciates employees who can think on their feet without having to come to them to set new rules.

The one outstanding thing that we've learned in our talks with women is that too much reverence for the past keeps them from adapting to the present. If you are so in awe of tradition that you accept it without question, you'll not only resist change, you'll never even consider it. If you make "what was" into "and ever shall be," you'll never invent a more efficient management program for IBM or come up with innovative promotional concepts for a new business.

Men are the creators. Women follow the rules. Women have not been conditioned to invent, organize, and combine information in new and exciting ways. Instead, women have been guided primarily to following the innovative new blueprints of man. Small wonder, then, that when confronted with the ever-changing demands of the business world, a woman who has previously known only the static condition of home finds it difficult to adapt.

It is much easier for a woman to adjust to change than to effect it. This has been her role throughout history, to adjust to rules but never to modify them. However, you must not be too much in awe of anything, to keep from revising and making it better. To be successful in business you must be able to both adjust to and change a system. Once you get used to creating new rules and systems you'll see how easily they're modified or eliminated according to how well they work.

For several months we worked with Roberta. She was 27 years old, recently divorced and worried about surviving on her own, not being able to support her two small children. She lived with her parents long enough to take some courses and land a job with a major advertising agency. But no sooner did she get her job than she began to worry about losing it. She just never seemed to be on top of things. First, her schedule was unorthodox: She worked from 3 P.M. to 11 P.M. Then, agency clients were popping in and out at all hours without appointments, making it difficult for her to focus. Next, there were times when management wanted her to switch duties or sub for other staff. Roberta was in a continual state of chaos. "I've always been a mess at work," she gasped. "Are you a 'mess' at home as well?" we asked. Roberta thought a moment. "No, I've got it pretty much together there," she said. "Funny," we mused, "how you can adapt to the strange schedules two small children must place you on at home, but you can't adjust to irregular client demands at work. What's the difference?" Roberta thought some more. Finally she said, "At home, what I say goes!" "In other words," we said, "at home you have no reservations making your own rules to fit the circumstances, but at work you *expect* to follow someone else's rules, whether they work for you or not." Roberta nodded in agreement. We told Roberta that she should stop seeing the home and work worlds differently, to use what she'd learned from being a mother with her clients. She was to set up a routine that was comfortable for her and then make the clients abide by *her* rules. She was, after all, in charge of the office just as she was the home. She also was to stop labeling herself a "mess" and start speaking in terms of what she was *now*. "Today I am in complete charge of the office."

Do whatever it takes to make a situation workable for you. Change what you can, adjust to what you can't. But under no circumstances do something simply because that's the way it's always been done before. Be creative. What you make yourself you are not in awe of. What you are not in awe of is easier to change. Use what you learned in the past not to lock you into a rigid way of doing things, but rather to make a better future.

The Problem of Equating the Past with What Is "Natural"

Dorene, a 46-year-old clerk in her husband Neil's hardware store and mother of three grown children, was raised in a small Ohio town to believe that it was only "natural" for men to take care of women. She told us, "I can still hear my mother say, 'From the beginning of time the woman's cleaved unto her man—that means he's gotta take care of her.' " As Dorene grew up she saw that what her mother said must be true—nearly every adult woman in town was married, and those who weren't were outcasts. "I remember how my father reacted the day I said I wanted to be a teacher," Dorene recalled. "I thought he'd be proud, but he turned white as chalk. 'Teaching's for old maids,' he said. 'Is that what you want to be? An old maid schoolteacher? It ain't natural.' So, rather than go against nature, I got married and let Neil take care of me, although I knew he never loved me. He even told me so once. Seems he only married me thinking it was the natural thing to do, too. And I never had a really natural feeling again. Thirty-six years living with a man 'cause I was afraid . . . afraid I couldn't be happy without him!"

The biggest block to change is the fear of not being able to find anything better. Dorene stayed in the old system because she was afraid she couldn't create a better one on her own. To eliminate the block of old conditioning, we had her tell herself for five minute periods three times a day, "It is natural to make things better. I can and will make things better." Four months later, Dorene left Neil to go to teachers college. Recently we received a letter: "Just wanted you to know . . . been teaching six months now . . . am the happiest 'old maid' in the world!" Doing what comes "naturally," in Dorene's case, had nothing to do with anybody's past but her own.

Whatever exists in your world at the time of birth is what you will interpret as being "natural." Robes were natural dress for men in ancient Rome, the rich naturally had slaves in the antebellum South and today it is only natural for men to make more money than women. However, there is nothing holy or absolute about what seems natural. Given a different upbringing, most of your "natural" tendencies would also be different.

It is a great ruse for anyone, especially men, to tell women to do certain things because it is natural or God's plan. For as feminist and author Mary Daly perceptively observes, " 'God's plan' is often a front for men's plans." The past is a world of men's rules. It seems natural because you were born into it. But nothing could be further from the truth. Today is tomorrow's past. Change today and you also change the eventual past. Only what you feel like doing today is natural.

One of our clients, Louise P., a 34-year-old book editor, told us of a recent victory over the "what is old is natural" trap. She hated cooking, wasn't any good at it, but felt it was something she had to master and endure. All her married life she had heard her husband, Patrick, insist, "All women like to cook. They've been doing it since the beginning of time. It's only natural." Not wishing to cause trouble, Louise continued to force herself into a daily activity she detested. Finally we proposed an alternative: We told Louise about another client of ours, Carol, who had just gone into business for herself, creating a Los Angeles based company called Home Dining Delight. "Carol provides an invaluable service to people who couldn't, wouldn't or didn't have the time to cook," we informed her. "Once a week a delicious menu is sent out and you can order by phone for a week's supply of food to be delivered in pouches that can be heated in boiling water or a microwave." Louise subscribed to the service, leaving her more time for herself, her children, and her husband. At first

Patrick objected but even he's happier now because the service lets him eat more whenever he wants.

It's interesting that Carol, when she first set this service up, observed an almost universal defensiveness in the women she approached for clients. "They were apologetic, usually eager to explain that they weren't buying the service because they weren't good cooks, but just didn't have the time," she said. "Many of them actually bragged about their cooking skills, claiming their friends had said they were good enough to go into business for themselves." These women were still clinging to the old belief that a good woman is a good cook.

To illustrate how arbitrary this old rule of woman as cook really is, consider the fact that cooking indoors, in the private sphere of home, is woman's work, while cooking outdoors is man's work. How often do you see women orchestrating the outdoor barbecue? Cooking is for women unless it entails a high profile or getting paid. Which explains why all the "great" cooks are men. The famous chefs cook in the public sphere for money. Our aim in this chapter is for you to see that many of your old roles that you think of as natural are more for the benefit of those who cast you in them than they are for you. With this added insight you will be able to move forward into a new religion that works for you!

The Trap of Thinking of Yourself in Terms of the Past

Whenever you think of yourself in terms of the past you are giving yourself a label. And while labels define, they also limit. All definitions limit. The word "woman" limits. It forces you to meet certain requirements, and while originally designed only to impart information, it soon leads to expectations. People soon come to expect certain attributes associated with specific labels such as "woman" and feel outraged or cheated if the expectations are not met. This is how stereotypes are made.

We want to help you lose your label, to learn you are what you do, not what you've done. You are not *absolutely* anything. You are a product of continual change. Looking back locks you in the past. And the action that brings change can only come in the present. Bette Davis spoke of the need to look only forward in her autobiography, *The Lonely Life.*

> I have always been driven by some distant music—a battle hymn no doubt—for I have been at war from the beginning. I've never looked back before, I've never had the time and it has always seemed so dangerous. To look back is to relax one's vigil.

Casting yourself in outmoded behaviors is not only backward looking, but also dangerous. A friend of ours, a 32-year-old gynecologist, in Los Angeles, recently had a terrific job offer on the East Coast. Irene enjoys her career very much and intends to pursue it all her life—"to die standing up," as she put it. She told her husband, Wes, that she had decided to take the job. Although work was not as important to Wes as it was to her and he could transfer without much hardship, he was shocked at his wife's decision. He believed in tradition. The woman always followed the husband across the country, pulling up stakes whenever he needed to move for a job. The idea of the man following the woman was preposterous. Our friend almost gave in to her husband's ways of thinking, but then she thought a moment. If she took this job, her earnings would double. Wes's work, though presently secure, was taking him nowhere and might someday be replaced by computer technology. Then where would they be? She couldn't afford to follow the old rule that says a woman always follows her husband—even if the rule did work two thousand years ago. She stopped thinking of herself in terms of the past and forged ahead into a new role of independence. She told Wes, "I love you with all my heart, but this is something I have to do," and accepted the job offer. When Wes saw that his wife meant what she was saying, he followed her to the far side of the country.

You cannot grow as long as you continue to think of yourself in terms of the past. Remove the limits of believing "what's old is best" and charge into the future!

The Real Trap: Not Only Having to Follow the Tradition but to Teach It, Too

Rosalie, 28, divorced, art instructor and mother to Meredith, 6, was amazed to learn that she unwittingly was teaching her daughter the old belief that men are better when she overheard Meredith in a conversation with one of the neighbors. "When I grow up I'm going to be a queen," Meredith enthused. Then she frowned. "Of course it's not as good as a king. But it's the best I can do." The neighbor laughed but Rosalie was shocked. "Why do you say a queen isn't as good as a king?" she asked her daughter. "You told me it wasn't, Mommy," Meredith answered. "A king always wins over a queen." Then Rosalie realized that Meredith had learned this from the game of cards she'd taught her. Kings were better in cards, so they must be in real life as well. The logic of childhood often finds its way into adulthood, and Rosalie asked what she could do to keep her child from being influenced by the old labels of the past. We told Rosalie that the best thing she could teach Meredith was to *question*. "Anytime you catch her believing someone else is better than she is," we said, "tell her to ask herself, 'Why?' If the answer is framed 'Because ____ says so,' she is being ruled by the past. Queen Meredith is *not* less than a king because the game of rummy says so. Tell her to say, 'I am equal to all because *I* say so *now*.'" Rosalie reported the advice is working very well. However, Meredith has now decided to be a king when she grows up. As Meredith put it, "*Who* says I can't be?"

Not only are you supposed to revere the male traditions, you may also find yourself, like Rosalie, passing them on to your children. The most important time in human learning is during ages 2 to 6. During these precious four years the core of your personality is formed. Events, conflicts, traumas during this segment of your life mold your future development far greater than experiences at any other time in your life. These are truly the "formative" years. They produce such a profound influence they are referred to in psychology as the "critical period."

This period, although much shorter, is also found in animals. Baby ducklings, for example, will relate to the first object they see as their mother. A duckling exposed to a cardboard duck, a dog or even the experimenter's hand during the critical period can form the same attachment toward them as it would toward its mother. In fact, there is a case of a peacock in an Austrian zoo that dutifully followed a hippopotamus, mistaking it for its mother because the hippo was its first contact after birth. Remember the story of the ugly duckling, the poor creature that didn't realize it was a swan because its only exposure was to a duck?

You're probably asking, "What does all this have to do with me?" Plenty, because you are the one most responsible for what your children are exposed to, and thus come to believe, during these early years. The woman usually spends more time with her child than her husband during these critical years. *You* have the greatest opportunity of all to mold the next generation toward equality and independence!

Begin by carefully examining the bedtime stories, fairy tales and nursery rhymes you read to your child during these tender, impressionable years of childhood. Tales of yore extol knights in shining armor, kings, wizards, gods and male forces that conquer all to protect tremulous female victims from destruction. Once upon a time, long, long ago, is the beginning of every fairy tale. It implies the past is better. The past was a time of magic and wonder, when gods walked the earth. The past was when men ruled the world absolutely. Be careful not to teach your children during the critical period that old is best, men are better and the old-time religion is the one true faith.

Kids may always want to read fairy tales, but try reading more than just these tales to your children. Make up your own stories to live by and tell your children. Tell a story of a world the way you would like it to be, a world you would like to have grown up in as a child, a world you would like your children to grow up in. Do you really want to live in a world where woman must wait a century for the kiss of man to wake her up, or where she must sweep the floor till rescued by a prince? Think about it.

Take your attention off the past by focusing on the future. Get a clear picture in your head of how you want life to be.

Then tell it to your children. Give them a dream of equality to follow. One in which we're all kings!

"My Man Must Be Better than I Am": *A Pitfall for the Liberated Woman*

As the women we've discussed in this chapter discovered, freeing yourself of the past clears your way to a brighter future. But getting rid of the past can be tricky. It has a strange way of creeping back and hitting you on the head when you least expect it. Women are so used to the old system they have a hard time shaking it, often believing they are liberated when, in effect, they have only reversed roles. A woman falling into this trap usually fears one of two things: (1) the tougher and more victorious she becomes, the harder it will be to find Mr. Right, a man who is even tougher and more victorious than she; (2) if she settles for a man who is not as strong as she is, she will end up having to protect him. Most women don't want to do this.

The core of liberating yourself is not becoming more like a man, but breaking free to become yourself. Where is it written that macho is better? It may be more masculine, but it is not better. If you are still pursuing these traits in men or trying to cultivate them in yourself because you're conditioned to believe they're better, you're still locked into the Good Girl Syndrome. You don't need a man who's tough and hard once you realize you can live without macho protection. Also, there's no reason why developing these qualities in yourself will make a man want you to protect him. Men are not victims of GGS. They're not looking for protection and they won't expect it, even if you have the power to give it.

A beautiful thing happens when you are freed from the Good Girl Syndrome. You can find and love a man for more satisfying reasons than his power to protect you. Your man does not have to be better than you. "Better" is a useless term in the new system you are creating. Love should not be based on competition, but liking and loving of the other person. Freedom gives you the power to love because you want to, not because you need to for survival. We will show you how to take what works from the past and combine it with futuristic vision to create a new system. A system that is both triumphant and nurturing. A system that allows you to build anew without forgetting the valuable lessons of the past.

Some Typical "Old Is Best" Behavior

Before you can build anew, you must set fire to the old city. Eliminate the rubble that blocks you from your happiness. Here are some common stumbling blocks that lock you in the past. Do you find yourself:

- Thinking of yourself in terms of the past, in terms of what you were as a child, an adolescent or just married?
- Labeling yourself or your behavior in any way? (Labels only limit you.)
- Using the past as a means of avoiding change? (Have you answered people with lines such as, ''Things have always been that way,'' or ''You can't beat the system,'' or ''You can't fight city hall''?)
- Truly believing that just because something is old, it is to be revered? (What was good enough for your mother may not be good enough for you.)

Charlene, 26, was ignored by her father as a child. ''I felt invisible,'' she told us. ''Nothing I did made any difference to him. I remember once, when I was 12, I spent my whole year's savings to buy him a very special birthday present, a pair of gold cuff links.'' Charlene was crying as she finished the story. ''All he said was, 'I don't wear French cuffs anymore.' Mother just smiled and said, 'I'll get you a shirt with French cuffs tomorrow.' She let him get by with everything.'' It was incidents like this one with her father that made Charlene give herself the label of ''unimportant.'' Today, in her marriage to Gabe and her work as a sales clerk in the household items section of a major department store, Charlene still thinks of herself in these terms from the past, where nobody cares if she's there or not. She feels so unimportant in her marriage, she never gives Gabe her opinion as to when they should entertain, who they should see or even how they should furnish their home. At work, she falls short of her potential sales because she doesn't think enough of her judgment to advise customers on purchases. "Whatever you like" is the most Charlene will commit to a shopper's asking for advice. We told Charlene that she was using her past and her label of "unimportant" to avoid change. Just because it was good enough for her mother to take what the world handed out, to be acted upon rather than doing some acting of her own, it was not good enough for Charlene. It was time for Charlene to stop being locked into the past by labeling herself and begin a new future of doing. We asked her to buy a notebook and, reserving one page for each day, write at the top of each page: "Today I'm going to _____." She was then to fill in the blank with a new behavior, something she had never done before. Charlene's first two pages were completed with, "Tell Gabe I want to serve dinner at 7:00 instead of 6:00" and "Push the brands I use myself, at work." As the days went by and the pages unfolded, Charlene eventually closed the book on the old label of feeling "unimportant" to open a new one filled with new self-actualizing *behaviors*. There are no labels in Charlene's life today, only positive action.

- Telling yourself that it's only "natural" for a woman to lack mechanical ability, be poor in math, possess traits of shyness and reserve, and lose her worth with age because women have always been like that? Remember, the past only explains the present, it doesn't determine it. *You* determine the present by what you choose to be.
- Feeling defensive and apologetic whenever you ask a man to assume "feminine" duties (dishwashing, grocery shopping or laundry)?
- Feeling threatened, unwanted or not needed if a man is a better cook, dishwasher, or housecleaner, than you are?
- Looking down on men who enjoy sewing, flower-arranging, interior decorating.

• • •

Liberation works both ways. Jeannette, 24, was surprised to find herself locked into many stereotypes from the past in her new marriage to Clive, an enlightened high school teacher who was more than willing to let Jeannette be herself if she could just get out of her own way. "I can't believe it," Jeannette told us, "I've been preaching women's lib since high school, and now I find I really don't even know what it is. I didn't realize it till Clive pointed it out. Like last week, when he got upset because I overdrew our checking account, I actually said, 'What do you expect from a woman?' and every time I ask him to do the dishes I feel funny, like I'm making a sissy out of him, even though he's happy to help out. And last night I let him make dinner, and the roast was better than mine. I can't believe the way I reacted. I was furious! Like he was infringing on *my* territory. Then this morning, when one of his friends brought over a quilt he'd spent all year on, I actually had to keep myself from laughing that a guy would spend so much time making a quilt. It's me. I'm not really liberated at all!"

We told Jeannette not to be too hard on herself. Awareness and a desire to change were the biggest part of the battle and she had both. The problem is that once these beliefs are conditioned they truly become a part of you. And if you're not careful, you automatically give them life. We asked Jeannette to keep a running list of every time she felt uncomfortable because she was doing something "masculine" or a man was doing something "feminine." We asked her to reread this list daily and really work on her reaction. No behavior is absolutely masculine or feminine. If you do it, it's feminine. If a man does it, it's masculine. Period. Happily, today Jeannette is practicing what she has been preaching all these many years.

- Hating football, basketball or baseball, but wondering what's wrong with men who share your same dislikes?
- Insisting that your man be better off than you in certain areas: feeling ashamed if he can't pound a nail straight, plane a door or fix a car?
- Refusing to date a man who is too "feminine"? The rules for what is masculine and feminine, who wears the dress and who wears the pants or who stays at

home and who makes the money are totally arbitrary and culturally defined. Why not look beyond the surface and decide to like a person for how nice he is, how kind, how caring, how considerate, how much he appreciates you, rather than forcing a man to play the very role of masculine supremacy you claim to detest.

Francesca, a 25-year-old photographer, was never able to find the right man. Currently she was seeing Damien, a producer of TV commercials whom she said she was "worried about." "He just doesn't seem like a real man to me," she informed us. "He's great in bed . . . loving . . . sensitive . . . compassionate . . . virile. He's sweet and understanding . . . always punctual, calls twice a day, never fails to say he loves me. He likes what I like. . . . He hates what I hate. . . . I guess that's what's wrong. He's so much like me he doesn't make me feel like a woman. I need that *dynamic difference!*" The "dynamic difference" Francesca was referring to was what had brought her last relationships to a screeching halt. "I'm even better at carpentry than he is," she interjected during one of her sessions where she was being particularly hard on Damien for his lack of "masculine" traits. "Good," we replied. "It'll be handy to have a woman around the house." Then, without pulling any punches, we gave Francesca the bottom line as we saw it. "If being able to pound a nail straight is more important to you in a man than how much he needs and cares for you, you have been getting what you deserve all along in your past relationships and you will only end up hurting Damien. The day you can appreciate those wonderful qualities of compassion, sensitivity, empathy and caring in yourself, you also will be able to appreciate them in your men." We asked Francesca to really start *questioning* all her old ideas about femininity and masculinity. Every time she was bothered by a trait of Damien's, she was to write it down and then asked herself, "*Who* says men should be _____ or shouldn't be _____ ?" The answer can only come from the past, and *your* time is *now*. Francesca decided to throw away the traditional rules that were dictating who she should love and let both Damien and her feelings be. She now loves him for what he is, not how well he fits the stereotypes of yesterday.

• • •

- Having trouble believing men can be sexy and non-sexist, not being aroused by the "good guys"?
- Finding yourself attracted to men who don't treat you as well as you deserve to be treated?
- Clinging to old setups because of inability to structure new situations with rules of your own? Do you need direction to the point where you can't think for yourself? Does a new job throw you for a loop until you're told how to handle it down to where to file the last note card? Managers report that they most appreciate employees who are able to think for themselves, who aren't continually pestering them with questions on how to do the job.

Vera, a 32-year-old art gallery curator, was so set in doing things the way they had always been done that she couldn't break her pattern of dating men who were wrong for her. She had read so many romance novels where the hero was "hard, arrogant and savage" that she couldn't stop herself from looking for the same "traditional" leading man in real life. If the guy was gentle, humane and kind, there was just no "sexual spark." This need to revere old stereotypes was also hurting her job, where she was required to create innovative new exhibits, and extend what was going on in the field of art. Our strategy for Vera was to have her repeat to herself three times a day, "Change is good. It is my objective. I assume full responsibility for restructuring a new life that works for me." Vera's sexual desires are no longer masochistic. She is aroused by men who are good to her rather than abusive. And she is brimming with lots of new ideas to set the art world on fire.

The Rewards for Insisting
on Tradition

A big help to your moving into a better future is for you to understand why you have held on to the past for so long. Here are some of the common payoffs for persisting in the old ways regardless of the consequences.

- Gives you a safe identity.
- Supplies a perfect scapegoat for failure.
- Allows you to avoid the risk of making new rules, ones that will work for you today.
- Provides an excellent substitute for thinking and tackling problems in a novel way. It's always easier to rely on old formulas, even if they don't work.
- You enjoy the fervor that comes from associating with like-minded individuals, fellow "good girls."
- Extreme worship or respect for anything raises it from the commonplace to the metaphysical. By worshipping male rules you thus force magic into an otherwise ordinary existence. Look what this kind of reverence did for the common cow in the Hindu religion.
- Total devotion implies that you will somehow be blessed for your strong support. If you receive no rewards, there is always the male-created loophole that you did not worship long, hard or earnestly enough.

Some Strategies for Combining the Past and the Now

Now, let's get busy. Primarily, cleaning up this problem involves cleaning house. Then looking forward. Get rid of all the old beliefs that stand in your way and find new ones to get you moving in a positive direction. Here are some strategies for removing hurdles and guiding you toward what you want.

- Refrain from labeling yourself. Labels come from the past. Simply say, as Roberta did to see herself in charge at work, "Today I am . . ." Finish the sentence with a piece of behavior that is the new you. You are what you do, not what you've done.
- Try to become more aware of labels you give yourself. Try, as Jeannette did to get over her stereotypic ideas

as to what is "masculine" and "feminine," to keep a running journal of every time you find yourself thinking you *are* something in particular. For example, if you catch yourself with the thought, "I'm too loudmouthed for a woman," record the label "loud-mouthed." Then ask yourself, "Would a man be labeled 'loudmouthed' if he exhibited the same behavior?" Probably not.

- Start questioning, as Francesca did to appreciate Damien more, and as Rosalie taught her daughter Meredith to do. Anytime an answer is couched in the terms "Because_____says so," you may be doing something because of reverence for the past. The past is important but it shouldn't rule you. Adults who continue their lives doing what Mommy and Daddy told them to do years ago, are buying into "old ways are best." TRADITION! Even *if* a rule worked in the past, it doesn't mean it should work now. The world is changing in a million ways every day. Think about how you can change with it.

- Just as Norma did to favorably impress her boss, deliberately try to act differently than before to see what it is like. For example, if you've always avoided foul language, swear once when something gets your goat. A woman salesperson we know said she doubled her sales to men when she started swearing because it immediately made them feel more comfortable.

- Make a list of all the things you would like to do. Then ask yourself why you haven't done them. If the answer to any of these items is, "Because it isn't proper," you are being blocked by male rules of the past. Paula had always wanted to be the one who paid the restaurant bill with their joint credit card, so one day she beat her husband to the draw, deriving great pleasure from this little show of economic power. Be "improper" (as long as it's legal) once in a while, and see what happens.

- Work at changing the system. If you wish to do something considered illegal by the male-dominated governing body, put forth effort for reform. Organize. Petition. Demonstrate. Run for office. A client of ours, Laverne, worked in a large office building in a part of town with a high crime rate. All the employees parked in a subterranean garage where the safest spaces, those closest to the entrance, were reserved for executives and upper management (most of them male). We encouraged Laverne to organize her female co-workers and petition the company for a redistribution of parking slots. It worked! Make your voice heard. Use the system in your favor.

- Respect the divinity within you. Trust yourself to do what's right, to create a bright, rewarding future without the imposed confinement of outside influences.

- Take time each day to clear your head of old thought. Inhale and exhale twenty consecutive times. Inhale as deeply as you can and hold it as long as you can before exhaling. Drive all old thoughts from mind by concentrating only on the *number* of each breath. Most thoughts are memories, messages that you recorded in your mind. When you listen to them, you are listening to the past. Put these messages on hold. A new reality may emerge.

- The best way to take your attention off one thing is to direct it to another. Free yourself of your past by focusing on your future. Don't look back. Strive to produce a very clear picture in your head of how you want your life to be. Make this image graphic, detailed in all five senses . . . taste, smell, touch, sound and sight. Make it specific. Imagine *exactly* what it is that you want. If it's a new home, be definite. How big? How many rooms? What style, location, color? Put yourself there. *Feel* the wood of the door as you enter. *Hear* your footfalls on the lush, soft carpet. *Smell* the clean freshness of woods and polishes. *Taste* the wonderful meals you will enjoy there. *See* the interior sparkle in the sunlight, vibrating with rich, radiant color. *Hold* this image till you *make* it happen.

- Like Vera did, give yourself a mental set for change. Repeat to yourself daily, *"Change* is good. It is my goal. I take full responsibility for creating a new life that works for me." Accept the responsibility for structuring and restructuring every day of your life. Refuse to rely on others to create your work space, schedule or entertainment for you. A client of ours was continually complaining that her husband was a crashing bore. He never bought tickets to a concert, suggested a new eating spot or invited friends over. In counseling we reminded her that while the man might be responsible for building the woman's life space in the old system, the new system of autonomy she was presently creating was different. Here, if something wasn't working out, it was her responsibility to fix it. We told her to buy the tickets, suggest the restaurants and invite the friends over herself rather than trying to remake her husband into something he wasn't.

- Do as Dorene did when she left Neil to go back to school, and eliminate the biggest of all blocks to change: the fear of not finding anything better. A woman stays in a loveless marriage for fear no one else will want her. She keeps a boring, unfulfilling job in anticipation of not finding a better one. She religiously abides by an ancient male system through sheer terror she will be unable to construct a more effective one of her own. Think positively. Whenever gripped by doubt and fear, repeat to yourself, "I *can* and *will* make it better."

Muriel, 40, a single, unemployed newspaper journalist, came to us in despair. "I have nothing to live for," she cried. "No family, no job, no future . . . the best years of my life are over." We knew from Muriel's first statement that what she was "looking forward to" was a future no one would want to enter. That was exactly the problem. Muriel's mind was so clouded with old thoughts, old fears, old expectations, that there was no room to conceive a bright new future. To set Muriel free of her past, we first had to build a positive, new future in *mind*. We asked Muriel to suspend her worries for the moment, to forget about the "impossibility" of her inferior position in a man's world, and to simply tell us what kind of future would make it worth her while to get out of bed in the morning. She was too depressed to think of anything good, so we helped. "Would you be married?" "No, I don't think so," she mused. "Would you be financially independent living on a desert isle?" we continued. "Boring," she said. "I like to work. But everyone says my stuff isn't fresh anymore. I'm too old." We smiled, "It's not you that's too old, Muriel. It's the thoughts in your head that are out of date." Together, using advanced imagery techniques we've developed for creating powerful thoughts, we created a scene of Muriel sitting in her own office at a major newspaper she always wanted to work for. The image was vivid, graphic. Muriel could see the furniture, feel the soft upholstered chair against her body, hear the typewriters clicking around her, smell the ink, taste the fruit juice she was drinking. She practiced this image daily, and soon it began to dominate her consciousness. "It's like a miracle!" she exclaimed. "I'm seeing a new future! I can't wait for it to happen." "Seeing" a new future lifted Muriel's depression and gave her the energy to start making it real. Two months after she began projecting her "new" future, she landed a job with a top newspaper. It wasn't the one she'd imagined, but her office did have the same color drapes! "It was all so easy once I decided to let go of the old," she told us.

If your life isn't working for you, change your program and move on. See a new future as Muriel did. This is exactly the time for you to do it. Keep reaching till you find the wonderful things you want. Your answers lie not in the past but in the future!

10

"Those Who Deviate Deserve To Suffer"

Why do I always worry and feel so guilty when I
don't do what a man says is "best" for me?

SUSAN T.
good girl group member

When Susan, a 22-year-old cocktail hostess, was a girl, her
father, an engineer on the railroad, called her My Little
Duchess. But when, at the age of 19, Susan went against her
father's wishes and moved in with Beau, a 20-year-old con-
struction worker, Susan lost her title. Her father didn't speak
to her for more than two years. "I feel so guilty," Susan told
us. "He worked so hard to support me all his life. It's not
much of a way to repay him, is it? 'I only want what's best for
you' he'd always say. But I love Beau so much, I don't care if
he's not 'best' for me." We told Susan that, first of all, her
father can't always know what's best for her. Only she could
know what was best by *first* trying out a new behavior. And
second of all, there was no reason to worry or feel guilty if she
didn't do what was best and made a mistake! Making mistakes
is only human. What is divine was the power not to punish
herself with guilt and worry, but rather to forgive herself so
that she could have the strength to try new experiences. In
Susan's case, we later discovered that her father objected to
her living with Beau, not because it wasn't best for her but

192

because it wasn't best for him. *His* friends didn't approve of unmarried couples living together, and it would have been easier for him if Susan simply had gotten married. Fortunately for Susan, who saved herself from a bad marriage by later learning by living with him that she was completely incompatible with Beau, her father wasn't able to make her feel guilty enough to get his own way.

In our introduction, we said that it takes a long time for a normal, healthy child to become a frustrated, unhappy "good girl." And now, in this chapter, we'll look at two of the deepest and longest-standing techniques that mold "good girls" and at how to work on bringing them within your control. The techniques we're talking about: guilt and worry.

Like Susan, most of us try to do what we think is best for us. But, it's not always easy to figure out exactly what is the best road to take. This is particularly true for women—"good girls"—who try to please everyone, especially men. You find you can't do everything at once; something has to give. And when it does, you probably feel that you've done something wrong. You feel guilty, and you start to worry. Guilt and worry—those are the two terrible by-products of thinking you have to follow someone else's rules, and that's what we will concentrate on in this chapter.

Men have brilliantly devised this program to cause you to punish *yourself* through guilt and worry for breaking their rules. This saves the men tremendous effort in law enforcement. It also assures that you'll be punished for *every* infraction, since it is impossible to get away with anything if you are the monitor of your own behavior. It's not necessary that Big Brother know your every thought, as long as you *believe* he does.

In this chapter you'll learn to stop punishing yourself for not living up to the rules of others. Like Susan, you'll create your own rules to live by and acquire the power to forgive yourself and start anew if sometimes they don't work out. You'll eliminate the needless guilt and worry that is so damaging to your self-image so that you will like yourself for being you!

Guilt: Punishing Yourself for Not Living up to Someone Else's Rules

As we've said, believing that you *deserve* to suffer when you don't act as you should leads to problems. Guilt is a feeling that comes when you think you have violated a law, done something "wrong." Wrongdoing in our society must be punished, if not by others then by yourself. Since there are so many people making so many rules, a truly "good girl" feels guilty nearly all the time. "It seems like no matter what I do," confides Leah, a 20-year-old chemistry major who has been seeing Aaron, a 23-year-old law student, "somebody doesn't like it . . . and then I feel guilty. Why can't I ever get it right?" Leah had a long history of suffering by her own hand through guilt. As a child she "bent over backwards" to win the approval of her loving, but demanding parents. She told us, "In grade school I was always upset 'cause I thought somebody didn't like me. It didn't matter who it was. If a kid in class didn't say hello or smile every time they saw me, I immediately felt guilty over what *I* must have done to offend them. By the time I reached high school I was a nervous wreck, I thought continually about what I was doing wrong with boys—Why weren't they nicer to me? . . . Why didn't I have more dates? . . . Why wasn't I more popular? Now that I finally have a relationship, I constantly feel guilty that I'm doing something that might end it."

We asked Leah, "What do you think all this guilt is helping you to avoid?" After a few moments of silence, we rephrased our question. "Let's put it this way," we said, "what do you think might happen if you didn't feel guilty all the time?" "People would hate me," she answered. "They'd think I was a terrible person if I didn't feel bad when I wronged them." "In other words," we said, "you believe that by punishing yourself with guilt you'll avoid disapproval and punishment from others." Leah thought a moment. Then she said: "That's silly, isn't it? I can't keep others from disapproving of me by beating them to the punch and disapproving of myself first, can I?" Once Leah realized how *useless* her self-punishment was, she began to ease off on herself. As she put it, "If

Aaron doesn't like what I do, he won't like it whether I feel guilty or not. So I think I'll save myself some grief!''

Leah couldn't get it right because she was trying to please others instead of herself. You can never please all of the people all of the time, and if that is your goal, you will *always* feel guilty. No matter how painful an incident, when it's over, it's over. Guilt, because it is self-generating, can be unending. It is a merciless taskmaster. But it's a wonderful tool for someone who wants to manipulate you. Plant the seed, set it in motion, and it can run eternally. If you were ever labeled "naughty" when you were a little girl and told you should be ashamed of yourself, you probably tried hard not to violate the rule again, in order to avoid the bad feeling of guilt and shame.

A typical connection between labels in childhood and adult problems can be seen in a former patient's recollections of her early life. Chance, a 42-year-old psychologist, recalls beginning nursery school. "I loved being with a large group of children for the first time and piped up loudly whenever I had something to say. But my teacher, Mrs. Stark, scolded me for being so loud and unladylike, and I began to blend into the furniture because I felt guilty and ashamed for being myself." Pretty soon, Chance was a shy, retiring, withdrawn "good girl." She maintained her shrinking violet behavior and, as an adult, wondered why she had difficulty speaking up to her husband, Simon, or at various professional meetings. When asked, she explained, "It just doesn't seem right. I've always been that way." But she hadn't—and that's the problem. She was taught to be this way by another woman who was carrying on the tradition that you should feel bad whenever you go against the system.

"What do you think would happen if you piped up at one of your meetings?" we asked her. "There'd be a lot of raised eyebrows," she said, "and they'd probably think I was being inappropriate." "Fine," we said. "Be inappropriate. In time they will adjust. At that point your behavior will be considered appropriate simply because they are used to it." Chance accepted the fact that some might object to her new behavior at first and plunged in. During the next meeting of her regional psychological association she spoke up seven times and refused to feel guilty for being "unladylike." Recently she told us, "You were right. It's amazing how fast everyone adjusted to the new me. In fact, at our last meeting I was tired and didn't say much, and one of the members asked if there wasn't something *wrong* with me 'cause I was so quiet!" In time, once they get used to it, others will *expect* you to live up to your own rules!

Worry: Punishment for Wanting to Break the Rules

Chance, like all "good girls," felt guilt when she went against the system of others. She even felt bad and worried if she even *considered* it! The message is simple: Not only shouldn't you go against the system, you shouldn't even *think* about it. This is as "bad" as putting it into action. While guilt is punishing yourself for breaking a rule, worry is torturing yourself for even thinking about it. These worries comprise all the "what ifs." "What if I save some time and fix a TV dinner tonight?" Or "What if I leave my husband home and go out by myself this evening?" Or "What if I say what's really on my mind?" All these "what ifs" can lead to your paralysis and continuance of the status quo, a system of others' rules. What if you just did what you wanted and forgot to worry about it?

The problem with both guilt and worry is they feel so unpleasant, that many women will give in to men's demands just to avoid experiencing these horrible emotions. "I'd rather do what he wants," said Leah, "than go through the hell of worrying about what'll happen if I don't."

Worrying over what will happen if you don't follow the male rules keeps many women imprisoned from childhood on. Erica C., a 27-year-old woman still living at home with her mother, is a perfect example. As she looks back on her life, she tells us that in the first grade, she was filled with the spirit of discovery, seeking out and exploring every nook and cranny of the schoolhouse. Mrs. Bloch, the teacher, informed her that it was very dangerous for little girls to strike out on their own and that she should not go out unless a boy was with her to protect her. It didn't take long before she began to worry. "What if I get caught alone in the dark?" Or "What if I get lost by myself?" Or "What if I'm not smart enough to stay out of trouble?" By the time Erica reached adulthood she had absolutely no confidence in her own ability to do anything. When asked why she so desperately wants to get married, she said, "I'd be worried to death if I didn't. How would I live?" She worries that she will perish without a man's "protection," even though she isn't sure what that protection means. And that worry makes her follow the *old* rules—rules that may relieve her worry, but end up making her more unhappy than she ever was before.

"I'm so bored at work, I could scream!" exclaimed Kitty, a single, 26-year-old junior executive in a large printing firm. "I thought I'd be doing something creative in this job, but all I do is routine layouts and comb the area for markets. I hate sales! I'm an artist!" When we asked her what was holding her in a job she hated, it didn't take long to spot the culprit as worry. "I can't afford to quit now," she told us in all sincerity. "I've put in five years at this firm. What if I can't find something better? What if I can't find something period? I'd have to get married!" Kitty had come from the same background as so many "good girls" we counsel—passive, fearful mother and strong, controlling father—but unlike most, she had rebelled. She was determined not to need a man for protection. So she set her sights on financial independence, and she succeeded—to a point. She managed to land a job in spite of her conditioning that men were better, but she was still not sure enough of her own equality to move out of this haven once it was indicated. Kitty was falling into the same trap at work that many women do in the home. "It's OK," we told her, "to leave your job for a better one. Your *place* is wherever you feel comfortable. You don't have to *stay* anywhere." But Kitty wasn't easily convinced. "All my friends say I'm crazy to give up my job security," she protested. "It isn't normal." We smiled. "Who ever said that being 'normal' brings happiness? In fact, it's been our observation," we continued, "that it is the 'normal' who are the most bored. Those who deviate, who take the road less traveled, are the ones most likely to find adventure and excitement." Kitty decided to risk deviating from the average expectations of others in order to end her boredom. She set up an office as a free-lance artist, and while she still has to find markets for her services, she also has the joy of creating her own product. There is no need to worry if you wish to break a rule that doesn't work for you. Instead, reward yourself for having the courage to forge a new path!

The Fall of the "Bad" Girl

As Kitty discovered, worry draws its strength from the imagination. The "what ifs" that keep you from going after your dreams work because they conjure up images of very negative consequences. The worst of these is the image of Hell—the ultimate resting place for the "fallen woman" and the "bad girl." For hundreds of years, literature, art and movies have sculpted and fed upon the image of the "good girl" who falls from man's (and society's) approval when she breaks one of the rules. The heroine of Nathaniel Hawthorne's *The Scarlet Letter* is physically branded for expressing her sexuality; Scarlett O'Hara loses the approval of Atlanta society for her business sense and fiery independence, among other things; Yentl loses her man because she must choose between love and knowledge—she can't have both. While it may seem that things have changed a lot today, they're still very much as before. We give lip service to pre-marital sex, living together, sexual openness, "doing your own thing," but the fact remains that when women do act independently they still feel guilty and worry about possible disapproval from others.

What we hope to show you here is a way out of your suffering. A way to prevent the only real kind of fall possible—the fall within *your own* eyes. Build your image of yourself and you can only rise!

How Guilt and Worry Damage
Your Self-Image

You probably already know that worrying and feeling guilty is being mean to yourself and damaging to your self-image. It relays the message that you are bad, and that you deserve to suffer. Feeling bad about yourself depletes energy, confidence and drive, which in turn perpetuates a vicious circle of feeling even more inadequate and unworthy. And it shows itself in many ways, for all different kinds of women.

Anita, 38, was so afraid she would lose her husband, Austin, to a younger woman when she turned 40 that she never said no to him. "What right do I have to refuse him anything when he makes all the money?" she asked us. "I just know I'll live to regret it if I don't give him everything he wants." Her worry about losing him turned her into a virtual doormat. The more she gave into his wants at the expense of her own, the less she thought of herself. And the less she thought of herself, the more she worried she would lose him! We taught her to end this downward spiral by doing some things for herself. One especially positive change was buying her own car. Even though she didn't directly make the money to purchase it, we helped her to realize that she was equally as deserving as her husband in the marriage relationship. And she didn't feel guilty.

Annie was in her mid 30s and was struggling with problems of her sexuality. She suffered desperately over her sexual attraction to other women, a worry that it would cause her to lose her job teaching in a private college. She believed devoutly in God, but could not understand how He could condemn her for something that was out of her control. She did not choose to be sexually aroused by women, but it had been part of her since puberty. She tried to go against these impulses, but nothing worked. With counseling, Annie began to stop hating herself for what was "unnatural." There was no need to feel unworthy simply because she was in the minority. Homosexuality has been "normal" in around ten percent of the population since recorded history. Sexual arousal is a genetic response, not one produced by logical deliberation that entails choice. Annie was no more responsible for her sexual preference than for the color of her eyes. She soon eased up on herself for not meeting external expectations and, after a few months, Annie came out of the closet. The very thing that she originally feared, public exposure of her gayness, made her stronger and bolstered her self-image. While Annie is far from free of guilt and worry, she has effectively vanquished some of the demons in her head by bringing them out into the light of day. Both Anita and Annie were suffering from worrying that they wouldn't meet the expectations of others. They got better when they tried, instead, to meet their own expectations and let others accept them for what they were.

Author Catherine Marshall exposes the evil of guilt and worry (self-punishment) in *Christy:* ". . . I learned that true forgiveness includes total acceptance. And out of acceptance wounds are healed and happiness is possible again."

When you can accept yourself for what you are, rather than what others want you to be, it will be a great day.

You are not good because you suffer. Nothing comes from your suffering but pain and disease. Guilt and worry only make you hate yourself. You deserve to grow, not to suffer. Be what you wish. Let others see you as you want to be—they will change! You don't need to expect any less! In the following sections we'll help you to grow by being good to yourself.

The Many Faces of Guilt and Worry

If you believe you deserve to suffer it's easy to spot. You'll see self-punishment popping up everywhere in yourself and others. Let's look at some behaviors that spring from your belief that you should be punished if you deviate from the rules. Do you:

- Feel guilt over rules—no matter how small—that you've broken?

- Worry over rules that might be broken?
- Worry that you just can't do what you want?
- Have a pervading fear that you really don't deserve to do or get what you truly desire? This takes many forms, from the simple "I'm not 'good' enough" (you won't be rewarded till you please everyone) to the "not untils," which are really the same thing—"I can't go to Tahiti until the car is paid off, the children are grown, my husband gets a raise, our payments are lower."

Andrea, 31, was obsessed by guilt if she deviated even the slightest from her household schedule. She couldn't leave the dishes unwashed for an hour, take time out to watch a soap or make a personal call to a friend in the middle of the day without turning into a "nervous wreck." "I constantly fret and worry about what I should be doing," she told us, "or what I should have done. I can never just sit and enjoy the moment." First of all, we pointed out to Andrea how useless these emotions were. All the worrying in the world never washed a single dish, nor did the same amount of guilt clean the bathroom that "should have been done yesterday." These self-destructive emotions changed nothing in the real world and robbed Andrea of her peace of mind. They certainly didn't make her a better person or add to her "goodness" in any way. Next, we asked Andrea to write down the consequences of the behaviors she felt so guilty about. What happened if there were dirty dishes in the sink a whole afternoon? What were the consequences of her taking an hour off to watch "General Hospital"? What was the result of chatting on the phone with a friend in the shank of her work day? In most cases, Andrea came to realize that there were no real consequences at all to the things she was worrying and feeling so guilty over. "The worst thing I could come up with," she said, "was I might end up having to do something later than I normally would." The sky won't fall on your head if you deviate from the rules that seem so natural to you. You only think it will. To prove us right, why don't you try keeping a journal of the consequences of the behaviors you feel guilty over like Andrea did? We think you'll be pleasantly surprised.

* * *

- Never enjoy the moment?
- Feel yourself an ingrate whenever you have your way over a man?
- Believe yourself one hundred percent responsible for a divorce, a bad marriage, or an unhappy romance—no matter what the situation?
- Hear the reprimanding voice of your mother or father (even if they have been dead for years) whenever you go against a rule they taught you as a child?

Cleo, 41, had been unhappily married to Teddy for 12 years, and during this time she always had done exactly what Teddy and her parents told her to do to keep the relationship going. They were continually expecting favors and taking advantage of her in countless small ways. Cleo's mother became very upset when Cleo's "baby" sister, Audrey, 35, announced her wedding plans to Dak, a man the whole family, including Teddy, thought was an opportunist who only wanted to get Audrey's house and savings. When Cleo told Teddy and her mother that she only hoped Audrey would be happy, they both set their jaws in disapproval. We already had schooled Cleo on how to deal with such a situation, and she handled herself beautifully when she asked, "Is that look to punish me for being bad and not agreeing with you?" Once it was clear to Teddy and Cleo's mother that Cleo was on to their manipulative behavior and could see it was only a means of getting what they wanted, they both stopped doing it. It had lost its effectiveness. Cleo had stood her ground and refused to let either her mother or her husband make her feel guilty. No matter what other people do, the ultimate responsibility for what you feel is yours. We know you'll be much happier if you choose to respond positively with calm and self-control.

- Hold yourself responsible for the well-being of others? Think or allow yourself to believe someone's upset, inconvenience or even physical illness is your responsibility?
- Worry about going to Hell, or not going to Heaven because you don't follow everyone's rules to the letter?

- Have a nagging sense of discomfort whenever you see a squad car, police or prison movie, even though you have done nothing wrong?
- Punish yourself by overeating whenever tempted to confront the system? First you think, "I'd sure like to call that man I met this morning." Then comes the anxiety for considering slipping out of the feminine role of the system. And you eat to buffer yourself from that anxiety.

Whenever Delia, 38, deviated from what her husband, Saul, 52, wanted her to do, he would clutch his chest and say, "You're giving me a heart attack! I can't take this stress. You're killing me!" Delia took full responsibility for Saul's health to the point her sleepless nights were filled with nightmarish visions of being cast into the abyss, stricken from the book of life and devoured by the beast every time she "caused" Saul even the slightest inconvenience. Her heart would thump whenever she saw a policeman, she was so certain her "evil nature" would be recognized and punished. Naturally—the police force had other things on their minds than a "good girl" displeasing her husband and since no one was about to punish her, Delia punished herself by overeating, until she was 40 pounds overweight. We told Delia that no one was responsible for Saul's upset but Saul. She couldn't give him a heart attack. Only Saul could do that to himself. However, since Delia was so determined to punish herself, we suggested that she get organized about it. Together, we scheduled three ten-minute periods a day as "suffering times." During these periods, Delia was to tell herself how terrible she was for not doing what her husband said. The magnification of her self-punishing behavior allowed her to see how really ridiculous it was. The scheduling allowed her to see how much control she had over it. Once she learned that self-punishment was both ridiculous *and* under her control, she stopped doing it. Delia no longer feels guilty for Saul's emotions and understands that they are *his* responsibility!

- Feel uneasy about sexual desires and fantasies?

- Have overwhelming guilt if you want to argue with your father or mother?
- Harbor obsessive guilt and worry whenever things go bad in your life, wondering, "What have I done to deserve this?" and believing that the right things happen to good girls and calamities befall the other kind?
- Always wait to be punished, a feeling that the ax is going to fall any minute, almost hoping it will so you can atone and stop worrying about it? This is a very self-destructive behavior because you actually seek out punishment in hopes that once it comes you will no longer have to worry about it. Unfortunately, guilt and worry are self-generating, and no amount of suffering is ever enough to eliminate them.

Cloris, 30, came to us with a terrible case of acne brought on by severe stress. When we asked her what was wrong in her life, she said, "Nothing. That's just the problem. Things are going *too* good. My marriage to Conrad is wonderful. My children are bright and healthy. I love my work as a lab technician." It took us several weeks to uncover that Cloris was feeling guilty because she found herself attracted to other men. Cloris believed that good things come to good girls and bad things come to the other kind, and she felt she was living on borrowed time. She knew punishment was on its way and she wanted to get it over with. So she *created* it in the form of her own skin disorder. We told Cloris that she probably wouldn't be as disapproved of as she surmised if she'd just air out her feelings. In a session with Cloris and Conrad together, we were able to get her to bring up her occasional sexual fantasies of other men and, to her surprise and relief, Conrad replied, "That's only natural. Just don't *do* anything about them!" Cloris was bringing all her unhappiness on herself because of *her expectations of other people's expectations!* Clear the air. Find out what people *really* expect of you. *Then* decide whether or not you want to meet them or deviate. In *any* event, don't waste your time and energy worrying or feeling guilty. It's totally self-destructive and never accomplishes anything.

• • •

We've now taken a brief look at what happens when you punish yourself in the form of guilt and worry. You can see that believing you deserve to suffer actually *causes* you to suffer. The only rule breaking you need concern yourself with are the deviations from the rules you make for your own happiness. Give yourself a hardy pat on the back for deserting the rules of others to travel the road to your own truth.

Why We Punish Ourselves

Your rewards for self-punishment generally involve atonement. You think that if you punish yourself then men will forgive you for disobeying them. This way you erroneously believe you are beating them to the punch, so to speak.

- Penance. Sufficient suffering in the form of guilt and worry can serve as penance, a way to cancel out all former wrongdoing. The problem lies in thinking that self-abasement could be the first step to self-improvement.
- Pity. Nothing wins pity faster than suffering. But nothing is more damaging to your self-image. Choosing to experience guilt and worry will cause you to think less of yourself.
- Pardon. Penance and pity lead to a sense of pardon and redemption.
- Suffering keeps you from expending energy and doing anything. It is easier to consume the present with guilt and worry over past rules broken and present ones yet to come than to make rules of your own.
- Suffering saves you from risking the dangers involved in change. Once the price of breaking a rule becomes too great, you may feel you have license to go back to the old system. The new rules just weren't "worth" it.
- Guilt and worry provide scapegoats for other sources

of unhappiness that are totally unrelated to it.

- Suffering sometimes lets you break the rules without losing anyone's approval. Even though you have left the accepted course, by worrying and feeling guilty you show the appropriate others that you know right from wrong and are trying to remedy yourself.

- Feeling guilt and worrying allows you to avoid the struggle of asserting yourself.

- You can label yourself "good" by suffering. The myths of our culture proclaim that "suffering builds character." Guilt and worry, two forms of self-punishment, contribute to the suffering necessary for martyrdom. You may find yourself a saint—but it will be at the price of satisfaction.

You can beat this reward system for self-punishment. You don't have to suffer. Give yourself unconditional forgiveness. We have a new plan to free you.

Strategies for Freeing Yourself from Self-Induced Suffering

The time has now come for you to say goodbye to guilt and worry—to take positive action. The strategies below will help you to wipe clean your need to cause your own suffering. Joy is on your horizon.

- Recognize like Andrea, who was concerned about deviating from her household routine, that guilt will not change the past. It cannot contribute to your "goodness" in any way.

- Try to understand, as Andrea did, that worry will not change your future. It cannot make you a better person, either. Worry does not mean planning: It refers to dwelling on projected negative outcomes with no intent to *do* anything about them.

- Ask yourself, as we told Leah to do, what all your present suffering is helping you to avoid. This is vitally important and may mean many hours of deep thinking. Do not be afraid, though, for only by working on your problems can you eliminate the need for guilt and worry.

- Accept the fact that some people are not going to like it when you make and follow your own rules. Realize, as we helped Chance to, that they are going to need a period of adjustment. In most cases, however, they will come around. Researchers in social psychology have long been plagued by the problem of reconciling differences in culture, behavior and genetics. The world is becoming smaller every day, and more and more, diverse populations of people are being forced to live harmoniously together. Studies show that you can spend years attempting to educate varying peoples to the beliefs of others without any positive results. *However,* once the peoples of different beliefs are forced to coexist, by proximity they soon adjust. You will seldom get someone to change by cajoling and coaxing. But change your behavior, and he will adapt.

- Keep a journal. Write exactly when, why and with whom you agonize for making your own rules. This will give you a heightened awareness of this particular problem. Are you really as opposed in the freedom to make your own decisions as you believe yourself to be? If so, define and isolate your "opponents." Recognizing them is half the battle.

- Record the real consequences of your behavior. What happens when you choose your own guidelines for life? Like Andrea, we think you'll be pleasantly surprised to find there are no real consequences to doing the things you worry about or feel guilty over.

- Tell people if they try to manipulate you with guilt as Cleo told her husband and mother. If a spouse gives you a dirty look every time you get home from the part-time job that you love, ask him, "Is that look to punish me?" Once he's made aware of his behavior, it's amazing how rapidly it usually decreases. You are helping to give him a heightened awareness, alerting him to behaviors he probably never saw in himself before.

- Do something that even you consider deviant and refuse to feel "bad" about it. Try ordering for the man when he takes you to dinner or refuse to enter a room before him. If he disapproves, ask him exactly *why* you can't order for him or he can't enter the room before you. If he answers that these things are not socially approved, that you are deviating from custom, laugh and say, "Good! The road less traveled is the most exciting." Then *reward* yourself by telling yourself you are being adventurous, blazing new trails. Get used to blatant, open, harmless deviation. Make a list of silly rules of etiquette that reinforce the roles of men and women. Then deliberately violate them. Stand when a man enters the room or ask men to get you coffee. This exercise can be a lot of fun and plays down the "sacredness" of the rules.

- Try the new strategy that worked so well with Delia in getting her to see how ridiculous it was to punish herself for her husband's bad reactions when only he was responsible for his emotions. Give yourself ten minutes, three times a day, as "suffering times," periods of deliberate self-flagellation for going against the rules of others. This concentrated effort may allow you to see the uselessness of self-punishment. It may also help you to see that if you have the power to bring on this behavior, you have the power to eliminate it!

- Be kind, loving and respectful to your parents, but understand that they can make mistakes, too. Their power is not absolute. It's all right to go against their advice; it does not mean that you don't love them— just that you are different from them.

- Realize, as Susan came to in going against what her father thought was best for her, that *error* is the reason most bad things happen. If you take the wrong lover, make a poor choice in marriage, a bad investment, it is not because somebody up there hates you. It's because you're human and subject to human error. Try to learn to forgive yourself.

- Make "deviation" a positive word in your vocabulary, as we taught Kitty to do when she left the boredom of her present job security to create something much more exciting. The road less traveled often leads to new, exciting lands.
- Be proud of your ability to turn away from the Establishment. It takes strength and courage and conviction to change. Give yourself credit for it.

The above are only a few beginning suggestions to rid you of guilt and worry over breaking loose from the male system. Be good to yourself and follow the path that suits you best. You will like yourself a whole lot more. And the surprising thing is that others will like you a whole lot more too! In Leah's words, "I finally realized that by worrying and feeling guilty all the time I was not only punishing myself, but setting myself up for others to punish me as well. It was almost as though others took my glum attitude as a signal I had done something wrong. When I cheered up, they treated me like someone who deserved to be cheerful!"

11

"Anger Is Unfeminine"

> I have the personality of a meek "goody-goody"
> while I'm really seething with rage within.
>
> Pam W.
> letter

Our first contact with Pam was a letter she wrote to us describing herself as a "forty-two-year-old housewife who was mad as hell and wasn't going to take it anymore." Her pent-up rage was giving her high blood pressure and her doctor said she was due for a cardiac arrest if she didn't "learn to control her anger." In our first session together we were able to determine that the primary source of Pam's anger was "selfish sex" in her relationship with her husband, Dexter. "Dex only wants it when he wants it," Pam fumed. "Well I showed him. I won't even let him touch me anymore."

The problem wasn't so much that Pam needed to "control" her anger as learn to *express* it constructively. We explained to her that while not being angry is the best state, you must *deal* with the anger you do have in a way that will produce a *positive* outcome. "Denying your husband sex," we explained to Pam, "will only result in your both being angry. Rather than trying to get even, strengthen your intention to get what you want. Initiate lovemaking when *you* want it. If he doesn't always respond, don't let that stop you. Continue initiating and you'll be surprised how many times you'll be able to change his mood." Once Pam felt free to keep pursuing her desires in spite of Dexter's occasional resistance, her anger subsided. The outcome was positive. They both ended up with more satisfying sex in their marriage. You should always *do* something about your anger. And what you do should produce a *positive* outcome.

In our last chapter, we talked about how the various reactions and feelings that go along with being a "good girl" can cause tremendous, and unending, guilt and worry. In this chapter, we'll talk about its counterpart: anger. How many of you have felt angry because you *couldn't* do everything that was expected of you or because you wanted to do something that "good girls" weren't supposed to do? But we'll bet that even if you were angry, most of you didn't show it. Why? Because anger is not feminine. "Good girls" don't show it.

Not being able to *do* something about your anger is a terrible bind to be in. Not only does it prevent you from taking constructive action, the anger turns inward to eat away at you, producing stress and disease. Other times it shows up as displaced. You do not allow yourself to deal with the source of your anger, so instead it appears in inappropriate situations. Someone may ask for one too many things at the office, such as to borrow your pen, and you explode. A passenger accidentally jostles you on the subway and you intentionally jab him or her back. You decide a car in front of you is going too slow and you lay on the horn, convinced he is deliberately trying to make you late. None of these incidents would provoke your anger if you weren't already on the brink, if you weren't already suppressing so much anger you are ready to burst.

So, since anger, aggressiveness, and assertiveness are traits reserved for men, the only way you can get any of your needs met is by bending the rules and using tactics commonly labeled "passive aggressive." These are the manipulations for which women have become notorious. While you may not be openly punished for "bending" a rule, you still won't get by with it. You'll probably be penalized with name-calling and labeling. Men are afraid that strong women may stand up to them and stop meeting all their needs on command, so they invent less than flattering terms for these so-called masculine women.

In this chapter we'll show you how to express your anger directly and in such a way that the results are positive. You'll learn the importance of making the first move and how to accept your anger without guilt. Most important, you'll see that anger is neither masculine nor feminine, simply human—and used correctly, it can be the driving force to vastly improve your life!

How This Idea Got Started

"I realize now," Pam later told us, "that Dexter told me women shouldn't get mad, that it was unfeminine, just so I wouldn't give him any static and he could get what he wanted!" Since women, like Pam, are not supposed to direct their anger openly, they often turn it inward on themselves to get high blood pressure or spells of depression. The worst part about it is that not only is this behavior nonthreatening and perfectly permissible, it is often thoroughly encouraged. "I remember telling Dex once," Pam said, "that I was so upset that I got headaches when we couldn't have sex regularly. You know what he said? 'At least you don't get mad about it.' Can you believe that? He was actually encouraging me to do nothing about my anger but make myself sick!" When anger is turned inward, it serves as another form of self-generating self-punishment much like guilt and worry. When you displace your anger from its cause, and turn it inward, you perpetuate the problem that is keeping you down. The anger that potentially could eliminate what is bothering you is held in check until it destroys or weakens you instead.

One of our clients, Gladys, was suffering from a terrible problem with rage. Gladys's main complaint was her extra weight: She was nearly a hundred pounds overweight. When we began discussing the weight problem, it soon became evident that Gladys was eating to punish herself. "The madder I get at myself, the more I eat," she said. For twenty "thankless" years she had slaved in a large shipping department in an unfulfilling position at lower management. She felt totally abused by the male personnel. They took her for granted, expected her to work overtime without advance notice, never appreciated her and shirked their own responsibilities by giving her their share of the work. The harder she tried, the more she was taken advantage of by those who wouldn't pull their full share. Gladys was painfully conscientious and even though she was well aware that she was criminally overworked, she took the stance, "Somebody's got to do it."

Gladys was paying a high price for being such a "good girl." Not only was she working harder than anyone else, she felt a great, unexpressed anger toward her tormentors that was coming back to her. It had no place else to go. She therefore attacked herself in pitiful binges of overeating. On occasion, the pent-up hostility was displaced onto her female colleagues whom she subconsciously hated for being as weak and ineffectual as she was. She lost her friends and was avoided by most of the women staff.

After some time with us, Gladys began to see that the reason she failed to stand up to the men at work was that she felt inadequate about her femininity. And her first insight came when she admitted that she felt it would be unladylike to raise her voice or express anger in any form to the men in her department. "They'll think I'm some kind of monster if I talk back to them," she said. She was not as concerned about blowing her stack to other women. Her identity, after all, was dependent upon how men, not women, saw her. Our first strategy was to change her definition of femininity from characteristics dictated by men to simply being herself. She *was* a woman. By definition, whatever she did was feminine. If she yelled at a man for mistreating her, that behavior was feminine. She thus resolved to express her anger toward men on the job. This usually took the form of simply telling a man that certain specifics of his behavior were making her angry. There was no need to yell, fume or turn red, not that there was anything unfeminine about those behaviors either; they just weren't particularly effective and didn't feel good. Once Gladys began revealing that particular conditions made her angry, she found that most men were willing to adapt to accommodate her, and instead of overeating and being angry with her friends, she found release and fulfillment in being herself. She is now thinner and happier, and she knows that no man has the right to tell her what she should feel. "It feels so good," she reported the last time we saw her, "to know it's OK to let someone know you're angry . . . especially to let a man know."

Whatever you as a woman feel is "feminine." Anger is every bit as feminine an emotion as love and nurturance. Accept this feeling in yourself and don't be afraid to let others see you express it constructively. *Use* it to make positive change in your life.

Passive Aggressive: "Bending" the Rules

While Gladys turned her anger onto herself, many women take a less self-destructive, albeit not the most effective, route and show their anger outwardly but in indirect ways. Since only men are permitted to show anger, assertion and aggression openly, many women resort to actions psychologists term "passive aggressive" in order to have their way. These are indirect methods of getting around rules without blatantly opposing them. They usually involve deliberate "sins of omission" in which a woman bucks the system through inaction rather than action. For example, even though she stays at home, she may grossly neglect the housework or, while always obedient, she is unresponsive during sex or, although she does what she is told at work, many of the necessary details she should do without being told remain undone.

Even though passive resistance won India its freedom from England and many a labor union higher wages for its workers, it will not help women; it only makes life tougher for everyone. That's because each of you is dealing with an individual problem that must be handled in its own way.

More important is the necessity of learning to express your anger directly. For anger to be effective it must be expressed in action. You must learn to change, not bend, the rules. The action must be positive and constructive and the change for the better. Anger is a tremendous force—an impetus for progress. Your anger at disease, ignorance, poverty, even death, can raise you ever higher. Express your anger at the blocks along the route to your personal success. Aim the energy of your anger directly at its source and destroy it, not by inaction and passivity but by pure action! In the sections that follow, we'll show you exactly how to do this!

The Importance of Making the First Move

As we've already discussed, anger is intense displeasure at something that stands in your way or that you feel is unjust. This feeling is good because it provides the driving force to break down the obstructions.

But while asserting yourself is terrific, it is not enough. You can make others understand that you are angry, but you will not become independent until you are also ready to turn your ideas into action. To do this you must be willing to make the first move. This is your key to power. Defensive anger can protect you, but only offensive anger can create and bring something new into your life. For your anger to be constructive, you must use it to forcefully take the initiative.

One of our clients, Alice, came to us with a lot of concerns. She was 36 years old and miserable in her marriage, but she felt that she could neither change things nor leave her husband, Reggie. "It wouldn't be right," she said. To complicate matters, she was unhappy that she had never been able to have a family because her severe tension caused her vaginal muscles to contract whenever she and her husband tried to have intercourse. Her rage had developed steadily over the years fueled by her husband's drinking and gambling problems. She would very much like to have a family and a good sexual relationship, but she shudders at the thought of attacking her husband with divorce papers. Instead, she grew older using passive aggressive tactics such as poor sex and long sulks, hoping in time *he* would leave her. Alice knew that unless she changed, it was more than probable that she would never have children. Her "femininity" was preventing her from making the first move to her own happiness. "You must first forgive yourself for being angry," we told her. "Being angry doesn't make you a bad person. It's your body's way of telling you that you have to *do* something to make you feel better.'' Once Alice was able to accept her anger as a valid part of her, she was able to make the first move so necessary to her happiness and leave Reggie.

It's good to feel anger if you *do* something positive about it. This entails your taking action and not waiting for others to act first. Exercise your power and make the first move!

Anger Versus Rage: Accepting Your Anger without Guilt

It's important that you be able to distinguish between the emotions of anger and rage. The difference is control. Rage is anger out of control. Anger can be used as a force for constructive action and removing blocks. Rage, on the other hand, like all uncontrolled emotions, is not only wasteful of energy and unproductive, it can often be dangerous. Many women equate anger with rage and are thus afraid to experience the first for fear the latter will also be present. However, there is nothing wrong with anger, no need to feel guilt for expressing it or fear of being destroyed by it. You have the license to show anger to your foes and exercise control of your own emotions.

Martha, who supplemented the family income by selling cosmetics door to door, saw us about a miserable marriage. Martha was in her 40s and had been married for over twenty years. As we got into the problem, it became apparent that the chief source of tension was her husband, Pete's, infidelity. "My friends always said I was overreacting," she explained in confusion, "that men are like that . . . but I just can't live that way anymore." We asked if she had spoken to Pete about his unfaithfulness and she confessed, "I can't. I'm afraid if I say one thing, all hell will break loose. If I get started I might end up doing something awful!" Twenty years of bottled-up anger at the male system and nothing had changed. Through a period of supportive counseling, Martha was able to see the need for her to tell Pete how angry she was over his infidelity. We told her she needn't fear losing control if she would begin by simply *labeling* her anger at Pete. Whenever the subject came up, she was to say "I feel really angry now" and then point out to him what he was doing to make her feel that way and what he could do to make her feel better. When Pete saw that Martha was truly upset by his infidelity he chose to be faithful.

Martha and her marriage is a classic case of holding in anger for fear it will come out as rage. She had stagnated in the paralysis of overcontrol out of terror she would lose *all* control. She chose to say nothing rather than risk saying too much. But Martha learned that saying nothing, damming up your anger, never makes things better. It only keeps you in a constant state of intense displeasure. To improve your life, you have to express your anger constructively in the form of attacking its source. This is not to say you should try to be angry, but that you should *use* it properly if it exists. True, it can be an unpleasant emotion, one you might feel better without, but the only way to get rid of it is first to face it! Use anger's energy to make changes. Anger is the most positive sign a therapist looks for in lifting depression. It shows that the stagnating apathy is gone and you care enough to feel again. Anger used productively is always good! You just have to learn how to face it.

Some Examples of Denying Anger

Now that we've discussed some of the places your desire to hold in your anger comes from, let's look at the shapes damming up this emotion can take. There are many forms. Here are some of the things you may do if you believe that anger is unfeminine.

- Show pent-up anger by kicking the dog, slamming the drawer, pounding your fist against the wall, screaming at your children.
- Always feel on edge, taking life too seriously, fighting tears, feeling strung out and nervous because of unvented anger.
- Not able to laugh at the funny, absurd things around you.

- Experience long periods of silence at home or with colleagues at work.

Ellen, a 26-year-old executive secretary to Harvey, a vice-president in a large architectural firm, found herself "going off the deep end." "I don't know what's wrong with me," she told us. "I get so angry in traffic I could kill anyone who gets in my way. If someone drums their fingers on the lunch counter I get visions of chopping them off with an ax. If someone accidentally jostles me on the street or in the office I want to slap their teeth out. I just seem to hate everybody. I even kicked my cat because I tripped over her trying to answer the telephone. I jump a foot if there's any unexpected sound. I'm constantly on the verge of tears. People at work say I need to lighten up, but I can't. Nothing seems funny anymore. So I just grit my teeth and bear it."

A little talking revealed that Ellen was angry over an expectation Harvey had of her that she couldn't bring herself to meet. Harvey expected her to take evening business dinners with him and prospective clients at fancy restaurants; he also expected her to accept social invitations from these clients "if the account was big enough." None of Harvey's male staff were ever asked to accompany him on these "meetings," and Ellen was feeling manipulated beyond the call of duty. Instead of dealing with her anger, she was letting it build, and we were afraid she might end up losing her job when her emotional dam inevitably burst. We taught Ellen three steps to effectively handle her anger: (1) she was to calmly tell Harvey she was angry with him; (2) she was to tell him what he did she was angry at. In this case his expecting to mix her business with his client's pleasure; (3) she was to inform him what he could do to eliminate her anger—stop inviting her to evening dinner with clients. Harvey protested, saying it was all part of the business. Ellen didn't get sucked in by arguing with him. She simply calmly repeated that this "part of the business" was making her angry and what Harvey could do about it. At the time, Harvey didn't give in. However, he never asked Ellen to another evening "business meeting," and her anger, once it was expressed constructively, subsided.

- Fear that if you say anything at all about what is

bothering you it will end in a fit of uncontrolled rage.
- Overreact, responding to situations not with just the amount of displeasure appropriate to the occasion, but with the addition of the vast reservoir of anger you are currently carrying around.
- Lie a lot for convenience (the dishonesty of denying your anger spills over into other facets of your relationship).
- Refuse to argue, a situation where you might be tempted to show anger (this can be deadly in any important relationship).
- Feel hatred because you're not able to clear the air by venting your anger.

Elsie, a 36-year-old housewife, said she hated her husband, Oliver, so much she "could kill him." Her anger toward him had been building for fifteen years, ever since he slighted her brother at their wedding, and she had a list of grievances against Oliver that could have filled a file cabinet. Elsie's feelings of dislike had become almost pathological because she had never expressed them constructively, never let Oliver know how she felt about all these "injustices." Instead, Elsie found herself constantly lying about her true feelings, saying "I love you" and "How nice" when inside she was boiling. The lid of her feelings was so tight she refused to argue for fear they might explode. Refusing to discuss important issues further contributed to the dishonesty of Elsie and Oliver's relationship. Since Elsie was not allowing herself to express anger at its source—Oliver—it was leaking out in bizarre outbursts to her friends and children. There was also a surprisingly large monthly bill for broken household items. From our discussions together, we learned that Elsie's mother, a self-effacing, submissive menial laborer, had instilled in her from childhood that "only men get angry." In trying to live up to her mother's ideal of womanhood, Elsie was ruining her health and her marriage. When she changed her definition of "feminine" to include the positive expression of anger to remedy what was bothering her, Elsie was able to tell Oliver how she was feeling and what he could do to help her.

- Gossip and backstab, two typically "feminine" behaviors, where, rather than expressing the unladylike emotion of anger to its source, you choose to say terrible things behind his back.

- Feel that nobody likes you because the guilt that you have over the "unfeminine" anger makes you feel like a terrible person, unworthy of love.
- Distrust others because the concealed anger in your own face to the world is a fraud.

Ellie Mae, 23, a clerk in a stationery store, was furious at her supervisor, Tammy, for all the "unnecessary restrictions" that were being placed upon her. To get even, Ellie Mae presented an angelic facade, all the time backstabbing Tammy with comments to other staff such as, "She sure gets off on her power trip" or "She's too incompetent to do any of this work herself so she tells us to do it." Ellie Mae was also the first to relay any dirt she could learn about Tammy, such as broken love affairs, expired credit cards, bank overdrafts —anything to discredit her. Unfortunately, Ellie Mae only came to hate herself for carrying around such vicious feelings, and since she was being so two-faced, she started distrusting the friendship of the rest of the staff. She wondered if they were as dishonest about their feelings toward her as she was regarding her anger at Tammy.

We told Ellie Mae that she could eliminate her need for backstabbing and gossip, feel better about herself and start trusting others again, if she would do just one thing: express her anger to its source by telling Tammy exactly what unnecessary restrictions were making her angry. "I can't do that," Ellie Mae gasped. "She's my boss." "That doesn't give her the right to make you miserable," we answered. "Nor does it mean you can't constructively express your anger toward her." Ellie Mae had been raised in a strict lower-middle-class family where you were never to "question an authority." We explained that there was an enormous difference between questioning someone's authority and telling them how their behavior made you feel. Her first strategy to deal with anger was to make a list of specifics, the job restrictions she was angry at Tammy for. When the list was completed, we asked whether she'd discussed any of the items with Tammy, and she hadn't. "I didn't want her to know I was angry," Ellie Mae confessed. We answered by saying, "It's good to let people know how you feel if you do it positively." Then we looked at the list. At the top was "I'm not allowed to leave work until 5:30 when I could easily make up the time by taking a shorter lunch break." We asked Ellie Mae to tell Tammy how this rule made her feel and how Tammy could help by letting her make up the time at noon. The result was good. Tammy respected Ellie Mae's feelings. "I want my workers to be happy," she smiled. "They do a better job that way." Ellie Mae had learned to use her anger positively to eliminate its source and make her life easier.

- Show meanness and deliberately try to hurt people to pay them back for the pain they caused you rather than honestly expressing anger to produce a change.
- Smile *all* the time and speak in soft, sugary tones.
- Never openly object to anything that *should* make you angry. If a man stands you up, talks down to you, cancels an appointment at the last minute, doesn't call you for days, brings home unexpected guests, never gets home till the food is cold, forgets your birthday and anniversary, raves about everyone's cooking but yours, fails to notice a new haircut or outfit, starts snoring immediately after making love, never takes you out, makes you cook on your vacation, ignores the children, expects you to continually pick up after him like a mother hen . . . you just smile as if it doesn't bother you. But inside, the anger keeps welling up.

Florence, a 26-year-old dental technician, was referred to us by her employer, Bernard, for stress reduction. Bernard told us by phone, "I really don't know what's the matter with her. She's one of the most qualified employees I've ever had, yet she acts so strange sometimes . . . doing little mean things to annoy me like cracking her gum when she knows I can't stand it or playing her radio too loud during lunch break. . . . Once I even caught her putting salt in my coffee. Yet she never seems to be mad at me, always smiling and sweet-talking. I don't think I've heard her complain about a single thing in the five years she's been working for me."

We asked Bernard how Florence reacted during the times

she should have been angry, as when things went wrong in the office, and he said she seemed to smile even more brightly then but it was "an eerie sort of grin, as if her jaw were set in determination not to react any other way." We learned from Florence that while she was upset by many things at work, she didn't want to hurt Bernard's feelings and risk making him think badly of her for seeing her angry. She didn't think this emotion was "appropriate" at work.

We told Florence that there was an appropriate way to express her anger in *any* situation. The important first step was to let Bernard know when she was upset so they could work together on remedying the situation. However, Florence was so deeply entrenched in her belief that anger was inappropriate and unfeminine, she continued to deny these feelings on the job. Finally we asked Bernard to help us out by using her telltale grin as a cue to tell her whenever he thought she was angry with him. Catching her in the act got Florence to see how much she really was denying her feelings and helped to draw them out so she and Bernard could then go on to pinpointing what he was doing to cause these feelings and what he could do to change. As it turned out, Florence's biggest irritation occurred when Bernard changed patients' schedules without informing her first. This was readily made right once it was brought out. In less than a month Florence was greatly relaxed at work due to the fact that she was now calmly revealing her anger to its source. "I was so afraid to let anyone know I was angry," she said, "I couldn't even admit it to myself. If you hadn't told Bernard to call me on these feelings, I'd probably still be denying my anger to myself today."

The Rewards for Not Showing Anger

As we've been saying, constructively expressing your anger begins with understanding why you bottle it up or displace it in the first place. Let's go over some of the payoffs for holding your anger inside so that you can begin to work toward expressing it properly.

•　　•　　•

- Not expressing anger contributes to the picture of sainthood.
- Winning approval and keeping sense of identity remains intact. Showing anger at the rules might make a man mad at you.
- The anger might work, and you might get your own way, but then you will have to expend the energy to decide what it is you desire. Figuring what you want out of life is work. It's always easier to let someone else tell you what you *should* want.
- Not showing anger keeps attention off of you and allows you to reinforce your low profile.
- It allows others to get their own way, making you feel more virtuous. You tell yourself that you are helping others by suppressing anger at the choices they make, even though those choices are harmful to you.
- You can indulge in endless self-pity because nobody understands you. How could they if they are never allowed to see how you truly feel?
- It validates the first program, "There is something wrong with me." An angry woman may feel, "There must be something wrong with me, or else I wouldn't feel so angry." The syndrome is a perfect self-feeding, self-reinforcing system for making you believe you are in the wrong.
- Not only do you retain male approval by not channeling anger to fight the system, you keep the approval of other women as well. Many "good girls" are particularly threatened by assertive, aggressive women who are not afraid to be honest with their feelings. They have a vested interest in "goodness" and do not like to see their choices invalidated by another woman who has created a better system for herself.

All the rewards for not expressing anger keep you static and prevent you from growing. They hold you within the status quo, the system of the others toward whom you're afraid to express your anger. Nothing is worth the price of this imprisonment. Break free! Use the energy of your anger to take you where you want to be!

Some Techniques for Expressing Anger Positively

One of the most basic points we've tried to point out in this chapter is that anger is human, and therefore it must be as "feminine" as it is "masculine." Everyone feels anger. But women especially have to examine the forms in which they show it. To effect positive change, you have to express your anger openly, honestly, and constructively. Here are some ways to positively express anger.

- Tell yourself, as we told Pam, that while not being angry is the easiest state to deal with, you have to express the anger that you feel. It is a hundredfold better than damming it up to make you ill, nervous and on the edge.
- Eliminate anger entirely by allowing yourself to take action against the rules that are provoking this destructive emotion. If you're angry, as Pam was, because there is too much "selfish sex" in your relationship, i.e., you only have it when he wants it, initiate lovemaking yourself when you want.
- As we taught Gladys to do in the shipping department, if a man does something you don't like, tell him so. If there is something you want, ask for it. If you are angry because men do most of the talking in your business meetings, speak up. Clock your time on the floor to make certain you are getting equal time.
- Show your anger, as we told Elsie to do toward Oliver, and label it clearly so that those around you can better understand the consequences of their behavior and learn to act to reduce the chances of angering you again.
- Don't delude yourself by telling yourself you are not angry when you are. It's very important to get in touch with these feelings and put them out for others to see. Really get in touch with these feelings at a physical level. Feel the physical sensations your body is experiencing. For ten minutes, turn off the thoughts in

your head, take a deep breath, and focus on the tightness in your abdomen, the difficulty in swallowing, the ache in your chest. "Feeling-focus," as we call it, allows you to realize how important it is for you to get the anger out so that you don't make yourself sick.

- Ask others to help you, as we asked Bernard to assist Florence. Instruct them to point out when you appear angry so that you can express it appropriately there on the spot at the time it is being felt.

- Tell people *exactly* what it is that is making you angry so that they can change *specific* pieces of their behavior. You may want to make up a list of these specifics as Ellie Mae did to change the behavior of her supervisor, Tammy. Explain these to them, both when you are angry and at later dates to reinforce the lesson, and let them know you were not only speaking out of anger, but really meant they should work at change.

- Begin expressing anger, the way we taught Martha to do, by labeling it. Say, "I feel really angry now." Then point out what behavior in the other person you have chosen to react to with anger. Ask him to eliminate or modify his disturbing behavior.

- Forgive yourself for being angry as Alice needed to do before leaving Reggie. While anger may not be a desired state, the experience and expression of it does not make you a "bad" person. Only behavior can be labeled "bad" and then only if it produces a negative result in the form of hurting another person.

- Tell someone precisely what he can *do,* as Ellen told her boss, Harvey, to dispel your anger. Sometimes labeling his anger-producing behavior is not enough for him to know how to correct it. A client of ours told her lover she was angry because he neglected her. He tried to remedy the situation by seeing her more often, but she still felt neglected. Finally, he asked her, "What can I *do* to make you feel less neglected?" It wasn't till then she realized she really wanted him to marry her. When they did talk about the possibilities of getting married, her anger subsided. Three steps lead to eliminating anger-producing blocks: (1) let the person know you are angry; (2) tell him what he did to cause you to react this way; (3) inform him of what he can *do* to appease your anger.

- Refrain, as Florence did with her boss, from worrying that you will hurt someone's feelings if he knows you are angry or you argue with him. You can easily follow the above three steps and be nice about it. In the long run, you are doing you both a favor by saving your relationship. Psychologist Joyce Brothers expressed the need to talk about anger when she said, "Anger repressed can poison a relationship as surely as the cruelest words." It's better to pass a sharp word here and there than to face the explosive consequences of repressed anger. Nothing you could say could be as devastating as that. Columnist Ann Landers, in *Ann Landers Says Truth Is Strange . . .* , gives advice on the importance of argument or battle in maintaining a healthy marriage.

  All married couples should learn the art of battle as they should learn the art of making love. Good battle is objective and honest—never vicious or cruel. Good battle is healthy and constructive, and brings to a marriage the principle of equal partnership.

Holding in your anger is dishonest. What's more, there can be no true equality as long as you deny this genuine emotion.

Everything we've talked about in this chapter points to the fact that you are what you do. The more you come to show your anger to produce positive change, the more comfortable you will become with it. In time, as you continue to develop rules that work for you, there will be fewer sources left from which anger can spring. And you will be much happier for it as well! As Florence put it, "Bernard no longer has to point out to me when he thinks I'm angry because I no longer am. Letting him know what he was doing to make me mad changed his behavior. Now there's nothing to be angry about!"

12

"Independence Is Dangerous"

Seems like my whole life I've always been afraid.
The question is: Afraid of what?

LINDA C.
radio-show call-in

Linda, a 30-year old, single social worker, told us that her whole life she'd always done what others wanted because she was afraid of them. "What are you afraid they'll do?" we asked her. "Fight if I don't give them what they want, I guess," Linda answered. "It takes two to fight," we replied. We then asked Linda to try something new. "Next time someone wants you to do something that you don't want to do, simply don't respond. If they lash out, make accusations, try to get you into an argument, refuse to get sucked in. Independently do what you want regardless of what others expect. Skip fighting or being drawn into their argument. You'll be delighted to discover there's really nothing to fear at all. Except the danger of believing there is."

Only dependence can be dangerous. Anything that keeps you from thinking on your own can lead to a life that benefits someone else rather than yourself. On the other hand, anytime you think for yourself, you have achieved independence. You can be independent in *any* situation. Whether just married, living away from home or your family for the first time, starting a new job, having a baby, going to a new state—the need for independent thinking is vital. Independence, like home, is a state of mind. A state in which you find your own answers rather than relying on others to make your decisions for you. We are all exposed to so many influences daily—from newscasters, ads, schools, government, family—that it is often easier to give into these pressures than face the imagined dire consequences of asserting your own independence. These imagined negative consequences of not giving into external pressure are the most powerful pull to dependency there is. We call it *fear*.

We've talked about anger, frustration, guilt and worry in past chapters. All are very strong emotions that can affect your entire personality and change the way you view the world, not just yourself. Now we're going to examine what may be the strongest force of all: fear.

Independence is dangerous and something to fear because men will do almost anything to make you dependent. They take advantage of the fact that you, like everyone else, regress under extreme stress or fear. When you have a difficulty to overcome, you first attempt to use the wisdom of your years for intelligent problem solving. If this fails, you revert to behavior that may have worked when you were younger. You might use adolescent strategies like flirting, charm or assuming various attitudes of "coolness" or "hipness" to achieve your aims. If the problem is urgent and adult or adolescent behaviors don't work, you'll probably regress to even earlier behaviors that were once successful. You might whine and plead and stomp like a pre-pubescent child. As your frustration at not being able to solve the problem finally overwhelms you, you would bawl like a baby, totally infantilized through the sheer frustration of not being able to achieve autonomy.

In this chapter we'll teach you how to eliminate your fear by intelligent action. You'll shed your childlike obedience to the system of others, an obedience born out of the fear of not being able to succeed on your own, to emerge a whole person who is not afraid to think and act for herself. Behaviors such as being "good" out of fear of being otherwise, believing others will take care of you because you're not able to take care of yourself, letting others act like they "own" you and compromising yourself for "protection" from those you consider your superiors will become things of the past. You will win the struggle that begins naturally from your birth, the struggle for independence. With this newfound autonomy you will begin to truly love yourself and be vastly more lovable to those around you as well!

Fear as the Reason for "Goodness"

Independence takes many forms. It is not the situation per se (whether you have your own apartment on the upper West Side of Manhattan or live with your parents) that determines whether you are independent, but rather, how you function in that situation. You can be independent in the home by not calling mother every time one of the kids gets a sniffle. You can be independent at work by not asking the whole staff for help every time you get a new assignment or by figuring things out for yourself without always having to ask. No woman or man is an island. You will never be independent of your need for love, companionship, and food. What we would like to help you become independent of, though, is fear. Fear that you won't be able to make it without male protection—without paying the price of following his rules instead of your own. In this case you are only "good" because you are afraid to be otherwise.

Many kinds of women are affected by this type of fear. Let's look at how it manifests itself so you can begin to recognize it and act to dispel it. Fear of independence takes two forms: (1) fear you will lose the "identity" and the "security" that you already have; (2) believing that you are right to let men make the decisions for you. Fear of man then becomes a "virtue." But what a troublesome one!

Let's look at one of the many ways that this fear of independence begins. In second grade, Marilyn was the smartest student in her class. By the time she reached junior high, she was on the debate team and a worthy adversary in any discussion. "But," Marilyn explained, "in high school, I lost my first love because he said I was too 'opinionated.' After graduation, I wanted to go to college, but I felt I would stand a better chance at holding a man if I stifled rather than developed my intelligence, so I married as soon as I could, when I was 19.'' By the time Marilyn was 40 her three children had left home and her husband, Stan, spent all his free time watching television and never talking to her. Marilyn was terrified. ''I blew my whole life,'' she said, ''I'm a loser.'' We told Marilyn, ''It's never too late to win.'' Then we asked her to ask herself, ''What am I *doing* to be dependent?'' and to jot these behaviors down. At the top of the list was ''I'm letting Stan keep me from getting a better education.'' We told her to work on this item first, and she did! Against Stan's opposition, she went back to school to learn data processing. He left her, but there's a happy ending. She found another man, one who could appreciate an independent woman!

You can never achieve identity or security by being dependent. And it is never virtuous or right to let others make your decisions for you. True identity comes from doing what is right not for someone else, but for *you.*

Why You Believe that Men Will Take Care of You

The danger comes when you believe that others know what is best for you better than you do, when you then entrust them to look out for your own welfare. The conditioning of Chapter 1, ''There is something wrong with me,'' contributes to your belief that you *need* to be protected. The answer as to who is going to protect you is supplied by Chapter 2, ''Men are better.'' The natural candidates for protection are superior beings. However, the only danger lurking for you in the Garden of Independence is you and your *belief* that you should be dominated. The only problem is you changing your mind. Just why is the work force so dangerous for a woman? Primarily because you believe you shouldn't be there. Why is independence dangerous? Because you're afraid men won't like you that way!

Psychiatrist Matina Horner, in *Women and Success: The Anatomy of Achievement,* writes of how women have been conditioned to fear achieving excellence, distinguishing themselves by superiority.

> Unusual excellence in women was clearly associated with them with the loss of femininity, social rejection, personal or societal destruction or some combination of the above.

No wonder women believe independence is dangerous. Excellence, achievement, autonomy and independence lead to rejection. But trading independence for protection is like exchanging your teeth for a toothbrush. Once the bite is gone, what is there left to defend?

Clara, 42, said she always was feeling put down by her husband, Swen, a farmer and man with very "traditional" beliefs. "Nothing I do as a housewife impresses him in the least," she said. "All he cares about is his crops. The chores I do he just takes for granted." "What are you good at?" we asked Clara. "Me? Why nothing," she said. "Then let's put it this way," we said, "what do you do *best*?" "I make great dill pickles," she smiled. "Then pickles will be your vehicle to excellence," we decided. We encouraged Clara to enter several contests, and soon her pickles were winning prizes. "I feel great!" Clara told us. "Is Swen impressed?" we asked. "Who cares?" Clara answered. "I feel so good about myself, I don't *need* him to tell me I'm good." Then she winked. "Besides, I think I'm getting through to him. He didn't say much to me, but I overheard him bragging on me to one of his friends." Develop your strengths. Learn to appreciate yourself. The stronger you become, the less you will feel like you need to be taken care of. As you appreciate yourself more, those close to you will appreciate you more also.

Rejection takes many forms. Society is not so blatant as it used to be, but the message is still there that you are not to excel. Few women make it past middle management. Few women rise to power in politics. And women who do are often labeled "hard" and, as we already quoted in the L.A. *Times* poll, "unladylike." It's all right for a man to be driving and hard, an achiever. But it's not all right for a woman because it's "unfeminine." The problem is not in getting the world to accept hard women, but in conceiving nurturing achievers! This is a lesson we all need to learn—how to be loving *and* successful, nurturing and achieving, kind and accomplished. Once you come to realize that "feminine" and "achiever" are not opposites but ideally compatible, you will absolutely know you can have both love and independence.

The Concept of Human Ownership

The concepts of dependency and ownership go hand in hand. The more you depend on someone, the more power you give them. As their power over you increases, so does their control—to the point where they in essence possess you. You have incorporated so much of them into you that your actions literally belong to them! There is no doubt—your dependency puts you in the possession of others.

You may be asking yourself how you personally became a victim of dependency. In many cases, parents are the first ones to pass on the idea of the dependency trap. They do this by making you think that not only are they responsible for you, they control you. "As long as you live under our roof, you'll do as we say," implies that to be supported is to be possessed. Whoever pays for your keep has a right to tell you how to live your life. But no one has the right to possess another soul, not even that of one's child.

For many women, slavery becomes formalized in the marriage contract. You may feel bound by law to work for your husband till the end of your days. While this is not really what "honoring" and "cherishing" mean, you may have the inaccurate idea that you are supposed to pay for this unique relationship with your freedom, as you in essence did with your parents. Since your husband, like your father, may support and protect you, it may seem only natural. Protection then assumes you're giving up your right to independence in exchange for "security." Ideally, marriage is a commitment to another person that you *want* to make. While in the old days, it may have made perfect sense to marry for financial security, today, fortunately, more women are marrying for love. And the concept of marriage is changing from one person owning another to a relationship of reciprocity, where two people share equally in the satisfying of each other's needs. In this kind of a relationship it's OK to take care of your man because it's your *choice*, not your duty. You are still very much your own person. Achieving this state of harmony with your mate begins with you.

What you must come to realize is that you have *value,* and that value is your key to independence. When you truly *believe* there is nothing wrong with you, that you are equal, and sometimes superior to, other people, you will sense your value. You have a great deal to give. When you come to fully realize this, you will see how really important you can *make* yourself to others.

To examine this truth in a more personal light, let's review the case of one of our clients, Judy, a young housewife who came to us because she was miserable—she felt she was falling into a rut. She explained that she had to follow a strict routine set down for her by her husband. This included breakfast at 7, lunch at noon, dinner at 8, laundry on Tuesdays (so he'll have clean shirts for dinner at his mother's every Wednesday), refreshments for his poker club on Mondays, companionship for all televised sports events, a bedmate whenever he's tired or amorous. It was a regimen designed exclusively to satisfy *his* needs. Judy was very unhappy because she didn't believe she was worth enough to make some demands of her own. It was not that she hated being a housewife, it was just that she'd like to be an *independent* one, a woman who runs the home to meet the needs of all its members, not only those of her husband. But Judy was afraid. She thought that making him fix his own dinner once in a while or leaving the house during a football game was swimming into dangerous waters. "He'd kill me if I wasn't there when he wanted something to eat," she said. She didn't want to lose her not-so-happy home.

Judy's real problem was she didn't realize how valuable she really was to her husband. We had her write down all the things she was doing to depend on her husband. At the top of the list: she was making her happiness dependent on his happiness. She couldn't be happy unless he was happy. And he couldn't be happy unless she did everything he asked. We next told her to stop doing *everything,* for a day. Naturally the household fell apart, but it was worth it. Her husband saw the magnitude of *his* dependency on her and developed an overnight appreciation. Her one-day strike led to a settlement, a list of things she would no longer have to do to make him happy. One was that she no longer had to feed his buddies during football games!

Estelle, 34, an assistant professor in chemistry, married to Charles, 35, a full professor of physics at the same university, considered herself a liberated woman until her best friend, Suzie, made an observation: "Why is it," Suzie asked, "that whenever something comes up, the schedule has to be rearranged around Charles's classes and not yours?" "I guess because he's a full professor and I'm not," Estelle explained. The following year, Estelle was raised to full professor, but nothing changed in her relationship with Charles. If time had to be taken to visit a bank, get the kids to a doctor, buy an appliance, it was still Estelle who had to rearrange her schedule and not Charles. "How does this make you feel?" we asked Estelle. "Like he's more important than me," Estelle said. "Like I have to let him make the major decisions in our lives. I hate to say it, but, dependent." "Then tell him about it!" we said. "Let him know how his behavior makes you feel. Be specific. Say something like, 'When I'm always the one who has to change my schedule to accommodate things we do together, I feel less of a person than you. And I don't like that feeling." Estelle followed our suggestion and was amazed at the results. "I can't believe how simple it was once I did it. Charles really wasn't aware of what he was doing. He said he'd be more than happy to rearrange his schedule once in a while now that he knew how I felt about it."

Sometimes in order to save a marriage or a relationship, you have to be willing to lose it. You have to stand up for your needs. If your partner values you, he will meet them. If he doesn't value you, perhaps the relationship is not worth saving. In any event, you must first value yourself.

The Danger of Trading Independence for Protection

We all want protection and security. It's only human. But as important as they can be to our lives if they are genuine, protection and security are often illusions. Does a marriage contract honestly assure you security against divorce, abandonment or welfare? When you trade freedom for protection, you may be giving up your rights to happiness in exchange for *nothing*. A need to never grow up and stay daddy's "good girl" forever could kill your chances for fulfilled, independent womanhood.

We know that you're not going to make the mistake of sacrificing independence for illusory protection or you wouldn't have read this far. You've made a terrific choice. Nothing is more exhilarating than independence! Shirley MacLaine writes of her desire for her daughter to experience the independence of freedom in *Don't Fall Off the Mountain*.

Freedom, with her front windows open and unlocked, with breezes and challenges blowing in. I wished that she would know herself through freedom. I wished that underneath she would understand that there is no such thing as being safe—there are no safe havens for anyone who wants to know the TRUTH, *whatever* it is, about himself or others.

We once had a client, Lissa, who was terrified of risking the protection of her present job for one that put her abilities to better use. Lissa had been trained for a professional position in business, but accepted a secretarial position in a data processing firm, primarily because she was afraid she would not be able to get anything more prestigious. She plainly did not believe she was worth anything more, even though educated for a superior level. Seven years later, there was a company merger and she was laid off. At this point she interviewed for a new position in keeping with her level of expertise. "We see your degree," said the personnel director, "but why did you stay so long as a secretary? I'm afraid we can't hire you." Not only was her secretarial haven insecure in that she lost her job, dependency on the easiest path was dangerous. It worked against her in the long run. We suggested to Lissa that she should assert her independence with a vengeance, to aim for a job that matched her qualifications no matter how many more interviews it took. We also suggested that she tell herself throughout the day, "I am worth $40,000 a year," the amount of the salary she had decided to shoot for. She was going to learn that she was worth whatever she *believed* her value to be. In three weeks she landed an excellent job with a salary commensurate with her worth. She had learned her lesson: the only real protection in life is a sense of your own self-worth and the independence to assert it. In Lissa's words, "If you don't believe you're worth it, neither will anyone else."

Real protection starts with yourself. There is no better security than being the best you can be and settling for nothing less. Independence is the best protection there is!

Fostering Independence: Everyone Needs It

Our entire life is a struggle for independence. We all need it. From birth, a baby struggles to gain autonomy from his parents. Parents learn to foster independence, to teach the child how to function on his or her own, in order to survive when the parent is no longer around. No adult is meant to be dependent throughout life. In fact, we come to resent people if we need them *too* much.

On the other hand independence leads to love—love of yourself and love of those from whose control you have freed yourself. Accept self-control and the power that goes with it.

Independence is glorious. It makes you the loving artist of your own fate. And, in time, it will make you infinitely easier to *be* loved. Independence makes you more lovable because you expect nothing in return. There is no higher form of love on earth.

Some Examples of Dependent Behavior

Now that we've exposed some of the sources that make you crave dependency, let's examine how to spot dependency in your behavior. What do you *do* that shows you are too dependent?

- Do things for men because it is expected, not because you really want to (feel resentment when you do them, and guilt when you don't)?
- Still bound to your parents in many ways, needing their approval for major decisions in your life, especially needing validation that you are still "good"?
- Live vicariously through your children, putting them first in your life over yourself, which only serves to foster their dependency on you?

Beverly, a 38-year-old housewife and mother of three girls, explained all rules of conduct to her children like this: "When I was a girl my father never allowed me to do _____ and I always did _____ ." To this day she still called her father, 78, whenever she needed to know whether she was making the "right" decision about something important in her life. Second in authority was her husband, Anthony, whom she consulted on less important matters such as what they'd be having for breakfast or where they'd buy the new sofa. By telling her children that they were to do what their father had told her to do and by going to Anthony for constant direction, Beverly was teaching her girls to look and talk up to men. We cured Beverly of this dependency of her father or husband, such as, "Do this because it will help others" or "because you will feel better" or "because you will learn from it," rather than "because _____ said that was how it should be done."

- Believe that relatives *owe* you something just because you are related? A blood relationship does not give someone the right to govern or live your life for you. You have a life of your own beyond being a daughter, a mother, a lover, and a wife. You don't own your parents, your children or your lovers. And they don't own you.
- Feel guilty whenever you "neglect" your husband or children by doing something without them or when you don't visit your parents as often as they would like?
- Feel you are always doing what you "should" rather than what you want?

Bernadette, a 24-year-old physical therapist, had been putting off her marriage to Ted, a 24-year-old sales representative, for more than two years. "It's not that I don't love him," she said, "I'm just scared to give up my freedom." Bernadette's mother had "lived for her children," sacrificing everything for them, and deep in her heart Bernadette saw the same thing happening to her if she married. We were quick to point out that marriage made you a slave only if you chose to let it. No relative, through blood or marriage, has the right to tell you what to do. There was therefore no reason to ever feel guilty for doing what *you* want to do. The fact that her mother did "everything" for her showed that her mother was a very dependent woman, *needing* her children to validate her own existence. Did Bernadette *want* to be equally as dependent by living totally for her future family to the exclusion of herself? We knew that she didn't and therefore suggested that she draw up her personal "independence plan" *before* she married. She was to write out specifically how she wished to live, pinpointing the things that were most important to her. She was happily surprised to discover that there was no reason that marriage should keep her from attaining any of these goals. Putting this down on paper gave her a greater sense of security and, determined to maintain personal freedom foremost, Bernadette was able to enter her marriage to Ted with a sense of inspiration rather than entrapment.

- Feel that it is always better not to make waves, that it's impossible to "beat the system" or "change the world"? Quite possibly. But you *can* make your own system, create your own world. It is not necessary that everyone follow the old rules.
- Need to let your partner believe he is your superior? (This stems from fear that he might leave you if he's not allowed to dominate.)
- Believe it is "natural" for women to be dependent? Independence is a natural, basic need in *both* sexes. From the moment of birth, animals and humans alike strive for autonomy. It was the cornerstone in the founding of our nation. No relationship can long endure in health when its members refuse one another the right to choose their own fulfillment. If the rules of men prevent you the joy of life, liberty, and the pursuit of happiness, they do not deserve to be followed. Remember, a bad rule can exist only as long as someone follows it.

Opal, a 24-year-old singer, was going through endless emotional turmoil in her five-month relationship with Warren, 28, lead drummer in the band she sang with. "I just can't get him to commit to me," Opal complained. "I really don't understand it. I do everything for him. I never try to change him. I agree with everything he says. I make him feel like a king. Sometimes I think he just thinks he's too good for me." "No wonder," we said. "You've done everything to make him a king but crown him! You've put him on a pedestal so high, you could never be deserving of him." Opal gasped. "What should I do?" "*Change* him," we said. "Begin by disagreeing when he does things that indicate he thinks he's too good for you." Opal had told us that one of Warren's put down behaviors was that he never liked to take her out in public. He said he was tired, but Opal believed he was ashamed to be seen with her. So we suggested, "Next time you mention you'd like to go out and Warren says he doesn't want to go, *disagree* with him. Tell him you definitely want to go out, whether he wants to or not. Forget about his 'reasons' for not wanting to.

Your only objective should be getting the two of you to your favorite club. Insist. Be willing to leave him if he can't accommodate you." Opal hesitated until we added, "Unless, of course, you don't think you're worth a better relationship." When Warren saw that Opal thought enough of herself to stand her ground and be independent *within* their relationship, he respected her wishes and gave in to them. "He still hasn't proposed," Opal told us recently, "but he sure does treat me a whole lot better since I started making a few waves and sticking up for myself."

- Avoid any kind of confrontation? Catch yourself saying, "I would do anything to avoid a fight"?
- Live in the reflected glory of your mate and are happy only when he experiences personal success at work or in his other activities?
- Allow men to boss you around?

Myrna, a 52-year-old director of a large hospital, sophisticated and independent as she thought she was, still needed to depend on a man who was better than her. When her husband, Denver, 63, a high-ranking government official, lost an important election and found himself out of power as well as out of a job, Myrna fell apart. "I feel like such a nothing," she complained. "What'll people think of me now that Denver's turned into such a flop?" "What do you think of yourself?" we asked. The question stopped Myrna cold. Then she began to cry. "I hate myself," she said. "Because Denver lost the election?" we asked. "No," she answered, "I hate myself for feeling this way. I never realized his success was that important to me. I want to love him for him, not his job." "That's great," we said. "We like you for saying that." "So do I," Myrna laughed. "I suddenly realize that I'd much rather be a woman who loves her husband under all circumstances rather than only when he was better than she was." With this shift in values, Myrna gained a new independence—love without contingencies. Once you release others from your expectations of them, you will suddenly find yourself a lot freer yourself!

While dependency takes many forms, the above examples

are the most common. As you can see, the opportunity for independence arises in every situation. It is not the circumstance, but the way you handle it that determines your independence. Think for yourself and you will have attained it!

Why We Continue to Be Dependent

You are close to independence. But you must first get a grip on the reasons you still have for fighting it. Here are some of your motives for remaining dependent.

- You don't make enemies of men. There's no worry that someone might not like you.
- There is no need for change, risk or responsibility. Whatever happens to you is a function of dependency on *their* rules.
- Others will love you. Your sense of "goodness" will soar.
- You have someone to worship, and nothing fosters worship more than dependency. Looking to a "higher" source than yourself for guidance is the ultimate action for shirking responsibility for your own fate.
- It is much easier to be dependent than independent. It's easier to behave than break with the past. The only problem is that it carries a terribly high price: your identity.
- You feel safe. As long as you have superior men to lean on, what could go wrong?
- There is often a great sense of belonging.
- You need never grow up. In a sense, dependency makes you feel eternally young.

Specific Recipes for Independence

It is undeniably possible to break free of someone's control over you and establish yourself as an independent person. It will require you to substitute action for fear, freedom for protection and power for slavery. Here are some definite strategies to make certain you achieve independence.

- Begin asking yourself, as Marilyn and Judy did, "What am I *doing* to depend on men?" Jot these behaviors down and work on them. Keep a journal if you'd like. Others only have as much power as you give them.
- Write your own "independence plan," as Bernadette did before her marriage to Ted, in which you declare your intentions for independence, how you wish to live. Be specific: don't be afraid to list your fears as well as your desires. Then try to pinpoint what is most important to you. You'll be surprised at how the writing of your thoughts will make you feel liberated!
- Talk to the men upon whom you consider yourself dependent as Estelle did with Charles. Explain how you feel in this type of relationship. This will give them an awareness of their *behavior* that causes you to feel dependent. One client said she felt like a dependent little girl whenever her husband patted her on the head before leaving for the office. Remember, men need training too. Their awareness is part of winning the battle.
- Watch yourself to make sure that you do not talk up to men. Do as we taught Beverly to teach independence to her children. In conversation, make definite statements as to how you feel, independent of what their expectations may be of you.
- Be careful, as we advised Opal, of agreeing too much with the men in your life. Don't do it just to be liked. Others may use it to take advantage of you. What's worse, you'll feel betrayed yourself.
- At work, when the boss enters the room, continue what

you were doing. (This applies whether your boss be male or female.) Refrain from dropping the letter you were writing or pretending exaggerated attention to your duties.

- If a man comes on too strong with you, give it right back to him. Dish out an equal measure of independence. If he overcriticizes, criticize back. If he raises his voice, fumes, demands, insists, mirror the same behavior back.

- Try, as we advised Linda, ignoring people's attempts to control by simply not responding to them. Skip refusing, questioning, or arguing; just don't reward their behavior with a response. Independently do what you want regardless of what the men in your life are up to.

- Know your stuff. There is no better preparation for independence than competence. If you are good at what you do, you have value and there is no need for dependence.

- Refuse to take anything less for your services than what you know you're worth. Do as we suggested for Lissa to up her position in the work force. Set the amount of salary you know you deserve and repeat daily, "I am worth _____ a year" until you come to *believe* it. Be prepared to go elsewhere if not fully appreciated. If you discover that a man is getting more pay for the same job as you're doing, tell your employer you want equal pay. If he refuses, quit!

- Try to appreciate yourself, as we taught Clara to do by making prizewinning pickles and Myrna by changing her values. Tell yourself that what you do you do well. To be appreciated by others, you must first appreciate yourself.

- On the job, be especially wary of men's request for "feminine" services out of keeping with your professional position, such as, fetching, running errands, relieving on the switchboard, or picking out presents for them to give to their wives. If they wouldn't ask a man in your position to do these things, then you needn't do them either. Simply ask him, "Would you

ask a man to pick up your shirts at the cleaners?"
"Buy earrings for your wife?" "Get you a cup of coffee?" or whatever it is he's asking you to do.

We know how easy it is to be afraid. We all have fears. But the only thing you really need to fear is your own dependency. It can keep you from being the terrific person we know you are. Chart an independent course and your way will be clear. You'll be out of the control of men and in your own hands. Steer a route that's true to yourself and the rewards will be great. We're betting on you! In the words of Victoria, "Independence gave me the chance to love without strings. That is the greatest love of all!"

13
The Clear

I only know one thing. I want tomorrow to be
different . . . better.

JANE K.
age 30

You are a clear! You are now free of the self-limiting myths we
have just explored. Your possibilities are limitless! More than
any other quality that distinguishes a woman who is no longer
a "good girl" is her zest for the future, her unbridled energy
to meet and tackle the challenges of tomorrow, her itch to get
out of bed in the morning and create a new and exciting day.

Portrait of a Woman Who Has Cleared
THE GOOD GIRL SYNDROME—YOU!

You are now free to be yourself, to find and express your
own identity. The limits of other people's belief systems are
gone!

You are no longer limited by barriers, either psychological
or geographic. You feel comfortable wherever you want to be.
You would be just as much at ease in the African bush or
the teeming markets of Marrakesh as you are in a Midwest
kitchen. While not foolhardly or brash, you don't let fear influence your decision making. You go for what you want in-

dependently of what others might think and revel in the glory of your independence. If you've never taken a college course, you take it. If you've never had a graduate course, you take it. If you want a Ph.D., you find a way to get it—outside financing or night classes, whatever it takes. You are loving and appreciative of things people do for you, but avoid being dependent. First of all, you are true to yourself.

You are a woman who has no compunctions about meeting her needs. You are assertive, aggressive, and often the one to make the first move. If you want something from a man you tell him. And when you are angry, you have no qualms about expressing it—directly and constructively—to its source.

Guilt and worry are little known to you. You are even able to put an extra item in your shopping cart in the express line of the supermarket without feeling you deserve punishment. You believe in following your own path and accepting responsibility for what happens to you. You are committed to self-direction. You accept mistakes as part of growth.

If the old ways of doing things work for you, you hold on to them. If they do not work, you search for new plans. You revere nothing simply because it is ancient. You look for meaning, goodness and utility. You want the best possible life for yourself and the ones you love and see no need to get stuck in the rut of doing things today just because they were done yesterday. If it works out better that your husband stay home with the kids while you go to the office, you follow this new system. If the man in your life prefers to cook while you attend to the carpentry, plumbing and electrical, that's fine too. You are more interested in seeing results from your efforts than paying homage to old systems.

Although you care how people see you, you are more concerned over how you see yourself. You never agree with someone simply because he or she wants or expects it. You get your identity from setting and achieving your own standards. Approval from others means little to you without self-approval. You enjoy sex and are not ashamed for others to know it—especially your partner. You know that you bring great joy to your partner by letting him see you satisfied.

As a woman cleared of GGS you live by the axiom that self-satisfaction, not self-sacrifice, is a virtue. If you think that someone is asking too much of you, you tell them so, and do not give in to their demands. You do not let yourself be manipulated by people who label your giving them what they want as "virtuous."

You are flexible. Change comes naturally to you. You recognize that rules are not "sacred" or inviolable, but makeshift devices to get you through a particular period in life. Then they are as outdated as the time that produced them. You are not afraid to take what once was or still may be considered a "man's job," such as driving a cab or being a law enforcement officer. Just as you are not in awe of rules, you also are not intimidated by people. You give no one the right to determine what is best for you. You reserve this right for yourself.

You beautifully realize that no one is any better than anyone else, and you treat everyone equally and with respect. And most important of all, you respect and accept yourself. You understand that you are whole and worthy and good just as you are. You are a child of the universe with a self-determined right to *be,* grow, and flower into magnificent independent adulthood.

We sincerely trust we've been able to help to show you the way to your own personal best. You may not use all the information we've given you in all the programs. That's fine. We wouldn't expect you to. If you use even one point, take *one* important step, you will make us joyously happy. We will have gotten through!

Some of this material you will act on right away. Some of it will take time to process. You may even have thought while reading it "This isn't me," and then suddenly you find yourself in a similar situation; only this time you know how to act the *effective* way, without compromising yourself. Pretty soon, much of what we've told you will become second nature, a part of you that guides you almost automatically. Then one wonderful day, you will know. You *are* a clear! It may hit you without warning, possibly months after you've finished the book, possibly right away. When you experience the clear, you'll have no doubt. The feeling of joy and exhilaration is unmistakable. You'll know it when it happens to you. And it *will* happen. One of our clients describes it. "It was the most incredible feeling. Everything just suddenly came together. I felt cleansed, free. . . . And I wanted to live!"

This is the start of your new life. There is wonderful news! You are finally you! We send you our love. Happy birthday!

List of Relevant Books

The books we've listed for you below relate to the causes and cure of the Good Girl Syndrome. Though there is certainly more we could have explored, we hope these readings will fill in some of the gaps for you. We especially hope they might give you more strategies, if you need them, for further clearing of GGS from your life.

Baker, Nancy. *The Beauty Trip: Exploring Woman's Greatest Obsession*. Watts, 1984.
> Explores women's desperate obsession with beauty, a dilemma rooted in a lack of self-confidence and independence. Once again, sacrificing self-fulfillment and autonomy in exchange for beauty leads to trouble.

Barbach, Lonnie, and Linda Levine. *The Intimate Male: Candid Discussions About Women, Sex and Relationships*. New York: Doubleday, 1983.
> Here we have the male point of view about sex and sexuality. The authors, who interviewed more than 120 men from various backgrounds, conclude that men are changing; they're trying to overcome stereotypes and achieve intimacy. They provide hope that men, at least some of them, will supply assistance in freeing women from the Good Girl Syndrome.

Beauvoir, Simone de. *The Second Sex*. New York: Vintage Books, 1974.
> The classic manifesto of the liberated woman. Probes every aspect of femininity—sexual, social, biographical and historical.

Blanchard, Kenneth, and Spencer Johnson. *The One Minute Manager*. New York: Berkley Books, 1983.

At first glance, this may seem a strange choice for our list, but managing the men in your life is not much different from managing a business. The authors' solid, simple behavioral techniques of one-minute goals, praising and reprimands can be very effective.

Boyd, Peggy. *The Silent Wound: A Startling Report on Breast Cancer and Sexuality*. Addison-Wesley, 1984.

This book provides much food for thought. With the causes of breast cancer still undetermined, Boyd, a psychiatric, medical-surgical nurse and public health specialist, conducted research among 180 breast cancer patients to test her hypothesis that a "silent wound" caused by the stress of unresolved sexual and social conflicts—notably in adolescence and at menopause—should be considered a major factor. She shows how improving self-image can help to reduce risk and diminish the impact on those who are afflicted with breast cancer.

Brownmiller, Susan. *Femininity*. New York: Linden/Simon & Schuster, 1984.

This book closely investigates how women fear that success will automatically cause loss of femininity needed to attract a man. The author describes many of the actions women have used in order to maintain their feminine ideal (corsets, bound feet, hoop skirts, veils, poisonous cosmetics).

Cameron Bandler, Leslie. *Solutions*. San Rafael: Future-Pace Inc., 1985.

The goal of this book is to show you how to use your own inner resources as a means to generate new behavior patterns. Based upon choice and the creation of new internal processes, this book focuses on couples' relationships, sexual problems, and general happiness.

Carnegie, Dale. *How to Stop Worrying and Start Living*. New York: Pocket Books, 1981.

Still the best book on the market for dealing effectively with worry.

Cassell, Carol. *Swept Away: Why Women Fear Their Own*

Sexuality. New York: Simon & Schuster, 1984.

Cassell, president of the American Association of Sex Educators, Counselors and Therapists, after ten years of research, examines this frustrating ambivalence from social, historical and behavioral perspectives. She discusses romance, bargaining, rules (old and new), contraceptions, expectations, fantasy, and the male point of view. She presents options for change, along with ways to direct one's own sexual destiny toward the ultimate goal of sexual equality.

Cole-Whittaker, Terry. *What You Think of Me Is None of My Business*. La Jolla: Oak Tree Publication, 1982.

An enlightening book that unlocks the doors to the qualities and potential that we all have. She talks about the faulty beliefs which we learn in our early years and says that people have freedom of choice and a personal responsibility to change. In Chapter 11 she presents new marriage vows that allow each partner to expand in their relationship, and to create a union that is a safe ground for individual expression of feelings, emotions, and thoughts.

Cunningham, Mary, with Fran Schumer. *Power Play: What Really Happened at Bendix*. New York: Linden/Simon & Schuster, 1984.

Written by Mary Cunningham, the vice-president for strategic planning at Bendix who resigned after front-page stories in the national press said that she was having an affair with company chairman William Agee, this book says a great deal about the vulnerability of executive women in corporate America.

Daly, Mary. *Pure Lust: Elemental Feminist Philosophy*. Boston: Beacon, 1984.

A particularly good book for liberating yourself from negative self-perceptions and anxieties based on how men judge you. Daly's "lust" is the feminine power that connects her with the rhythms of nature and ties instinct and intuition to reason.

Daniell, Rosemary. *Sleeping with Soldiers: In Search of the Macho Man*. New York: Holt, Rinehart & Winston, 1984.

This book may not be for everyone, but it does produce material not found in other sources. It is one woman's sexual odyssey and resolution of her love-hate feelings toward the earthy, dominating, aggressive stud. Sexual randomness and the repercussions it brings are discussed with refreshing candor.

Dowling, Colette. *The Cinderella Complex.* New York: Pocket Books, 1982.

Dowling's book is a classic in aiding women to recognize their hidden fear of independence. A must reading for all women who believe that independence is dangerous.

Fezler, William. *Breaking Free: Ninety Ways to Leave Your Lover and Survive.* Washington, D.C.: Acropolis Books, 1985.

Ninety tried and true techniques to help clear your head and get over an impossible relationship, whether it be one where you left because your needs simply weren't being met or your partner left you through choice or death.

Fezler, William, and William Kroger. *Hypnosis and Behavior Modification: Imagery Conditioning.* Philadelphia: J.B. Lippincott Co., 1976.

This is a professional book that will be understandable to the informed layperson. It adds considerable substance to the popular books written in the fields of hypnosis, behavioral psychology, and goal achieving with imagery and visualization. For those who wish to understand how and why our thoughts can be reprogrammed.

Fezler, William. *Just Imagine: A Guide to Materialization Using Imagery.* Los Angeles: Citrine Press, 1984.

Gives thorough instruction in how to clear your head for stress reduction, deep relaxation, and reprogramming. Twenty-five specific images of ascending complexity teach you to rise above self-destructive ideas and reach a new awareness in which you can form new rules that work for you.

Fishel, Elizabeth. *The Men in Our Lives.* New York: William Morrow, 1984.

An excellent primer on how women are shaped by the significant men in their lives. Particularly revealing is the detailed examination of the first primal relationships with several types of fathers (patriarch, pal, bystander, charmer, the absent father) and the ways they affect later attitudes toward men and choice of mate.

Forster, Margaret. *Significant Sisters: The Grass Roots of Active Feminism 1839–1939*. New York: Knopf, 1984.

Profiles eight women, representing various points along the grass roots spectrum of the women's movement. Inspiring, passionate reading about women who made a difference.

Fraser, Antonia. *The Weaker Vessel: Woman's Lot in Seventeenth-Century England*. New York: Knopf, 1984.

A best-selling, superbly readable study of women in England from the death of Elizabeth (1603) to the accession of Anne (1702). This comprehensive survey provides many good models of spirited, determined women, high and low, who braved censure and took risks.

Gallese, Liz Roman. *Women Like Us: The Women Who Had the First Chance to Make It to the Top*. New York: William Morrow, 1984.

Focuses on six women from the class of 1975 at the Harvard Business School and contrasts the image of their corporate successes with the reality. What it takes to make it to the top, the compromises and the ensuing alterations in self-perception are especially illuminating to women wishing to break free from traditional, male-inflicted roles.

Gaylin, Willard. *The Rage Within: Anger in Everyday Life*. New York: Simon & Schuster, 1984.

In this absorbing and accessible study, Dr. Gaylin explains how anger not expressed directly is diverted self-destructively through psychosomatic symptoms from acne to rheumatoid arthritis.

Giddings, Paula. *When and Where I Enter: The Impact of Black Women on Race and Sex in America*. New York: William Morrow, 1984.

A prime sourcebook of the black woman's struggle for equality and independence, beginning with the 1892 anti-lynching campaign launched by Ida B. Wells and Memphis journalist Mary Terrell up to the civil rights struggles of the 1960s.

Gilligan, Carol. *In a Different Voice*. Cambridge: Harvard University Press, 1982.

Thought-provoking research on women, men and the

differences between them. Gilligan develops her observations that men and women have two ways of speaking about moral problems, two ways of describing the relationship between other and self. Women may not fit existing models of personal growth because psychology has limited these models to men's experience.

Howard, Jane. *Margaret Mead: A Life*. New York: Simon & Schuster, 1984.

An engrossing biography of the woman who probably did more than any other to shatter the preconceptions concerning the "rightness" of male and female roles. Anthropologist Mead's books on sex in the South Seas taught us that different cultures have equally valid ways of coping, that no one way is absolutely superior to any other, and that rules must be judged by their results.

Kassorla, Irene. *Nice Girls Do*. Los Angeles: Stratford Press, 1980.

An informative, no-nonsense book for all the "good girls" who still feel "bad" at the thought of enjoying sex. Kassorla presents a detailed program for overcoming guilt-producing childhood messages concerning sexuality and achieving sexual happiness.

Kiley, Dan. *The Wendy Dilemma: When Women Stop Mothering Their Men*. New York: Arbor House, 1984.

Shows how an excessively mothering, overly protective woman is refusing to take responsibility for her autonomy. Kiley provides good suggestions for achieving what Kiley terms the independent "Tinkerbell."

Marshall, Megan. *The Cost of Loving: Women and the New Fear of Intimacy*. New York: Putnam, 1984.

Excellent reading for the woman who wishes to investigate seriously the costs and gains of independence. Marshall describes a number of women and the ways they have responded to the new possibilities of clearing, pointing directions to resolutions in a period of transition.

Memmi, Albert. *Dependence*. Boston: Beacon Press, 1984.

The brilliant French sociologist explores the constituents of dependency and gives techniques to cope with them.

Minton, Michael, and Jean Libman Block. *What Is a Wife Worth: The Leading Expert Places a High Dollar Value on Homemaking*. New York: William Morrow, 1983.

Countless descriptions of landmark cases (primarily divorce), charts for determining the dollar value per hour of homemakers' work (from nurse to cook to hostess), plus a discussion of the legal and monetary advantages of marriage make this a very helpful book for the women struggling to determine her worth and raise her self-image in the home. Explanation of new marriage laws in America as influenced by the 1970 Uniform Marriage and Divorce Act, which requires courts to include a wife's homemaker contribution as part of marital assets, is particularly enlightening.

Newman, Mildred, and Bernard Berkowitz and Jean Owen. *How to Be Your Own Best Friend.* New York: Ballantine Books, 1971.

A wonderful psychiatric pep talk on how to stop putting yourself down. The authors warmly explore how to get on friendlier terms with yourself, the best possible antidote for loneliness and low self-esteem. A must for any woman who chronically believes there is something wrong with her and men are better.

Oakley, Ann. *Taking It Like a Woman.* New York: Random House, 1984.

Rather than accepting mothering and the woman's role in the family at the expense of your identity, it would be better to reestablish them as "authentic and unalienated labour." Oakley describes how she contradicts woman's traditional role of self-sacrifice in the service of men "to surpass my femininity," to create "lasting, loving reproductive relationships which bestow freedom instead of confinement."

Pelletier, Kenneth R. *Mind as Healer—Mind as Slayer.* San Francisco: Robert Briggs Associates, 1977.

A powerful book that deals with the importance of stress and life style on the delicate interplay of mind, body, and spirit. Includes comprehensive descriptions of techniques for stress reduction and life style changes to stay well and keep the immune system from breaking down.

Peters, Thomas J., and Robert H. Waterman, Jr. *In Search of Excellence: Lessons from America's Best-Run Companies.* New York: Harper and Row, 1982.

Learn how the big boys get what they want and how to

copy it to the letter. One of the best books out on the
"male" qualities of action, autonomy, enterpreneurship
and making *lots* of money.

Phillips, J.A. *Eve: The History of an Idea*. New York:
Harper and Row, 1984.

    According to this brilliant study, Eve's creation, *not*
her disobedience in the Garden, spells humanity's down-
fall. This is must reading for anyone interested in docu-
mentation of the Genesis legend as a woman-hating myth
that continues to shape our biases toward the sexes.

Price, Susan. *The Female Ego*. New York: Rawson, 1984.

    Presents an in depth picture of the role of childhood
programming on the female ego, then offers compassionate, clear-eyed advice on how women might develop and
strengthen their traditionally weak egos. Great for building self-image.

Ray, Sondra. *The Only Diet There Is*. Berkeley: Celestial Arts,
1981.

    This book is concerned with loving and forgiving
oneself, focusing on pleasure, along with doing what
makes one happy.

Remoff, Heather Trexler. *Sexual Choice: A Woman's Decision*. New York: Dutton/Lewis, 1984.

    Several intriguing methods are elaborated for *initiating*
sexual affairs. Particularly beneficial for "good girls"
who still believe it is the man who should make the first
move.

Rubin, Nancy. *The Mother Mirror: How a Generation of
Women is Changing Motherhood in America*. New York:
Putnam, 1984.

    A thorough and contemporary look at women pulled
between two desires: to nurture or to be independent.
Rubin is skillful at identifying and illuminating conflicts
inherent in today's mothering and probing new ways such
as single mothers, late-life motherhood and surrogate
mothers.

Sanford, Lind Tschirhart, and Mary Ellen Donovan. *Women
and Self-Esteem: Understanding and Improving the Way
We Think and Feel About Ourselves*. New York: Anchor
Press-Doubleday, 1984.

    A big help to anyone who thinks "there is something
wrong with me." The authors see many women's prob-

lems as due to low self-esteem similar to that ascribed to religious and racial minorities. Their extensive study seeks to determine which personal relationships and social and cultural influences contribute to a woman's negative or positive self-image. They offer exercises in self-analysis and suggestions designed to control negative images and behavior.

Schenkel, Susan. *Giving Away Success: Why Women "Get Stuck" and What to Do About It*. New York: McGraw-Hill, 1984.

This book examines the roots and manifestations of the "learned helplessness" often found in women, and its more masculine counterpart, "the mastery orientation." Behavioral strategies are presented to conquer women's internal barriers to achievement.

Schwarzer, Alice, translated by Marianne Howarth. *After The Second Sex: Conversations with Simone de Beauvoir*. New York: Pantheon, 1984.

Six lively, intelligent and provocative interviews conducted over a ten-year span, with Simone de Beauvoir, author of *The Second Sex*.

Shaevitz, Marjorie Hansen. *The Superwoman Syndrome*. New York: Warner, 1984.

This is a smart, practical book for women needing help juggling a job, home, husband, and children. Hansen gives concrete, organized advice for improving the quality of life through management techniques.

Shainess, Natalie. *Sweet Suffering: Woman as Victim*. New York: The Bobbs-Merrill Company, Inc., 1984.

The roots of masochism (self-punishment) are explored intensively along with detailed portrayals of its manifestations. This is a helpful guide that will enable you to pinpoint your own self-punishing behavior patterns and take steps to overcome them.

Steiner, Claude M., Ph.D. *Scripts People Live*. New York: Grove Press, 1974.

An outstanding explanation of the influence of parental conditioning on the way of life. Based on what it takes to gain recognition, love, and nurturing from his or her family, a child develops a way of life or Life Script in order to comply. Steiner describes a number of Scripts relating to women such as Creeping Beauty, Plastic

Woman, Mother Hubbard, and Cinderella.

Warschaw, Tessa Albert. *Rich is Better: How Women Can Bridge the Gap Between Wanting and Having It All: Financially, Emotionally, Professionally.* New York: Doubleday, 1984.

  Provides instructive techniques, strategies and self-assessments for women to recognize their psychological power and dissolve their "pervasive poverty mentality." Insightful ways to enlist the support of men are also described.

Weber, Eric. *The Divorced Woman's Guide to Meeting New Men.* New York: William Morrow, 1984.

  This is a practical, comfortable guide to finding and impressing the right man. It is Weber's belief that there's a man for every woman, so be what you want to be, then find the man who can appreciate you.

Index

If they can do it, so can you.

But first find out *how* they did it.

Develop your success potential with these books written by and about people who have discovered the secret of getting ahead. If you want more out of life, these books are for you!

__10000-6	**THE WINNER'S EDGE** Dr. Denis Waitley	$3.50
__08530-9	**THE DOUBLE WIN** Dr. Denis Waitley	$3.95
__07456-0	**BELIEVE!** Richard M. Devos with Charles Paul Conn	$2.95
__10170-3	**THE ULTIMATE SECRETS OF TOTAL SELF CONFIDENCE** Dr. Robert Anthony	$3.50
__10067-7	**I WOULD IF I COULD AND I CAN** James H. Hoke	$3.50